ENGLISH CONSERVATISM SINCE THE RESTORATION

ENGLISH CONSERVATISM SINCE THE RESTORATION

An introduction and anthology

Robert Eccleshall

London
UNWIN HYMAN
Boston Sydney Wellington

Published by the Academic Division of
Unwin Hyman Ltd
15/17 Broadwick Street, London W1V 1FP, UK

Unwin Hyman Inc.,
8 Winchester Place, Winchester, Mass. 01890, USA

Allen & Unwin (Australia) Ltd,
8 Napier Street, North Sydney, NSW 2060, Australia

Allen & Unwin (New Zealand) Ltd in association with the
Port Nicholson Press Ltd,
Compusales Building, 75 Ghuznee Street, Wellington 1, New Zealand

First published in 1990

British Library Cataloguing in Publication Data

Eccleshall, Robert
English conservatism since the Restoration: an introduction and anthology.
1. Great Britain. Political ideologies: Conservatism, Theories, history
I. Title
320.520941

ISBN 0–04–445773–1
ISBN 0–04–445346–9 pbk

Library of Congress Cataloging in Publication Data

Applied for

Typeset in 10/11 point Bembo
Printed by Billing & Sons Limited, Worcester

Contents

Preface

This book is an introduction to a style of political thinking rather than a history of a political party. It begins therefore with the emergence of a recognisable Tory creed during the seventeenth-century Restoration, and not at around 1832 when the modern Conservative Party came into existence. There is little mention, either in the chapters or in the extracts which conclude them, of party leaders (Winston Churchill, for instance) unless their speeches and writings happen to convey, in a cogent and illuminating manner, aspects of conservative thinking (as is the case with Peel, Disraeli, Macmillan and Thatcher). Too many historians, I argue in the introductory chapter, have written a retrospective account of the doctrine from the standpoint of how people of a sensible conservative disposition ought to think. The effect has been to produce a laundered version of the doctrine that includes writers who cannot properly be regarded as conservatives (David Hume, for instance), while excluding others who do not fit the argument – even though they were associated with the party and typified a pattern of thinking. But the task of the historian of political ideas, in my view, is to tell a coherent story by re-creating the beliefs, intentions and methods of argument of writers, minor as well as major, who represented a tradition of political discourse. The story should not include thinkers merely because they are judged to be sound from the ideological perspective of the historian, or ignore a host of figures simply because they made little impact on the practice of politics. In this particular story the number of obscure but interesting characters - Offspring Blackall, John Reeves, Michael Sadler, Lord Henry Bentinck, Sir Ernest Benn, to mention a few – is larger than the great names of the Tory party who usually capture the historian's attention. When reading the writings of some of these neglected characters, I must confess, I found myself in less uncongenial company than anticipated.

I should like to express my gratitude to Dr Vincent Geoghegan, Professor Cornelius O'Leary and Dr Christopher Shorley for reading an initial draft of the text and suggesting various stylistic and other improvements; and to Dr Rick Wilford for commenting on the introductory chapter. My thanks are also due to Ms Betty Donnelly and Ms Judith Graham for deciphering my scrawl and typing much of the final manuscript.

Robert Eccleshall
Belfast, January 1990

1 *Principles galore*

Conservatives are by temperament cautious and prudent. Aware of the frailties of human nature, they are suspicious of grand schemes for improving society: indeed, they regard any such fanciful design as not only pernicious in its aim of sweeping away constraints upon potentially unruly behaviour, but also as a manifestation of human vanity and imperfection. Instead of speculating about an unattainable earthly paradise, conservatives cherish existing social arrangements as a repository of the accumulated wisdom of the past. Politics for them is a practical activity in which the task is to maintain a settled way of life not by the pursuit of theoretical certainty, but through experiential adjustment to changing circumstances. Sceptical by nature, reluctant to embrace intellectual abstractions, mistrustful of missionary zealots who would transform society according to some visionary blueprint, and anxious to preserve the organic unity of a nation in which people may conduct their affairs in a customary manner, conservatives favour the kind of gradual, piecemeal reforms that are periodically required to keep the ship of state afloat on an even keel.

This is how the doctrine is usually characterized. As a description of how conservatives think, it is not entirely inaccurate: no more so than the depiction of socialists, for example, as Utopian dreamers intent on leaping into a propertyless community regulated by a mutual instinct for co-operation instead of the coercive apparatus of the state. Both are abstractions in so far as relatively few conservatives or socialists conform to their respective stereotype. British labourism hardly passes the test of boundless optimism and theoretical sophistication. Most of its adherents, far from seeking to smash the state by the application of speculative reason, are pragmatists concerned to use the benevolent power of government to tame rather than annihilate capitalism. The rarefied description of socialism is easily recognized as a caricature, and only the most partisan observer is likely to confuse the perspective of the British left with the unsullied essence of the ideology. The pure theory of conservatism, by contrast, is often presented as an abridgement of the actual views of those who subscribe to the doctrine and not, as is the case, as an ideal-type which fails adequately to convey the outlook of the English right.

Part of the explanation for the prevalence of this stereotype is that sceptics are admittedly not as sparse on the British political landscape as are revolutionary socialists. A cursory search can soon reveal various figures who, combining respect for tradition with an awareness of the limits of human knowledge, exemplify what is reputed to be the conservative temper. Historians of conservatism, themselves in the main sympathetic to the doctrine, are adept at rummaging through the past in this fashion. Their technique is to retrieve a moderate and defensible conservatism by using a brisk and necessarily random method of exclusion and selection. The process entails the posthumous excommunication of avowed conservatives who cannot be comfortably accommodated within the canon, the recruitment of thinkers who died before the emergence of an identifiable Tory creed during the Restoration, and the re-christening of others who when alive either eschewed any party label or else belonged to the political opposition. Hence, for instance, Richard Hooker, who defended the Tudor state and church as the outcome of an evolving collective wisdom, is installed as the founding father; the Marquess of Halifax, a Restoration statesman and pamphleteer who never joined any political group and who despised the Tory belief in divine-right monarchy, is commended for his pragmatism; while the eighteenth-century Scottish historian and philosopher David Hume, who stood aloof from party conflict, is celebrated as an exemplar of the conservative mistrust of rationalism in politics.

By this reshuffling of the historical pack, too, the anti-Jacobin Edmund Burke is transformed from a Whig into the crowning embodiment of everything that is valuable in conservative thought. Nineteenth-century conservatives, discouraged by the young Burke's espousal of causes such as Catholic emancipation, looked elsewhere – particularly to Bolingbroke – for their ideological antecedents. There were, moreover, other writers (the neglected John Reeves, for instance) who elaborated a genuine Tory response to the ideas associated with the French Revolution. Yet by an audacious twentieth-century trick, so successful that no serious student of the doctrine would now dare ignore him, Burke has become the principal occupant of the Tory pantheon. His exposure of the metaphysical follies of the French Jacobins and their English allies, his claim that historical experience is a surer guide to political practice than deductive logic, his deprecation of the 'private stock' of individual reason when isolated from 'the general bank and capital of nations and of ages', and his endorsement of the 'prescriptive' authority of a settled constitution – these are said to constitute the ingredients of an articulate and thorough conservatism. The canonization of Burke is central to the retrospective task of establishing the continuity of doctrinal scepticism. The effect is to portray modern conservatives as heirs of a robust intellectual tradition which, spurning facile optimism, has continually made a virtue of the 'politics of imperfection'.[1]

The tendency to equate conservatism with doctrinal scepticism has been reinforced by the enormous influence on postwar English political philosophy of Michael Oakeshott. Politics, for him, 'is not the science of setting up a permanently impregnable society, it is the art of knowing where to go next in the exploration of an already existing traditional kind of society'.[2] Politicians do not consult rule books or govern according to principles of universal validity regardless of the circumstances of time and place. Instead, like experienced cooks, they practise the acquired skills of prudence and intuition. People of a conservative disposition, being sensitive to the diversity and limitations of human conduct, appreciate that politics is the art of attending to social arrangements by the pursuit not of some grand enterprise, but of the 'intimations' of an intricate evolving process. Hence, unlike their opponents, conservatives neither retreat into abstractions nor pretend that there is an ultimate purpose in politics beyond ensuring the continuity of a particular way of life.

The British academic right, seemingly spellbound by Oakeshott's distinction between technical and practical knowledge, have in recent decades produced a spate of books arguing that conservatism is not a systematic theory for improving the human condition. It articulates instead the concreteness of political activity, and in doing so reveals the folly of any attempt to manipulate society according to preconceived ideas. A common argument of Oakeshottians is that conservatism is not an ideology. This claim, taken at face value, implies that conservatives either lack a distinct view of society or else are incapable of thinking intelligently about politics. Philosophical sceptics, of course, do not imagine that they belong to what J. S. Mill called 'the stupid party', and their intention is to denigrate other political doctrines by characterizing ideology as a negative mode of thought. Conservatives refrain from ideological speculation, it is said, because they do not succumb to the illusion that individuals can be delivered from the trials and tribulations of present society into some future golden age. Those of other political persuasions, by contrast, construct political ideals in the false expectation of changing human nature by social engineering. The message being transmitted, with only a little deciphering, is: 'You liberals and socialists are starry-eyed extremists who indulge in a perverted form of knowledge in the vain hope of eradicating human imperfection; we are sane pragmatists who attain genuine understanding of the political order because of our attachment to experience.' As such the insistence that conservatism is non-ideological belongs to the rough-and-tumble of political argument. Polemics of this sort are an ideological exercise in themselves which, though often entertaining, do not require serious consideration.[3]

A less rumbustious, though hardly less fatuous, aspect of this style of thinking is its parochialism. It is alleged, for instance, that 'true conservatism' – the kind which shuns political ideals and is disinclined to set the world to right – 'is a decidedly English doctrine with little appeal and no following in other countries [because] only English and hence British political institutions have ever been decent enough to allow a decent man to be conservative'.[4] Another author, having expended a deal of energy demonstrating why conservatives are averse to the rationalist temper in politics, reaches the banal conclusion that children should be compelled in certain circumstances to play the quintessentially English game of cricket. The justification for this restriction of individual liberty is said to derive not from a priori speculation, but from an observation that cricket is the kind of activity which makes life meaningful for the inhabitants of a specific political culture.[5]

At its best, however, philosophical scepticism transcends Anglomania to make some trenchant criticisms of modernity. Here the intention is to lament the decline of genuine conservatism rather than defend the views and practices of its contemporary adherents. Although conservatives once sought to maintain a limited state, Noel O'Sullivan argues, they have now embraced the heresy that social progress can be consciously planned. O'Sullivan's characterization of the doctrine as a commitment to limited government seems odd in so far as liberals – not conservatives – have traditionally wished to erect constitutional barriers against arbitrary power. Whereas conservatives have tended to mistrust the 'private stock' of individual reason when undisciplined by law and social convention, liberals have generally supposed that the relatively unimpeded exercise of private judgement is both morally desirable and of benefit to the community. Hence the concern of liberals to identify a preserve of individual rights within civil society from which the state is prohibited.

What O'Sullivan has in mind is a distinction made by Oakeshott between two types of political society: in one, that of a civil association, the state is restricted to making and enforcing rules which enable individuals to shape their own lives; in the other, government is an instrument for implementing a shared vision of happiness. The function of conservatism, according to O'Sullivan, is to maintain a civil association through a limited style of politics. But since 1945, he claims, the civil philosophy which once sustained authentic conservative practice has been almost eclipsed by a conviction that the state is an enterprise for promoting consumer affluence and capitalist efficiency. And he therefore urges conservatives, in a mood of nostalgic resignation rather than confidence, to resolve a crisis of identity by rediscovering their intellectual heritage.[6]

Oakeshottism of this sort is remote from the perspective of modern conservatives and also, though O'Sullivan is reluctant to admit this, from much of their ideological tradition. In a sense it matters little for O'Sullivan's purpose whether conservatives once avoided visionary politics: the concept of a civil association serves as an ideal type, providing a backcloth against which he can highlight allegedly undesirable features of the modern polity. It does matter, however, in that O'Sullivan has also written a history of conservatism, a lucid and subtle work, in which he again associates the doctrine with a preference for limited politics.[7] The problem, of course, is that he is hard pressed to find more than a handful of English thinkers who fit the description before the twentieth century, and precious few thereafter. In contrast therefore to more promiscuous historians, who seize upon some unlikely figures, the fastidious O'Sullivan excludes from the conservative camp many who properly belong there.

To find conservatives who, from the perspective of philosophical scepticism, have strayed deep into alien ideological territory, one need look no further than the New Right's crusade to cleanse Britain of every trace of socialism. What is Thatcherism if not a visionary scheme to transform society according to the inescapable science of political economy? And where, in its mixture of abrasively theoretical market economics, uncompromising anti-egalitarianism and fervent patriotism, are the ingredients of what Oakeshottians judge to be authentic conservatism? Thatcherites are no less disposed than the wildest of socialists to promise the moon. There was little apparent hostility to abstractions in the glee with which free-marketeers seized the intellectual initiative during the mid-1970s, little sense of the limits of human reason or of the wisdom of piecemeal reform in the zeal with which they eventually set about dismantling collectivism, little sign of loyalty to a settled way of life in their contempt for the postwar consensus, and little appreciation of the intricacies of an organic community ('There is no such thing as society', Margaret Thatcher pronounced, 'there are only individuals') in their impatience to loosen constraints upon competitive individualism: nothing, in short, to indicate that 'conservatism bases its appeal on existing fact or on historic record [because] it has the prosaic and unexciting duty of displaying the merits of things as they have been and are'.[8]

In a sense, of course, Thatcherites do not break decisively with tradition. Often they contrast the economic and cultural torpor of postwar Britain with the achievements of a more glorious past. The intention is to summon the nation to advance not into an untried future, but backwards to the Good Old Days of Victorian enterprise and, in Mrs Thatcher's case, beyond – to the first Elizabethan age when merchant adventurers carried English values and commerce around the globe. This counter-revolutionary appeal to the 'historic record' is nevertheless based upon a clear conception of how society should be organized: a Brutopia of capitalist prosperity offering little protection for those unable to compete in the struggle for survival.

Right-wing radicals, notwithstanding nostalgia for a lost golden age, have been energetic in their efforts to release market forces throughout society. From 1979 they unsettled the British way of life by assaulting many of the institutions and ideas which, from the perspective of philosophical scepticism, constitute the conservative nation. In a period when the avowed custodians of tradition have been more ruthlessly dynamic than any Labour government, the citizen does not have to be a conservative to cherish the irenic spirit of Anglicanism, to admire the collegial ethos of universities, to take pride in that symbol of British decency, the National Health Service, to wish to preserve the relative autonomy of the civil service and the BBC, to be grateful for the particular rights and liberties that have been deposited down the centuries in common law, and to favour constitutional safeguards against arbitrary power. In these topsy-turvy times, indeed, guardians of the organic community are more likely to be found in the 'people's party' than in the new model army of the 'patriotic party'.

Some moderate Tories, including Lord Pym and Sir Ian Gilmour, believe that Thatcherites have placed themselves beyond the pale of conservatism by their passionate disregard for institutions hindering market capitalism. The Conservative Party, they complain, has been hijacked by sectarians intent on substituting the infallible laws of economics for the art of prudent statecraft. There is nothing new in this sort of charge. It was made by patrician Tories against Peelites early in the nineteenth century, by tariff reformers against the acolytes of Herbert Spencer who at the end of the century vindicated *laissez-faire* with a science of social evolution, and from the 1930s by advocates of a mixed economy against recalcitrant individualists within the party. Conservatives, always prone to ideological quarrelling among themselves, have frequently accused one another of heresy in discarding pragmatism for doctrinal simplicity.

They are happier, however, when castigating the theoretical excesses of their opponents. A favourite ploy is to suggest that support for progressive causes signifies the intrusion of foreign ideological influences into a native empiricist tradition. It has long been fashionable, for example, to depict British socialists as Bolsheviks in lounge suits. 'Conservatism is the very breath of English history', Harold Begbie wrote in a little book first published in 1924. 'Modern Socialism is a mushroom forced by Russian atheism on the dunghill of German economics. The one is at least an element in every Englishman's patriotism; the other, the poisonous vodka with which international enthusiasts stimulate their blissful vision of a world proletariat in chains to a world bureaucracy.'[9] Polemics of this sort are a populist version of philosophical scepticism. Even Michael Oakeshott, who should have known better, sometimes indulged in the smear tactics of Little Englandism. 'With eyes focused upon distant horizons and minds clouded with foreign clap-trap', he grumbled at the time of the immediate postwar Labour administration, 'the impatient and sophisticated generation now in the saddle has dissolved its partnership with its past and is careful of everything except its liberty'.[10] A fevered imagination must have been needed to suppose that Major Attlee, the most sober and quintessentially English of Labour leaders, embodied the spirit of Jacobinism.

Oakeshott's dislike of rationalism in politics is based upon the assumption that England has been relatively immune from the belief, prevalent in continental Europe after the Renaissance and especially from the Enlightenment onwards, that deliberate action can lead to social progress. Tories, in fact, have always called for vigilance against pernicious ideas that are likely to float across the English Channel. And they have frequently accused domestic radicals of being infected with the bug of European rationalism. Sir Robert Filmer blamed an unlikely conspiracy of Romish Jesuits and Genevan Calvinists for introducing the doctrine of popular sovereignty into seventeenth-century England; John Reeves believed that all eighteenth-century reformers were the intellectual descendants of those same Protestant sectaries; and Benjamin Disraeli rebuked nineteenth-century Whigs for steering the ship of state into turbulent waters by navigating according to 'cosmopolitan' rather than national principles. This island race will remain a conservative nation, is the persistent message, only so long as it maintains a fortress against extraneous ideological missiles.

There are two major flaws in this image of a nation largely insulated from political abstractions. First, England has long been a nursery of ideas for subverting the established power structure. Indeed, because the nation-state was thrown into turmoil at a relatively early stage in its formation, republican and democratic ideals flourished there before they took root in other parts of the world. The fiction that political society is a contract between mutually consenting adults, which underpinned demands for manhood suffrage, the abolition of monarchy and aristocratic privilege, and for an extension of individual liberties, was elaborated during the Civil War period of the seventeenth century. And the doctrine of natural rights, the core idea of contractualism, subsequently became the clarion cry of American and other colonists in their struggle to escape from the clutches of the British Empire, as well as of French Jacobins. Margaret Thatcher had a point, though not the one intended, when she informed the French at the bicentenary celebrations of their Revolution that the concept of human rights had been conceived on the other side of the Channel. Dreams of a fairer, less hierarchical community are as intrinsic to English political culture as sceptical reluctance to challenge the prescriptive authority of existing social arrangements.

Conservatism itself, secondly, is awash with abstractions. Those in the party hostile to extensive government have continually been tempted by what a nineteenth-century Tory called the 'theoretic folly' of political economy. W. H. Mallock, a prolific writer at the turn of the century, spent forty years formulating a 'scientific conservatism' to demonstrate that unrestricted capital accumulation is the prerequisite of social progress. Even Burke, who is supposed to epitomize the conservative mistrust of deductive logic, repudiated Jacobin egalitarianism by asserting that market forces are 'the laws of nature, and consequently the laws of God'. Nor is the penchant for speculative reason confined to conservatives who believe that the laws of supply and demand are as inevitable as those of gravity. Toryism originated with a doctrinal flourish: the extravagant claim, made in the aftermath of the Civil War and Interregnum, that the restored dynasty had been divinely conferred with unqualified power through lineal succession from Adam. Disraeli, though critical of Whigs for succumbing to continental rationalism, also reproached the Peelite Conservative Party of the 1840s for degenerating into an unprincipled faction. And Robert Peel himself, though disinclined to adopt the principles of beneficent social hierarchy favoured by Disraeli, was a dogmatic free-marketeer. Only rarely have conservatives refrained from the intellectual sins which they commonly impute to others.

One reason why conservatives may appear suspicious of abstractions is their habit, as it is sometimes described, of stealing Whig clothes: their tendency initially to resist innovation but, once change is forced upon them, to defend the new arrangements as an aspect of traditional society. In constitutional matters, for example, Tories have consistently opposed reforms before subsequently accepting them as means of strengthening the political fabric. Having vindicated the absolutism of divine-right monarchy, they soon adjusted to the Glorious Revolution of 1688, which established the principle that sovereignty ought to be distributed between the crown and the two Houses of Parliament. Viscount Bolingbroke, the most prominent of eighteenth-century Tories, traced the origin of this concept of power-sharing back to the mists of English history in order to condemn the executive despotism of the Whig Establishment. Evoking the same idea of a co-ordinate authority of the three estates of the realm during the debates leading to the great Whig Reform Act of 1832, conservatives warned that an extension of the franchise would precipitate mob rule. Once the Bill was enacted, however, Peelites welcomed it as an opportunity of consolidating the alliance of upper and middle classes against the threat of democracy. In these ways Tories have contrived to depict themselves not as constitutional die-hards, but as prudent custodians of the ancient framework of government.

In doing so, however, they have been inclined to 'utopianize the present'.[11] They have frequently countered proposals for innovation by claiming that the British political system is, in the words of an eighteenth-century Tory, 'the best in the whole World' and 'as Perfect as a Humane Constitution can be'. J. S. Mill, writing in the aftermath of the 1832 Reform Act, noted the peculiar affection of avowed pragmatists for theoretical purity. 'There are people who talk to us of standing up for ancient institutions', he commented with regard to the determination of conservatives to withstand the democratic tide, 'and the duty of sticking to the British Constitution settled in 1688! What is still more extraordinary, these are the people who accuse others of disregarding variety of circumstances, and imposing their abstract theories upon all states of society without discrimination.'[12] Sometimes conservatives have been driven by their ideal of the inviolable constitution to adopt some remarkably unconstitutional tactics. During the Ulster crisis of 1912, for instance, some of them sanctioned armed resistance against the Liberal government as a means of maintaining the political integrity of the British Isles. Conservative deference to the practical wisdom of a settled way of life easily ossifies, paradoxically, into doctrinal rigidity.

Wherein then lies the identity of conservatism? Not in an avoidance of abstractions, as philosophical sceptics imagine, but in a particular conception of the political order. Conservatives, notwithstanding their differences, have been consistent in selectively using principles to construct a distinctive image of the social order. They have emphasized, on one hand, the military virtues of duty, obedience, loyalty, and submission to the authority of the state. Toryism originated in response to the contention that the rights of naturally free and equal individuals might, on occasion, nullify the obligation to be governed. Restoration royalists repudiated the alleged right of the 'body of the people' to resist arbitrary government by confirming the Pauline injunction to obey the powers that be. And whereas contractualists believed that the constitutional safeguarding of certain liberties – providing, in effect, a zone of self-governing existence largely immune from state interference – would secure individual autonomy and encourage civic virtue, Tories warned of the potentially subversive consequences of too much exercise of private judgement. From Restoration absolutism to the Thatcherite preoccupation with law and order, conservatives have always been fearful of social indiscipline.

They have persistently argued, on the other hand, that discipline requires authoritative leadership. And political leadership, conservatives suggest, is connected with the substantial ownership of property, whether inherited by birth into a 'territorial aristocracy', or acquired by entrepreneurial success. It would be a relatively simple task to compile an anthology of statements by conservatives affirming the necessity and desirability of social hierarchy, and the consequent futility of egalitarian schemes:

> There must always be an inequality of talent and skill just as there will always be those who lead and those who are led.

> All human experience proclaims that an equalitarian society in the purely economic sense is an illusion. Let us imagine that by some political alchemy it had been possible to make all men equal, to abolish all class distinctions, to pay equal wages and to award each man complete freedom of action. Within a very short space of time this new equality will have vanished into the mist. Some men will be rich, some will be poor. Some will be masters, some will be servants. A few will lead, the rest will follow. In a free society material inequality is natural and fundamental. Mutual equality would be a drag upon progress, for progress would be dependant upon the pace of the slowest.[13]

And again:

> If a society is to prosper, its political, social and economic arrangements must be such as to stimulate and satisfy those with most to contribute to the common good. In any society, at any time, there are some citizens who have more to contribute than others, and it is in everybody's interest that this outstanding minority should exercise more influence over public affairs than the untalented majority; should form, that is to say, a ruling class.[14]

The conservative image of the properly constituted political order is of a chain of social command linked by deference to authority, respect for the rule of law, sentiments of allegiance and patriotism, an anti-egalitarian ethos, aversion to class conflict, and the mixture of restraint and guidance provided by a minority.

Just how selective conservatives can be in using principles is illustrated by their fondness for the Christian doctrine of the Fall. Individuals are inherently depraved and predatory, they often claim, and would soon relapse into savagery without the restraint of law and morality. Anxiety about the destructive potential of fallen human nature explains the enthusiasm of many conservatives for such forms of social control as extensive police powers, corporal and capital punishment, firm action against truculent workers, the prohibition of pornography and sexual heterodoxy, and the censorship of what is published and broadcast. Mrs Thatcher, for example, has occasionally justified strengthening the authority of the state by referring to the sinful condition of mankind. In its implications the doctrine of original sin is profoundly egalitarian, because everyone is in need of both divine grace and social discipline to approximate to the decent human existence intended by the Creator. But conservatives stand the doctrine on its head. We may all be

> Frail children of dust
> And feeble as frail

yet a few, according to them, are able to shake off the dust to lead particularly praiseworthy and socially useful lives. This is so for two reasons.

There are, first, the particular habits and privileges associated with the differences of class. Burke, when condemning the levelling spirit of Jacobinism, noted the influence of socialization upon raw human nature. 'The legislators who framed the ancient republics', he commented in *Reflections on the Revolution in France*,

> had to do with men, and were obliged to study human nature. They had to do with citizens, and they were obliged to study the effects of those habits which are communicated by the circumstances of civil life. They were sensible that the operation of this second nature on the first produced a new combination; and thence arose many diversities amongst men, according to their birth, their education, their professions, the periods of their lives, their residence in towns or in the country, their several ways of acquiring and fixing property, and according to the quality of the property itself, all of which rendered them as it were so many different species of animals. From hence they thought themselves obliged to dispose their citizens into social classes, and to place them in such situations in the state, as their peculiar habits might qualify them to fill and to allot to them such appropriate privileges as might secure to them what their specific occasions required.[15]

Conservatives have long believed that the operation of this 'second nature' serves to protect a minority from many of the frailties which commonly afflict people. The argument, which took root in the relatively fixed hierarchy of a predominantly agrarian society, is that those born into a élite can, in an unusual degree, acquire knowledge and wisdom, cultivate taste and virtue, and engage in civilized conversation, as well as being imbued from an early age with the responsibilities of public service. They are therefore less likely to be corrupted by power than those untrained in its exercise.

Owning large amounts of property, moreover, they are unlikely to be excited by the passions which often prompt the poor to embrace intemperate schemes of political reconstruction. Social breeding, then, counteracts the post-lapsarian human condition by creating a governing class equipped, as Burke put it, to be the 'soul' of the body politic.

Some conservatives, secondly, appear to believe in what one of them disparagingly called 'the immaculate conception of the rich'.[16] This argument, which took shape amid the rapid expansion of nineteenth-century industrial capitalism, is that some individuals make an exceptional contribution to society through their own efforts rather than the accident of birth. Entrepreneurs achieve success by energy, ambition and flair. These 'wonderful people', as Margaret Thatcher once called them, allegedly possess rare qualities of moral vigour and economic dynamism. And from their leadership is said to flow the prosperity and progress without which society would stagnate. So while conservatives are convinced that evil is abroad in the world, they do not believe in an equality of wickedness. The officers aboard the ship of state appear in conservative imagery as rather splendid chaps, even though they must sometimes batten down the hatches on an unruly and possibly mutinous crew.

Conservatives have generally been in agreement about the means of selecting the officers. 'They agree that the final object of a social organization is to see that wealth and power are distributed in accordance with fitness', wrote a Tory publicist,

> and that the ultimate justification of all privilege is that it is the means of service. They recognize three chief methods of selection. The first, that of competitive examination, implies that it is the duty of the State to give exceptionally talented subjects the opportunity of a full education . . . The second method of choice, that of Liberal capitalism, or the survival of the fittest in open competition, has the advantage that those who prove their fitness by satisfying actual demands are automatically rewarded. Its disadvantage is that the rapid fluctuations of personal and social prosperity which it involves destroy stability. It is therefore the object of Conservatism to preserve as many of the virtues and as few of the defects of Liberal capitalism as possible by means of a judicious combination of authority and liberty. Finally, within reasonable limits, the Conservative approves of hereditary selection.[17]

The 'natural aristocracy' envisaged by Burke, for example, consisted of professional and commercial groups, besides proprietors of inherited wealth. On occasion, however, conservatives have censored one another for wishing to recruit inappropriately qualified people into the governing class. A complaint of landed Tories against the Peelite party was that it had fallen under the sway of industrial capitalists lacking an ethos of public service; Edwardian Tories regretted the corruption of their party by a new breed of plutocrats; while Peregrine Worsthorne, one of the most interesting of contemporary conservative thinkers, argued in 1987 that Thatcherism had become too closely identified with 'bourgeois triumphalism': hard-nosed financial 'yuppiedom', which was undermining 'the high traditions of Britain's governing order'.[18] Thatcherites, in contrast, are the heirs of nineteenth-century individualists opposed to the complacency of the British Establishment. Mrs Thatcher's frenetic campaign against so many public institutions was to some extent motivated by a conviction that wealth creation had been inhibited by the cosy paternalism of the traditional élite. Her intention was to reinvigorate the economy by enabling entrepreneurs to assume a more prominent position in the nation's leadership.

Differences among conservatives are more visible on the issue of how the officers should pacify the crew. Tory paternalists have wished to attach the people to what Disraeli called their 'natural leaders' through a judicious combination of authority and benevolence. They have argued, from a fear of popular unrest as well as from a sense of *noblesse oblige*, that the privileged classes should attend to the condition of those placed in their charge. 'I wish for reform', announced Robert Southey in the spirit of early nineteenth-century Tory philanthropy, 'because I cannot but see that all things are tending towards revolution, and nothing but reform can by any possibility prevent it.' Tory Democracy, which blended themes of patriotism and social amelioration, was conceived as a strategy for securing allegiance to the party at a time of working-class enfranchisement; and the post-1945 commitment of the Conservative Party to full employment in a welfare state was often justified as a continuation of this late nineteenth-century tradition of One Nation Toryism. Paternalists believe that political economy absolves the wealthy from their protective responsibilities, and have frequently objected that the Conservative Party is being blown off course by free-market dogma. This was a complaint made against Peelites by Tory reformers, who hoped to curtail the spread of acquisitive values by strengthening the social ties binding the unenfranchised masses to the landed classes. In recent years dissident Tories, echoing the charge levelled at Peel by Disraeli, have accused Thatcherites of re-creating two nations of rich and poor.

Others prefer to combine the authority of the state with the discipline of a market economy. Public provision of extensive welfare entails excessive taxation of wealth-creators for the subsistence of the poor, according to free-marketeers from Burke to Thatcher, and thereby impedes social progress by deterring entrepreneurship. In addition, the pampering of subjects by an indulgent government is said to weaken self-reliance by creating an ethos of dependence upon the state. The effect is to undermine political stability by putting pressure on government to assume functions it cannot adequately fulfil. When the state appeases the citizenry by tampering with market forces, it cannot discharge the primary responsibility of securing law and order. Burke feared that the spirit of Jacobinism would subvert ordered hierarchy in England by arousing unrealistic expectations of social amelioration. And some conservatives suggest that postwar managed capitalism not only inhibited economic growth, but also made the nation ungovernable. Rising crime rates, the militancy of workers accustomed to inflationary pay increases, and the unruliness of a citizenry corrupted by moral permissiveness – these were allegedly symptoms of the general disintegration of authority into what Worsthorne called 'riotous disorder'. Thatcherites are fond of contrasting the indiscipline of the welfare state with those habits of independence, thrift, moral sobriety, and respect for authority said to be characteristic of the Victorian enterprise culture. Their intention on assuming power in 1979 was to restore the authority of the state by confining government within its legitimate sphere: the preservation of a stable currency and the maintenance of public order.

Differences of this sort among conservatives tend to condense into two contrasting views of the political order. In the one, society is a hierarchy of privileges and obligations in which wealth is held in trust for the common benefit; while in the other it is a fluid structure of competitive individualism where the successful are not plunderers of the poor, but creators of prosperity which trickles down to everyone. Observers can usually recognize the distinctive characteristics of the former, but sometimes fail to identify the specifically conservative features of the individualist conception. This is so for two reasons.

The first has to do with the ideological preoccupations of the observers. For R. J. White, for instance, the character of conservatism derives from 'the alluvial deposit' of aristocratic society, with its ethos of responsible proprietorship and legislation on behalf of the poor.[19] Occasionally the doctrine has been tainted with *laissez-faire* dogma, but was soon purified by Tories eager to protect the masses from the 'thraldom of capital' by reaffirming the principles of beneficent social hierarchy. Free-market ideas are thus depicted as an alien intrusion into the conservative tradition, which culminated, in White's account, with Disraeli's furbishing of feudal ideals for a democratic age, only to collapse within a few decades amid a sordid quarrel about tariff reform. His anthology of the tradition, indeed, is more of a requiem for Merrie England than an attempt to capture the diversity of conservative thought.

W. H. Greenleaf, in contrast, has no difficulty in conveying the diversity of conservative thinking, and is certainly not inclined to excommunicate those who subscribe to the science of political economy. In his concern to identify genuine differences within the doctrine, he is reluctant to concede that its two major strands are linked by any unifying themes or common concepts. He prefers instead to reveal the essential ambivalence of conservatism by highlighting the opposing views of its adherents with regard to the legitimate functions of the state. The tensions embodied within conservatism, according to Greenleaf, reflect a debate which has dominated the political scene for more than a century. And his immensely rich and detailed study of the British ideological heritage is intended to illustrate how all the major doctrines have attracted both libertarians and collectivists – the former favouring limited government in order to safeguard citizens against arbitrary rule, and the latter wanting the state to pursue some common purpose which transcends particular interests. He admits that collectivist conservatism is 'authoritarian' in emphasizing the role and responsibilities of a governing élite.[20] When considering libertarianism, however, he has little to say about the fixation of individualist conservatives with entrepreneurial leaderhip, or about their desire for a state strong enough to discipline individuals who fail to respond to the moral and economic imperative of market forces. He dwells instead on their anti-statist concern to preserve individual freedom and private enterprise by restricting government to a minimum.

Libertarianism and collectivism are alternative expressions for the distinction which Oakeshott makes between two conceptions of the state, a civil association protecting individual liberties through the rule of law, and an enterprise promoting the common welfare. In using the typology to characterize the two strands of conservatism Greenleaf, unlike Noel O'Sullivan, is at least prepared to admit into the conservative fold people not committed to limited government. Nevertheless he is an admirer of Oakeshott, about whom, indeed, he has written a book.[21] So it is not surprising that, sharing his mentor's distaste for rationalism in politics, he should depict libertarian conservatism as a far from ignoble attempt to combat collectivism by securing a civil association in which individuals can run their own lives. Like White, though from a different perspective, Greenleaf allows his ideological sympathies to cloud his historical judgement. The effect is to obscure the coherence of conservatism by representing its various strands almost as distinct, even rival ideologies.

The second reason why observers mistake the identity of individualist conservatism is their tendency to characterize it as liberalism in disguise. Thatcherism, for example, is often described in the literature on the subject as 'classical' or 'economic' or 'neo-' (whatever that may mean) liberalism, because of its intention of 'leaving society and the economy alone'.[22] Conservative politicians themselves in recent years have sometimes located themselves in the tradition of nineteenth-century liberalism. In 1976 a number of conservative intellectuals, worried by the Thatcherite emphasis on emancipating people from the clutches of government, formed a group to counter the 'liberal' rhetoric of the market. Conservatives should be wary of the concept of economic freedom, according to the Salisbury Group, because it obscures the need for a stratified society disciplined by a state which is 'large and strong'.

The accusation that free-market conservatives are closet liberals is not novel. Tory Democrats at the end of the nineteenth century feared that the party would be diverted from attending to the welfare of the people by the infiltration of 'Manchester School liberals'; while conservatives who favoured economic planning and greater social welfare in the 1930s believed that the party was inhibited, by the presence of too many unreconstructed liberals, from following a middle way between unbridled capitalism and socialist regimentation. Long before the advent of Thatcherism, moreover, conservative proponents of competitive individualism were not unhappy to acknowledge their debt to the founders of what is usually known as liberal political economy. Peel, for instance, claimed to be following the economic doctrines prevalent 'from the days of Adam Smith'. The history of conservatism discloses a sort of conspiracy between libertarians and collectivists to depict the former as liberals of the classical variety.

After two hundred years, however, the suggestion that *laissez-faire* is a congenitally or inherently liberal idea is wearing a little thin. The free market is one of those ambiguous or contestable concepts amenable to diverse political purposes. Its meaning is fixed or decontested, as is that of other elastic concepts such as individual liberty and social equality, by ideological usage. Radicals who opposed the Corn Laws, for example, also condemned the balanced constitution, beloved of Tories for its co-ordinate authority of the three estates, as a bastion of the privileges and patronage of a predominantly landed élite. Unlike Peelites, therefore, they linked their demand for free trade to a campaign to establish democratic and other rights against an overmighty state. In doing so they resorted to the language of political economy, in the same way as contractualists had previously used the rhetoric of natural rights, to advocate a sphere of self-governing existence within civil society where government was prohibited from entering. At the end of the century, when their party committed itself to securing welfare rights, most liberals discarded the ideal of a market economy for that of an interventionist state.

From Burke to Thatcher, in contrast, the concept of a free economy has been used to vindicate rather than undermine the authority of the state. Conservatives who at the turn of the century flocked into the Liberty and Property Defence League and the British Constitution Association – organizations which waged a rearguard ideological battle on behalf of economic individualism – were not intent on diminishing the authority of government or on subverting ordered hierarchy. Their fear was that the state would be prevented from securing the inequalities of property by the ineluctable demands of an enfranchised working class for programmes of social amelioration. And the intention of Thatcherites, in rolling back the state from the economy, has been to restore a disciplined society where government is released from the pressures of the postwar period to injure potential wealth-creators by embarking upon egalitarian schemes.

In conservative usage, then, the free economy has been consistently attached to an argument for firm government. It is the persistent image of society as a command structure in which the responsibilities of leadership can be exercised within the framework of a strong state – manifested in divine-right royalism, the Tory conception of mixed sovereignty, anti-Jacobinism, the doctrine of the survival of the fittest, One Nation Toryism and so forth – that distinguishes English conservatism from rival ideologies.

NOTES

1 Anthony Quinton, *The Politics of Imperfection: the religious and secular traditions of conservative thought in England from Hooker to Oakeshott*, London and Boston: Faber & Faber, 1978.
2 Michael Oakeshott, *Rationalism in Politics and other essays*, London: Methuen, 1962, p. 58.
3 An example of this approach is Kenneth Minogue, *Alien Powers: the Pure Theory of Ideology*, London: Weidenfeld & Nicolson, 1985.
4 Gordon Graham, *Politics in its Place: a Study of Six Ideologies*, Oxford: Clarendon Press, 1986, p. 188.
5 Lincoln Allison, *Right Principles: a conservative philosophy of politics*, Oxford: Blackwell, 1984, pp. 170–1.
6 Noel O'Sullivan, 'Conservatism', in David Miller, Janet Coleman, William Connolly and Alan Ryan (eds) *The Blackwell Encyclopaedia of Political Thought*, Oxford: Blackwell, 1987, pp. 97, 101; idem, 'Conservatism, the New Right, and the limited state', in Jack Hayward and Philip Norton (eds) *The Political Science of British Politics*, Brighton: Wheatsheaf, 1986, pp. 21–36.
7 Noel O'Sullivan, *Conservatism*, London: Dent, 1976.
8 F. J. C. Hearnshaw, *Conservatism in England: an Analytical, Historical, and Political Survey*, London: Macmillan, 1933, p. 7.
9 'A gentleman with a duster', *The Conservative Mind*, 2nd edn, London: Mills & Boon, 1924, p. 9.
10 Michael Oakeshott, *Rationalism in Politics*, op. cit., p. 50.
11 The phrase is used by Vincent Geoghegan, *Utopianism and Marxism*, London: Methuen, 1987, p. 4.
12 John Stuart Mill, *Essays on Politics and Culture*, Gertrude Himmelfarb (ed.), New York: Doubleday, p. 53.
13 Bernard Braine, *Tory Democracy*, London: Falcon Press, 1948, p. 67.
14 Peregrine Worsthorne, 'Too much freedom', in Maurice Cowling (ed.) *Conservative Essays*, London: Cassell, 1978, p. 141.
15 *The Works of Edmund Burke*, Vol. 2, London: George Bell, 1894, pp. 454–5.
16 Christopher Hollis, *Death of a Gentleman: the Letters of Robert Fossett*, London: Collins, 1957, p. 33.
17 T. E. Utley, *Essays in Conservatism*, London: Conservative Political Centre, 1949, p. 46.
18 Peregrine Worsthorne, 'Bourgeois triumphalist threat to Mrs Thatcher', *The Sunday Telegraph*, 7 June 1987, p. 22.
19 R. J. White, *The Conservative Tradition*, 2nd edn, London: Adam & Charles Black, 1964, p. 13.

20 W. H. Greenleaf, *The British Political Tradition, Vol. 2: The Ideological Tradition*, London: Routledge, 1983, p. 198.
21 W. H. Greenleaf, *Oakeshott's Philosophical Politics*, London: Longmans, 1966.
22 Kenneth Minogue, 'Introduction: the context of Thatcherism', in Kenneth Minogue and Michael Biddis (eds) *Thatcherism: Personality and Politics*, London: Macmillan, 1987, p. xii.

2 *From the Restoration to the French Revolution*

Toryism unfolded during the Restoration as a vindication of a hierarchical and deferential society in which the absolute power of a hereditary ruler was allegedly conferred by God. No sooner had the doctrine taken shape, however, than Parliament removed a royal tyrant in the Glorious Revolution of 1688, and in doing so abrogated the principle of absolute hereditary kingship. This assault upon divine-right monarchy left Tories floundering, according to conventional historiography, and inaugurated a century of political and ideological ascendancy for their Whig opponents. It is true that the Tory Party was in almost permanent opposition for the first half of the eighteenth century, and became practically invisible during subsequent decades. Yet eighteenth-century Toryism was not the incoherent, defensive and backward-looking ideology often portrayed by historians. Tories soon adapted to the Revolutionary settlement by transferring the attributes of sovereignty from unlimited monarchy to the three estates of Crown, Lords and Commons. In doing so, they could accuse Whigs of disturbing constitutional equilibrium by their despotic ambitions; they could also preserve the authoritarian tenets of Restoration absolutism by claiming that subjects were bound by a divine injunction to obey those who exercised sovereignty within an admirably balanced political system. This ideal of ordered hierarchy within the framework of a model constitution received fresh impetus at the time of the French Revolution; and, in the nineteenth century, it was to be the basis of an appeal to the propertied classes to support the new Conservative Party.

Political debate in the early part of the seventeenth century focused on the issue of whether royal power derived from divine appointment or arose from the consent of the community. Rulers exercised an absolute authority, according to royalists, because kingship was 'not a *Deriuation*, or *Collection* of humane power scattered among many, and gathered into one head; but a *participation* of Gods owne *Omnipotency*, which hee neuer did communicate to any *multitudes* of men in the world, but, *onely*, and *immediately*, to his owne Vicegerents'.[1] For proponents of limited monarchy, by contrast, kings were not entitled to levy taxes, for instance, without parliamentary approval, and some theorists contended that God had originally lodged sovereignty in the multitude rather than a single person – thereby leaving the choice of an appropriate form of government to the people's discretion. In this view, the extent of royal authority had been determined at the time of the initial transfer of power from the community, which meant that rulers were circumscribed by the conditions imposed upon by their ancestors. The theories of absolute and limited monarchy were refined during the English Civil war of the 1640s. During this period, moreover, there was an outbreak of radical populism in which condemnation of royal absolutism was extended into an offensive against every form of ecclesiastical and secular hierarchy. Protestant sectaries, who believed that individuals could apprehend scriptural truths without guidance from the bishops of the established church, used a consensual theory of the origins of legitimate political power to demand a written constitution ratified by popular approval and enshrining individual rights.

Radicalism diminished after the execution of Charles in 1649, and more or less disappeared with the Restoration of monarchy in 1660. The early years of the Restoration took the form of a counter-revolution which reimposed censorship, revived most of the pre-Civil War prerogatives of the Crown, removed Parliament's right of regular assembly, and prohibited dissent from a reconstituted Church of England. Theoretical underpinning for the new regime came largely from Anglican clergy, who reaffirmed the ideal of a social hierarchy integrated by religious uniformity and by unconditional obedience to a divinely commissioned monarch. Their immediate task was to eradicate the ideological legacy of the previous twenty years. This was a formidable enterprise in so far as the collapse of traditional patterns of authority had prompted absolutists to make two significant concessions to their opponents.

First, some royalists had conceded that the king could not enact laws without the sanction of Parliament. Even Charles I, in *His majesties answer to the xix propositions of both houses of parliament*, published on the eve of Civil War, had admitted that the nation possessed a system of mixed government, because the legislative functions of monarchy were shared with the Lords and Commons. Parliamentarians, seizing on this retreat from absolutism, had extended the argument by suggesting that sovereignty resided in three co-ordinate estates of the realm, which entitled the two Houses of Parliament to preserve the public interest by overriding an arbitrary monarch. For Restoration propagandists, however, the admission that England was a mixed monarchy had been a blunder on the part of royalists, which had given their opponents a pretext to depose and eventually execute Charles.[2]

Secondly, some absolutists had appropriated the idea that legitimate government is based upon the people's consent. Unlike radicals, they intended not to emphasize rights which individuals could exercise against an overmighty church and state, but rather to reach the authoritarian conclusion that a ruler should be vested with unfettered power for the sake of peace and stability. Individuals were equally endowed by nature with a right of protection – so ran the argument – but, given their inclination to clash with one another, they could secure their particular interests only by mutually agreeing to surrender the right of self-defence to publicly constituted authority. People were therefore obliged by considerations of self-interest to obey the commands of established government. Such contractual justifications of political obligation were expounded by a few royalists during the Civil War, developed after 1649 to vindicate the authority of the new republic, and received their most conspicuous elaboration in Thomas Hobbes's great work, *Leviathan*.[3] But Restoration royalists were appalled by this attempt to ground obedience in self-interest rather than in a divine injunction. By conceding that political authority derived from the consent of individuals who were naturally free and equal, they believed, absolutists had strayed into alien ideological territory, where instead of being reminded of their duties to obey those whom God had set over them, the people were urged to be vigilant in case government encroached upon their rights.

One of the first Restoration writers to repudiate the ideas spawned by the 'late sad Troubles and distractions' was Robert Sanderson, the new Bishop of Lincoln. In a preface to *The Power Communicated by God to the Prince, and the Obedience Required of the Subject*, written by Archbishop Ussher and published posthumously in 1661, Sanderson attacked the concept of mixed monarchy, and ridiculed the suggestion that the Crown was but one of three co-ordinate estates. He reserved most of his scorn, however, for the contention that political authority derived from the mutual accord of free and equal individuals in a state of nature. How could a pact have been made between individuals in an anarchic situation lacking settled rules of procedure? Was everyone, including children, women and the insane, equally involved in the decision to constitute public authority? Did the social contract bind persons who either had withheld their assent or were absent when the agreement was ratified? And why should subsequent generations accept the terms of an ancestral agreement in which they had not participated? Writers who speculated about a fictitious natural human condition became entangled in a web of contradictions, according to Sanderson – especially when they sought to determine whether or not private property pre-dated the establishment of government. Clarification was provided by scripture, particularly *Genesis*, which revealed that the dominion conferred upon Adam over creation was the origin of both property rights and political power. After the Flood, moreover, the unlimited sovereignty divinely entrusted to Noah had been the source of subsequent proprietorship and kingship. Scripture, then, did not record that God had sanctioned a social contract between naturally free individuals, but rather disclosed a story of how the patriarchal authority which Adam and Noah possessed as heads of their respective families had been gradually extended until polities existed throughout the world. Here was proof enough of the illegitimacy of any form of government except absolute monarchy.[1]

Restoration absolutism was not seriously challenged until the 1670s, when a nascent country party, led by Lord Ashley, the first Earl of Shaftesbury, attempted to arrest the drift to authoritarianism in church and state. His *Letter from a Person of Quality to his Friend in the Country*, issued in 1675 and probably written with the help of John Locke, highlighted the threat posed by an emerging court party, consisting 'of the high episcopal men, and the old cavalier' which was intent on consolidating both Anglican uniformity and the executive tyranny of the Crown. Clergy – ' the most dangerous sort of men alive, to our English government' – were held to be principally responsible for justifying arbitrary power, because they fostered the pretence

> that priest and prince may, like Castor and Pollux, be worshipped together as divine, in the same temple, by us poor lay-subjects; and that sense and reason, law, properties, rights, and liberties, shall be understood, as the oracles of those deities shall interpret, or give signification to them; and never be made use of in the world to oppose the absolute and free will of either of them.

The preface and text of *The Power Communicated by God to the Prince*, as well as a sermon which Sanderson had preached at Hampton Court in 1640 when a royal chaplain, were among the works cited in the *Letter* as evidence that clerics wished to sacrifice individual liberties on the altar of the divine right of kings and prelates.[4]

The rift between court and country parties widened with the Exclusion Crisis of 1679–81, when Parliament attempted on three occasions to disqualify the Duke of York, the future James II, from succession to the throne. The controversy, coupled with a suspension of censorship, precipitated a torrent of literature in which the doctrines of absolute and limited monarchy were debated to an extent unprecedented since the Civil War. Towards the end of the Crisis, moreover, the protagonists began to affix the labels Tory and Whig to one another. The former was a nickname for Irish brigands now transferred to the royalist court party, and the latter an epithet for Scottish Covenanters now attached to the exclusionist country party. The terms soon entered common usage, largely through the effective propaganda of a staunch monarchist, Roger L'Estrange.[5]

Whigs, anxious to exclude James in order to avert the twin dangers of popery and absolutism, used consensual arguments to demonstrate that Parliament might legitimately prevent someone succeeding to the throne who would jeopardize Protestant rights and liberties. Tories retorted with the familiar claim that hereditary kingship was an inviolable gift of God, and not a conditional delegation of power from a sovereign people. One Tory ploy was to suggest that their opponents, for all their raucous anti-popery, were in ideological collusion with Catholic writers of earlier times, who had also endowed the community with authority to correct or depose arbitrary rulers. It was in this context that Sir Robert Filmer's *Patriarcha: or the Natural Power of Kings*, which had been written before the Civil War, was published in 1680 for the first time, and immediately became the emblem of Restoration Toryism.[6]

Filmer's political theory was doubly useful to Tories during the Exclusion Crisis. First, like Sanderson, he portrayed kingdoms as families writ large. Using extensive scriptural and historical evidence, Filmer sought to demonstrate that the absolute familial dominion bestowed upon Adam and Noah had been transmitted to successive monarchs through the principle of primogeniture, whereby the eldest son inherited his father's authority and estates. The community, being devoid of sovereignty, was not entitled to participate in the legislative functions of monarchy, or to depose a ruler who breached the terms of an imaginary social contract; and though the two Houses of Parliament were valuable intermediaries in advising the king of the people's grievances, they did not share a co-ordinate authority with the Crown. *Patriarcha*'s message in the context of the Exclusion Crisis was that Whigs lacked authority to alter the succession to the throne. Second, the book opened with an assault upon Catholics and radical Protestants alike for arousing popular dissension against established government. By claiming that rulership originated through a conditional grant of power from naturally free individuals, wrote Filmer, both Jesuits and Calvinists had connived to undermine political stability.[2] Here was ammunition for Tories eager to accuse Whigs of conspiring with papists to sow the seeds of anarchy.

The Whig response to the publication of *Patriarcha* indicates the extent to which political opinion had polarized since the restoration of monarchy. Filmer was savaged in *Patriarcha non monarcha: The Patriarch Unmonarch'd*, written by James Tyrrell, grandson of James Ussher and editor of *The Power Communicated by God to the Prince*, who had now become a fierce opponent of absolutism and a supporter of the campaign to exclude James. The most famous rebuttal of Filmer, however, came from John Locke, who in two early Restoration tracts had cited extensively from Sanderson's lectures, *De Obligatione Conscientiae*, to demonstrate that there were few grounds for either religious dissent or political disobedience.[7] But in *Two Treatises of Government*, written during the Exclusion Crisis and published in 1689, Locke used *Patriarcha* as a peg on which to hang a condemnation of both ecclesiastical and political authoritarianism. The ideas of Filmer – 'the great champion of absolute power, and the idol of those who worship it'[8] – were exposed in the first treatise as a recipe for slavery. In the second treatise, Locke justified resistance to arbitrary power by formulating a doctrine of sovereignty not dissimilar from that which Filmer had attributed to Calvinists and Jesuits. Political power was held in trust from the community, not conferred upon kings through lineal succession from Adam, and rulers were therefore bound by the terms of an original contract to preserve the rights and liberties of their subjects. Government could be overthrown if the legislature or executive behaved tyrannically, and authority was then returned to 'the body of the people', the original source of political power.

Whigs failed in their objective of excluding the Duke of York, who succeeded to the throne in 1685. Instead of consolidating the alliance of Crown and church, however, James offended the Tory Anglican Establishment by tolerating Catholics and dissenters in his bid to govern with their support. This was a disastrous policy, and, opposed by Parliament and the bishops, James fled the country in 1688. The Glorious Revolution – in which Parliament disregarded the principle of indefeasible hereditary monarchy by installing the Calvinist William of Orange, son-in-law of James, on the throne – used to be portrayed as a victory for Locke's contractualism, and the death-knell of cherished Tory convictions. It was neither of these.[9]

Whigs were transformed by the Glorious Revolution from a subversive faction into a respectable party which wished to distance itself from the turmoil of the Exclusion Crisis. Forming part of the propertied élite, moreover, they were not anxious to embrace a doctrine which appeared to give 'the body of the people' authority to remove tyrannical power. Whigs therefore side-stepped the radical implications of Lockean theory by pretending that James had vacated the throne. In so far as Parliament had filled the vacancy, they argued, a constitutional breach had been repaired without either the government dissolving or the community exercising a right of resistance to an arbitrary ruler.

The offensive against divine-right monarchy posed a more acute dilemma for Tories. Some of the clergy refused to acknowledge William's legitimacy, and one of these non-jurors, Abednego Seller, collected the church's arguments against resistance into a volume, *The History of Passive Obedience Since the Reformation*, which he introduced by acclaiming Sanderson's 'admirable Preface' to *The Power Communicated by God to the Prince.*[10] Other Tories, glad to be rid of James, resorted to various tactics to justify the events of 1688. One was the fiction of the vacant throne, which made it possible to deny that resistance had occurred. Another was to suggest, in the fashion of some absolutists during the Civil War period, that the mere possession of power entitled a ruler to obedience from his subjects. This was a rather flimsy basis of political obligation, however, which aroused suspicion among their opponents about Tory allegiance to the new regime. Why, asked a pamphleteer, trust a Tory who, proclaiming 'the Divine Right of Succession', must be 'in Principle and inclination for K. *James*, and believes K. *William* a king *de facto* only, without a Rightful Title, and in plain English, an Usurper'?[11] The writer had a point. Before Tories could provide firm ideological support for the Revolutionary settlement – in which the new king had accepted the throne on terms agreed with Parliament, and enshrined in a Bill of Rights – they had first to concede that the community was competent to determine the extent of legitimate royal power.

This concession was soon made. Maybe James's assault upon the privileges of the Anglican Church had made Tories aware of the shortcomings of a doctrine which enjoined obedience to the Crown. Perhaps, too, they were persuaded of the desirability of constitutional safeguards against arbitrary government by the efforts of Whigs (in office between 1695 and 1702) to strengthen the executive. By the turn of the century some Tories were certainly emphasizing the capacity of the constitution to curb abuses of power. They did so by retrieving the Civil War concepts of mixed monarchy and co-ordinate authority which had been denounced by Restoration absolutists. The distinctive feature of English polity, wrote Sir Humphrey Mackworth in 1701, was its 'prudent distribution of power', which secured both the prerogatives of the Crown and the rights of subjects. Constitutional equilibrium was preserved through the co-ordinate authority of monarch, Lords and Commons, which, as Charles I had acknowledged in his *Answer to the xix proposition of both houses of parliament*, constituted a system of 'mutual checks' against overweening ambition by any of the three estates of the realm.[12] Tories had invented that ideal of the balanced constitution which historians usually associate with eighteenth-century Whiggism.

In extolling this constitutional trinity, Tories did not abandon the whole of their ideological legacy. The accession in 1702 of Anne, the daughter of James and a solid Anglican, helped to dispel doubts about the legitimacy of the Revolutionary settlement, especially as Tories were the governing party from 1702 to 1704, and remained in office until 1708. In confident mood, therefore, some publicists reaffirmed the authoritarian tenet of old-style absolutism that subjects were bound to obey established government. This they did by using patriarchal arguments to demonstrate that rulership and subjection were integral to the divine scheme. Yet eighteenth-century patriarchalism, contrary to the impression given by some historians,[13] was not a slightly diluted form of Filmerian absolutism. Tories recast non-resistance in a post-Revolutionary mould by discarding not only the principle of indefeasible hereditary succession, but also Filmer's belief in the divine right of unlimited monarchy. Patriarchalism was used instead to remind subjects of their duty to submit to those who exercised authority within the beneficial constraints of a balanced constitution.

An early exponent of this type of hybrid Toryism was Offspring Blackall. In an Accession Day sermon preached before the Queen in 1708, the year following his appointment as Bishop of Exeter, Blackall located the origin of sovereignty in the Garden of Eden. Rulership might have arisen by way of contractual gift from the '*Aggregate Body of the People*', he admitted, if

> this Multitude had sprung together out of the Earth; or if they had been all Created by God at one and the same Time: But it can't be true upon Supposition that they all descended from the same first Parents, *Adam* and *Eve*; for it being so, no Man, except only the first Man of all, ever came into the World, but he was naturally, at the very instant of his Birth, in a state of Subjection to some other Men: No Man, since the first, was ever, properly speaking, Free-born. For in his Natural Capacity, he was born a Subject to his own Parents, and in his Political Capacity to the King, or other Chief Governour of that Kingdom or State of which, at his birth, he became a Member. The People could not therefore give to any Man that Authority over either themselves or others which they themselves never had; They could not give to another what was not their own to give; they could not give to one Man what another Man was then in the Lawful Possession of. Thus, I hope, it appears, that Government is of Divine Institution, and that the Authority of those that are plac'd in Government, is from God.[14]

Blackall's doctrine of *The Divine Institution of Magistracy* was condemned by Benjamin Hoadly, an ardent clerical Whig, as a licence for tyranny.[15] Yet Blackall was no Filmerian. Scripture recorded that people were born into subjection, he admitted, but it did not prescribe absolute monarchy through lineal succession as the only legitimate form of government.

Blackall had already elaborated this argument in another Accession Day sermon, *The Subjects Duty*, in which he reminded his congregation of the biblical injunction to submit to those in authority. But though magistracy was 'Absolute, Unlimited, and Uncontroulable', the manner of its exercise varied between communities. The English nation was fortunate to possess an impeccable constitution, which inhibited arbitrary power by involving the three estates in legislation. Recently the government had prudently altered not the framework of the constitution, but the succession to the throne, and had imposed conditions upon its occupants – a legitimate exercise of sovereignty because the law of primogeniture did not apply rigidly even within families, and there was no reason why it should be an inalienable principle of monarchy.[3]

The Subjects Duty was repudiated by some on the right, who were astonished that its author, previously considered an orthodox High Churchman, should jettison the doctrine of absolute hereditary monarchy. Blackall had 'perplex'd the *Monarchy* with *Democracy* in his New Systeme of *Active* Obedience', it was said, and in doing so had 'Despoyl'd God's Vicegerent of his Chief Prerogative'.[16] But others recognized the advantage of attaching to a trinitarian legislature those attributes of sovereignty formerly associated with absolute monarchy. Blackall had expressed standard Anglican political theology, according to one writer – responding to Hoadly's broadside against *The Divine Institution of Magistracy* – because he 'pursu'd the true *Golden Mean*' between the extremes of arbitrary kingship and popular sovereignty.[17]

The advantage of following this *via media* emerged during the trial in 1710 of Henry Sacheverell, arraigned for preaching that English government was 'founded upon the *steady Belief* of the *Subjects Obligation* to an *Absolute*, and *Unconditional Obedience* to the *Supreme Power*, in *All* Things *Lawful*, and the utter *Illegality* of *Resistance* upon any *Pretence* whatsoever'.[18] By impeaching Sacheverell, a farcical but nevertheless formidable exponent of High Church views, 'for high crimes and misdemeanours', Whigs intended to discredit Toryism by revealing that it was still rooted in Restoration absolutism. But the trial backfired, even though the judgement went against Sacheverell, when the Whig prosecution justified the Glorious Revolution with contractual arguments, and in doing so invited the accusation that they approved of popular resistance to arbitrary power. Tories, on the other hand, emphasized the capacity of the balanced constitution to deal with the threat of tyranny. The Tory defence spent much time citing churchmen such as Ussher, Sanderson and Blackall to establish the orthodoxy of Sacheverell's doctrine of non-resistance.[19] More significantly, they denied that the doctrine was relevant in forming a judgement about the events of 1688. 'It can't be pretended', said Sir Simon Harcourt in his opening remarks for the defence, that 'there was any such Resistance used at the Revolution; the Supreme Power in the Kingdom is the Legislative Power; and the Revolution took effect by the Lords and Commons concurring and assisting in it.'[20] In this way Tories could depict themselves as the guardians of that 'prudent distribution of power' which secured the rights and liberties of subjects within an ordered hierarchy, and also, like their Restoration predecessors, smear

Whigs as crypto-anarchists who were willing to mobilize the people against government of which they disapproved.

Their skilful handling of the Sacheverell trial helped to secure electoral victory for Tories in 1710. With the death of Anne in 1714, however, the failure of Tories to unite in favour of the Hanoverian succession undermined their credibility as a governing party, and initiated half a century of exclusion from office. During this prolonged period of one-party government, Whigs promoted the interests of landed and financial capital through a corrupt and oligarchical political system, which weakened Parliament's control of the executive by a combination of extensive patronage and managed elections. Although the Whig Establishment did not share a monolithic political outlook,[21] its members rejected Lockean contractualism which endowed the people with a right of resistance to arbitrary power. Court Whigs adopted an ideological position not dissimilar from that of Tories in Anne's reign, who had professed to walk a middle way between tyranny and populism. Unconditional allegiance, according to Whigs, was due to the sovereign authority within a finely balanced constitution precluding abuse of power. Some Whigs now abandoned the claim that constitutional equilibrium had been restored by the Revolutionary settlement, arguing instead that the Bill of Rights had inaugurated an era of ordered liberty for the English nation – the inference being that Whigs were the custodians of a new golden age.

The Tory Party was marginalized rather than destroyed by the long Whig ascendancy, and much of its support came from the squirearchy, dismayed by the increasing subservience of Parliament to the executive, and disgruntled because their taxes were contributing to the success of creditors and speculators.[22] How many of them wished to restore the Stuart dynasty (excluded from the throne when the son of James II failed to succeed Anne) has been the subject of fierce controversy in recent years. While some historians suggest that most Tories were loyal to the Hanoverian regime,[23] others contend that the survival of post-1714 Toryism 'had much to do with Jacobitism both as a tactical option and as an ideology'.[24] The issue is obscured partly by the paucity of reliable evidence, but also because the attempt to discover a flourishing Tory Jacobitism is part of a larger project to demolish the Whig interpretation of history – which in turn is linked to the political project of burying modern socialism.[25] It may be that the apparently indissoluble connection between triumphant Whiggism and the Hanoverian monarchy kindled affection for the exiled Stuarts among many Tories; but again, there is little firm evidence that a substantial number were willing to place the Pretender James on the throne by means of domestic insurrection and foreign invasion. Jacobitism as a political tactic, moreover, did not necessarily imply belief in the divine right of absolute hereditary monarchy. One ideological option, favoured by Jacobites in the years preceding Anne's death, was to locate sovereignty in the co-ordinate authority of the three estates, and thereby turn the ideal of the balanced constitution against the Whig Establishment by alleging that it had showered the executive with prerogatives as mighty as those once claimed by royalists on behalf of kingship.[26]

The most renowned advocate of 'oppositional constitutionalism' during the Whig ascendancy was the former Tory minister, Henry St John, Viscount Bolingbroke, a political adventurer who had damaged his party by intriguing with James at the close of Anne's reign.[27] In the late 1720s and early 1730s (a period sandwiched between two spells of enforced exile in France because of his Jacobite sympathies) Bolingbroke elaborated a theory of the balanced constitution in a bid to lead the extra-parliamentary opposition to Robert Walpole's Whig administration. Bolingbroke was a patriarchalist in so far as he located the source of political authority in familial dominion, rather than in a pact between free and equal individuals inhabiting a state of nature. Magistracy was of 'divine appointment', he argued (using the same phraseology as Blackall) because 'there must be an absolute, unlimited and uncontrollable power lodged somewhere in every government'. Unfettered sovereignty did not have to be vested in indefeasible absolute monarchy, however, and Bolingbroke denounced Filmer as 'that ridiculous writer' who had 'advanced the silly and slavish notion of royal fatherhood'.[28] Particular forms of government were a matter of discretion, and the founders of the English nation had sensibly decided to establish a system of parliamentary monarchy. Citing the sixteenth-century cleric, Richard Hooker – as did many Tories and Whigs[29] – Bolingbroke claimed that the superiority of English polity derived from this ancestral agreement to involve the community in the legislative functions of the Crown.

This theory of the co-ordinate authority of the three estates was developed in *A Dissertation upon Parties*, published in 1735 shortly after Bolingbroke had written it in the fanciful hope of building a broad alliance against the Whig Establishment headed by Robert Walpole. Party labels were obsolete, argued Bolingbroke, because the bulk of the nation rejected both the 'obscure remnant' of divine-right Tories and the 'mercenary detachment' of Walpolean Whigs. Moderates from both parties should therefore support a revamped country party in opposition to a corrupt court oligarchy. Such unity was feasible because the ideological differences separating Whigs and Tories had not inhibited a common front against royal despotism in 1688. Whigs, then, had no legitimate claim to be the exclusive heirs of the Revolutionary settlement, especially as a faction of them were busily subordinating the legislature to an exalted executive. English history was depicted by Bolingbroke as a perennial struggle to restore the constitutional equilibrium bequeathed by the founders of the nation, when they framed a constitution in which sovereignty was lodged in the monarch-in-parliament. Frequent remedial action had been taken to seal the covenant between Crown and community which was implicit in a system of mixed government. In the Revolutionary settlement, moreover, the balanced constitution was restored on even firmer foundations, in so far as the Bill of Rights had both circumscribed the royal prerogative and clarified subjects' liberties. These foundations were now being eroded by a new form of executive despotism, however, which made it imperative for constitutionalists to unite in defence of parliamentary independence.[4] Bolingbroke had turned the post-Revolutionary ideological consensus into an assault upon Whiggism in office.

The 'broad bottomed'opposition party favoured by Bolingbroke failed to emerge. Instead the Whig oligarchy was removed from office by George III who, succeeding to the throne in 1760, perhaps fulfilled Bolingbroke's eventual dream of a 'patriot king' by surrounding himself with politicians lacking firm party affiliation. Historians tend to depict political strife in the second half of the eighteenth century as a contest between various Whig factions. It is true that few people described themselves as Tories. Although opposition Whigs often branded the governing party as Tory, allies of the court, anxious to counter the charge of being subversient to the Crown, either eschewed any political label or else accepted the appellation Whig. Despite the semantic confusion of politics in this period, it is not implausible to suggest that Toryism survived even without many overt adherents.

First, the parliamentary gentry of the old Tory party 'largely went into regular support of the successive ministries acceptable to George III',[30] and some of them obtained government posts. In the second place, the arrival of a monarch eager to free himself from dependence upon the Whig Establishment gave fresh impetus to the traditional ideal of a social hierarchy unified by religious uniformity and by passive obedience to divinely instituted government. This ideal was reinforced by the emergence in the 1760s of an extra-parliamentary reform movement, which condemned the Revolutionary settlement as a conservative arrangement for entrenching the interests of property at the expense of the rights and liberties of common subjects. Radicals used Locke's theory of the popular origins of legitimate political authority to demand both a wider franchise and the elimination of Anglican privileges. Churchmen responded by reaffirming a divine injunction to accept the established order. According to George Horne, who was to become Bishop of Norwich, subjection was natural in so far as rulership was rooted in familial relationships rather than in a Lockean social contract. Horne nevertheless used his patriarchal account of the source of political power to urge acquiescence not to unbridled monarchy, but to those who exercised sovereignty within the restraints of a finely balanced constitution.[31] In sanctifying the nation's trinitarian legislature, 'Old Tories' could confront a growing left-wing challenge to church and state by claiming, like their predecessors, to follow a middle course between arbitrary government and popular sovereignty.[32]

The gulf between radicals and conservatives widened with the French Revolution of 1789, which made a dramatic impact upon British public opinion. Numerous organizations sprang up to campaign for political reforms, including repeal of the reviled Test and Corporation Acts, which excluded religious dissenters from public office. Radicals now used contractual arguments to demand a transfer of power from the propertied élite to the community at large. Tom Paine, the leading publicist of the ideals of the Revolution, advocated the establishment of a British democratic republic, in which religious liberties and the other 'rights of man' would be safeguarded by a written constitution. Defenders of ordered hierarchy responded by ridiculing the doctrine of inalienable rights. In their anxiety to remind subjects of their duty of obedience, moreover, Tories sometimes repudiated the principle of the co-ordinate authority of the three estates, and in doing so discarded the ideological legacy of the eighteenth century. But a new form of conservatism took shape within the apparently atavistic shell of counter-revolutionary Toryism – one which emphasized the organic nature of society so as to demonstrate the superiority of historical experience over the abstract logic of the 'rights of man' as a guide to current political practice. This defence of the *ancien régime* at home, which was elaborated by some Whigs as well as Tories, underpinned a political alliance against republicans and democrats from which a more visible Toryism was eventually to emerge.

The most interesting Tory of the period was John Reeves, a staunch Anglican who endorsed discriminatory legislation against dissenters and Catholics. Reeves has attracted the attention of historians because of his efforts to suppress radicalism. Frightened at the prospect of both domestic insurrection and a French invasion, the government attempted to curtail the spread of English Jacobinism by a 'reign of terror' including mobilization of the militia, prohibition of meetings, rigorous enforcement of the libel laws, prosecution of leading radicals for treason and sedition, and the suspension of habeas corpus. This repressive policy was assisted by a wave of patriotism, in which loyalty was affirmed to the Crown and the established church as the pillars of constitutional stability. If the surge of authoritarian populism was to some extent spontaneous, it was nevertheless channelled by more than a thousand loyalist clubs, which emerged from the officially sanctioned Association for the Preservation of Liberty and Property against Republicans and Levellers – launched by Reeves in November 1792 amidst a blaze of publicity. The clubs were organized by the clergy and the propertied classes, but harnessed the energies of a rabble, whose members sometimes expressed their loyalty harmlessly, as when they burned effigies of Paine, but often did so by intimidating radicals. The Association also mounted an effective propaganda campaign by disseminating cheap counter-revolutionary prints, songs, tracts and handbills, (with titles such as *One Pennyworth of Truth from Thomas Bull to his brother John*) which exalted the king as a symbol of law and order. The loyalist clubs mostly vanished within a year, after successfully suppressing the organizations of their opponents.[33]

Historians have given less attention to Reeves's political ideas and to the controversy which they aroused.[34] His *Thoughts on the English Government* were conveyed in a series of *Letters*, in which he captured the fervent royalism of the time by locating sovereignty in the Crown. In the first *Letter*, published in 1795, he suggested that the tree of monarchy would survive even if the two branches of the legislature were 'lopped off'. The second *Letter*, which appeared four years later, was still more explicit in rejecting orthodox constitutionalism:

> The Idea of *Co-ordination* takes away all Relation of King, and subject, and every principle of derivation and dependence

> between the King and his two Houses . . . It contributes to make the King in Parliament, and the King out of Parliament distinct persons. It makes the Parliament a distinct thing from the King, and not a Council, belonging to him. It sets up a divided, multiform supreme power, contrary to both Law and practice, which only acknowledge one, entire, supreme head of the Government, exercising its functions, sometimes in Parliament, sometimes in Council, at other times by the Ministers and Officers of its own appointment, and known to the Law; to which supreme authority every body is subject, and owes allegiance.[35]

This inflation of the royal prerogative caused a furore in which many of the arguments of the previous century and a half surfaced once again. Charles James Fox, the leader of a minority of Whigs who welcomed the French Revolution and opposed the repression of English Jacobins, blamed the Association for the Preservation of Liberty and Property against Republicans and Levellers for provoking an authoritarian backlash which threatened subjects' rights and liberties. Some of the Association's publications would have been prosecuted as treasonable Jacobite tracts earlier in the century, he told Parliament in 1792, because they revived the doctrine of divine-right monarchy.[36] Fox was among those Whigs who in 1795 persuaded the Attorney-General to prosecute Reeves for 'libel on the British Constitution', and a parliamentary committee was established to authenticate the authorship of the first, anonymously published, *Letter*.

Whigs were outraged that someone who had formed his association with official connivance, and who remained in such intimate contact with ministers as to appear the 'mouthpiece of government', should have denigrated the Glorious Revolution as a 'fraud and farce', and depicted those claiming to be its heirs as imposters who, since 1688, had either been in the pocket of the court or in league with agitators. The charge of libel concerned the passage in the *Letter* in which Reeves had described the two Houses of Parliament as dispensable branches of the royal trunk. During the parliamentary debates and subsequent trial, Whigs condemned the *Letter* as a product of the 'school of Filmer', and contended that Reeves had done more than Henry Sacheverell to undermine the legitimacy of mixed government. In fact, Reeves had little sympathy with the proposition that monarchs derived their authority by divine commission through lineal succession from Adam. Filmer's doctrine of 'the divine indefeasible Right of Kings' was a mirror image of that of the rights of man, according to him, because both were speculative theories divorced from political reality.[37]

The government was embarrassed that one of its staunchest supporters had, largely because of a careless literary style, laid himself open to the charge of a belief in absolutism. In using the metaphor of the tree of monarchy, it was said in his defence, somewhat ingeniously, that Reeves had not implied that the Crown might legislate without the co-operation of the Lords and Commons. He had merely confirmed that government was not dissolved during a temporary suspension of Parliament. It was historically true, moreover, that the other two estates had been drawn into the legislative process at the Crown's initiative, and the sessions of Parliament were still summoned by royal writ. This attempt by the defence to remove the sting from Reeves's exuberant royalism succeeded, to the extent that he was acquitted of libel – though the jury censured him for issuing a 'very improper publication'.[38]

The row provoked by the *Letter* was a rumbling from an almost extinct volcano, not a warning of eruptions to come. Few now disputed the legitimacy of a system of mixed government: indeed, nineteenth-century Tories were to invoke the principle of co-ordination against Whig measures to extend the franchise. Moreover, the clamour over Reeves's apparent reversion to old-style absolutism concealed the novel and more interesting feature of his thought: the fact that he repudiated the doctrine of popular sovereignty by depicting an organic community gradually unfolding through accumulated wisdom. The essence of English government, according to Reeves, was to be discovered, not by abstract speculation or deductive logic, but through an understanding of the mass of statutes and minutiae of administrative practices which had emerged from experience over a long period of time. At crucial historical moments such as the Reformation and the abdication of James II, remedial action had been taken to preserve the traditional pattern of politics rather than fundamentally to alter the ancient framework of government. Whatever their ideological complexion, successive ministries had kept the ship of state afloat, not by steering it towards beguiling horizons, but by guiding public affairs according to convention and precedent. When in office even Whigs had abandoned the preposterous principles which they professed in opposition. So it was hardly surprising that the majority of people had now set aside their political disagreements to defend the established order against republicans and democrats.

Since its inception, however, the stability of the English nation had been periodically threatened by rebellious factions which discarded historical experience and pragmatism for fanciful political schemes. The doctrine of popular sovereignty, initially imported from France under the aegis of Calvinism, had prompted sectaries to challenge the Elizabethan state, precipitated Civil War in the seventeenth century, and misled some Whigs after 1688 into speculating about Revolutionary and constitutional principles; and it was now being used to demand radical change as a means of implementing the fictitious rights of man. Reeves urged his compatriots to remain steadfast against the modern heirs of a doctrine which had always been subversive. And this required the nation to deal firmly with an unholy alliance of dissident aristocratic Whigs and working-class radicals, who were intent on destroying ordered hierarchy.[5]

One of Reeves's admirers hailed the *Letter* as 'the finest panegyric on good order and subordination; the happiest defence of Executive Government at this period of seditious quixotism; and the ablest refutation of Sectaries'.[39] Notwithstanding the hyperbole, there is a kernel of truth in these remarks. If Reeves's enthusiasm for monarchy had briefly rekindled the political debates of a bygone age, his *Letter* also contained the ingredients of a forward-looking and sturdy conservatism: his vindication of kingship and the established church, endorsement of strong executive government, approval of political pragmatism and historical wisdom, detestation of egalitarianism and the doctrine of popular sovereignty, sanctification of social hierarchy, and his censuring of the Whigs for their tendency to behave as a faction by indulging in theoretical abstractions and forming alliances with lower-class radicals – all were eventually to feature in a reinvigorated Toryism.

The new Toryism was to emerge from a process of political realignment already well under way in 1795. When he referred in his *Letter* to 'the *Refuse* of the *Whig Club*', Reeves had in mind the Association of Friends of the People, which had been founded in 1792 by parliamentary Whigs who believed that enlightened men of property should lead the lower classes in their campaign for reform. The formation of the association widened the rift between a Foxite minority (for whom the government's proscription of civil liberties was an exercise in executive despotism) and establishment-minded Whigs who were inclined to support stern measures against agitators. In 1794 some of them were led by Portland into a coalition with the governing party, leaving Fox in charge of an oppositional rump. William Pitt, who called himself an independent Whig, believed that he was heading a loose grouping, temporarily united in the face of domestic subversion and the prospect of foreign invasion. In fact, Pitt's government of national unity laid the foundations for the Tory party's eventual reappearance.

This fragmentation of Whiggism into rival factions explains why the epithet 'father of modern conservatism' is often attached to Edmund Burke, whose spirited promulgation of counter-revolutionary ideas played a part in causing the schism. Burke, a Whig, was dismayed that the French Revolution had been welcomed by Fox, his close friend, and appalled by the comparison made between its assault upon social hierarchy and 'the glorious event, commonly called the revolution in England', when William of Orange (he told Parliament in February 1790) 'was called in by the flower of the English aristocracy to defend its ancient constitution, and not to level all distinctions'.[40] His *Reflections on the Revolution in France and on the Proceedings in Certain Societies in London Relative to that Event*, published later in the same year, castigated the doctrine of popular sovereignty, and linked the legitimate exercise of political authority to the ownership of substantial property. Existing institutions embodied the wisdom of the past, according to Burke, and practical experience was a guide in public affairs infinitely superior to the cold abstractions of the French revolutionaries and their English allies. The political message was similar to that of Reeves five years later, though the *Reflections* was a more skilful rhetorical performance than *Thoughts on the English Government*.

The *Reflections* provoked numerous responses from radicals, notably Paine's *Rights of Man*, but received little public endorsement from Whigs, who at this stage were reluctant to split their party, however much they were disturbed by Fox's enthusiasm for the Revolution.[41] The disagreement between Burke and Fox came to a head in May 1791, when the latter argued in Parliament that a 'rational constitution' must be founded on those 'original inherent rights of the people' which had been derided in the *Reflections* as 'visionary and chimerical'. Why, he asked, should someone known for his liberal opinions (Burke had formerly championed the rights of Catholics and condemned British colonial policies) now denounce the overthrow of tyranny in France? Burke, infuriated by the accusation that he had discarded Whig principles, caused Fox to weep by renouncing his friendship with him.[42]

Burke repudiated the charge of inconsistency in *An Appeal from the New to the Old Whigs*, published in August 1791, in which he argued that mainstream Whigs had always refused to acknowledge a right of subjects to dissolve and reconstitute government. The prosecutors at the Sacheverell trial, whom Burke cited extensively, had not suggested that the contract implicit in a system of mixed government entitled the 'body of the people' to exercise sovereign authority against arbitrary rulership. Instead, they had justified the Glorious Revolution as a remedial measure by the two estates of Parliament to secure the balanced constitution against royal tyranny. Burke, anxious to demonstrate his Whig credentials, could hardly ridicule constitutional principles in the manner of the Tory Reeves. He had no need to do so, however, because his evocation of the Whig inheritance enabled him to vvindicate the established order unambiguously. The conservative message of the *Appeal* was most eloquently conveyed in Burke's description of natural society as a chain of command rather than a structure of equal rights: one in which 'chieftains' – primarily owners of inherited wealth, but also men who had succeeded in commerce and the professions – guided, protected and disciplined the people.[6]

Burke, an independent MP since his quarrel with Fox, hoped that his *Appeal* would persuade conservative Whigs to enter a coalition with the Pitt administration. But most still wished to avoid schism, and a facade of party unity was retained until radical Whigs formed the Association of Friends of the People. In 1793 a parliamentary group sympathetic to Burke's views established a third party led by William Windham, and in the following year Portland Whigs joined the government.

Although Burke retired from Parliament in 1794, he continued to be preoccupied by the spread of Revolutionary principles. Towards the end of 1795 he urged his former parliamentary allies to impede the prosecution of Reeves on the ground that the charge of libel was a pretext for the propagation of Foxite views. Reeves should have avoided the 'slovenly' metaphor of the tree of monarchy and refrained from castigating eighteenth-century Whigs, according to Burke, yet he was a person of 'considerable Abilities' whose political theory, 'with a commonly fair allowance, is perfectly true' and 'neither more nor less than the Law of the Land'.[43] The irony of the case, Burke wrote to Windham in November, lay in the fact that Reeves was berated for elevating monarchy by men whose ideas threatened all three estates:

> *Heraldry* of the constitution! Whether the Lords and Commons or the King should walk first in the procession! Which is the

> Root, which the Branches! In good faith, they cut up the Root and the Branches! A fine Business of Law Grammar, which is the Substantive, which the adjective. – When an author lays down the *whole* as to be revered and adhered to, – at any former time would any one have made it a cause of quarrel, that he had given the priority to any *part*? especially to that part which was attacked and exposed? My opinion is, that, if you do not kick this business out with Scorn, Reeves ought to Petition and to desire to be heard by himself and his Council.

Burke concluded a letter to Captain Woodford with 'An Exordium' which, he suggested, Reeves might use to 'put the house into good humour' if he was permitted to petition the Commons. This satirical address – couched in the form of an apology by Reeves for using 'depraved *metaphors*' and 'theoretical abstractions' – was a thinly disguised stricture against the doctrine of the rights of man. Once the decision had been taken to proceed with the prosecution, Burke sent a note to the Attorney-General, Sir John Scott:

> I trust, that the Royal Oak will long flourish, and shed its Acorns, in plenteous Showers, on us the honest quiet swinish Multitude below; whilst the barren bloody pole of Liberty set up by Revolutionary Societies, is burnt, to singe the Bristles, and to smooth the heads and Hams, of the wild Boars of the Gallick Forests, who would come hither to root up and to trample down the British harvests.

Reeves himself was gratified by Burke's endeavours on his behalf.[44]

A few weeks before he became interested in the Reeves affair, Burke had expressed his views on economic policy. After complaining to Windham that 'there is no Rank or class, into which the Evil of Jacobinism has not penetrated', he advised him to obtain a 'Copy of the Memoire I delivered to Mr Pitt' (on the 7 November 1795).[45] The memorandum was written in response to a parliamentary debate about the high price of grain following a bad harvest. Burke, fearing that the government might be tempted to alleviate economic hardship, wanted to dissuade Pitt from meddling with the laws of supply and demand. Such pressure to tamper with market forces arose, he believed, from the rebellious spirit of the age, which fostered an illusion that every social ill was amenable to instant political remedy. A principal cause of the French Revolution had been an 'officious universal interference', he later wrote to Arthur Young, Secretary of the Board of Agriculture, which addled 'the brains of the people . . . with every sort of visionary speculation'. The memorandum to Pitt, along with fragments of the letter to Young, was published posthumously in 1800, as *Thoughts and Details on Scarcity*. Although ostensibly concerned with economic issues, the tract was a further expression of Burke's dread that egalitarian ideals would erode habits of deference and submission, and thereby do irreparable damage to the structure of social discipline which he had vindicated in *Reflections* and *An Appeal*.

Burke's obsession with the spread of radicalism explains the vehemence with which he denied that government was competent to control economic forces. For several decades Whigs had sought to emancipate trade from political constraints by campaigning to eliminate tariffs on imports and exports. An '*Englishman*, notwithstanding his boasted Liberty is, in regard to Commerce, still NOT FREE', Josiah Tucker had written in *The Elements of Commerce and the Theory of Taxes* (1755), 'and we still want the GLORIOUS REVOLUTION in the Commercial System, which we have happily obtained in the Political'. The most systematic case for a 'system of natural liberty' was made by Adam Smith, who argued that government should attend to law and order, and refrain from intervening in commerce. Smith, it was claimed in the preface to *Thoughts and Details on Scarcity*, paid the 'greatest deference' to Burke when writing *The Wealth of Nations*, published in 1776. How far Burke and Smith influenced one another is a contested area of scholarship.[46] Burke claimed to be a disciple of Smith and an early student of the science of political economy. Yet there was an ideological gap between the passionate entreaties of *Thoughts and Details* and the more reflective tones of *The Wealth of Nations*. Whereas Smith was careful to emphasize the unfortunate – albeit unavoidable – effects of market forces upon ordinary people, Burke developed the tenets of political economy into a robust justification of inequality.

Burke discredited proposals for relieving poverty by depicting labour as a commodity within a capitalist market operating in accordance with 'the laws of nature, and consequently the laws of God'. The interests of labour and capital were ultimately identical, in so far as the lower classes depended for subsistence upon the profits made by the rich. In any case, the poor were too numerous to benefit from redistributive policies, and any attempt artificially to raise wages would either inflate prices or else cause unemployment by reducing the demand for labour. A government which cushioned the poor against natural hardship, moreover, would engineer its own downfall by arousing extravagant expectations amongst the people. The state, then, had no business interfering with those immutable laws of supply and demand by which the pursuit of self-interest was transformed into a mutually beneficial system of production and consumption. During temporary periods of scarcity, therefore, those who were indigent should be offered private charity rather than public assistance, and taught to find consolation in the precepts of Christianity.[7] Whereas in his *Appeal* Burke had used the traditional vocabulary of paternalism to argue that authority should flow from a propertied élite to the mass of people, the same message was transmitted in *Thoughts and Details on Scarcity* through the new language of political economy. The effect was to sanction capital accumulation within an ordered hierarchy where rank and wealth – whether conferred by birth or achieved by economic competition – carried a responsibility to attend to the chain of social command. And this required all men of property to withstand the 'Evil of Jacobinism'.

After the fall of Pitt in 1801 there was a decade of unstable government, followed by a succession of ministeries led by Lord Liverpool between 1812 and 1827. Party labels came back into fashion during this period, and the Liverpool administrations were eventually described as Tory by their supporters and opponents alike. Early nineteenth-century Toryism was not avowedly Burkean. The liberal opinions of the pre-Revolutionary Burke offended many Tories, particularly in the 1820s, when, with a growing demand for Catholic emancipation, popery rather than Jacobinism was perceived as the principal threat to the *ancien régime*.[47] Liverpool's formula for a sound polity was nevertheless similar to that of Burke: a firm policy of law and order, on one hand, which upheld the institutions of church and state by suppressing agitation for constitutional reform; and a preference for a self-regulating economy, on the other, manifested in measures to reduce both taxation and restrictions upon commerce.[48]

By the 1820s, however, a conflict was taking shape between those anxious to preserve the values of traditional society and the advocates of market capitalism. The aristocratic language of paternalism and the concepts of political economy, blended by Burke into an assault upon radicalism, were now separated into alternative images of society. And the new Conservative Party, as the Tory Party became known in the 1830s, was soon to be torn apart by the rivalry between its paternalist and free-market factions.

NOTES

1 Roger Maynwaring, *Religion and Alegiance: in two Sermons Preached before the Kings Maiestie . . .*, London: Richard Badger, 1627, p. 11.

2 On the principle of co-ordination, see C. C. Weston and J. R. Greenberg, *Subjects and Sovereigns: the Grand Controversy over Legal Sovereignty in Stuart England*, Cambridge: Cambridge University Press, 1981; and Michael Mendle, *Dangerous Positions: Mixed Government, the Estates of the Realm, and the 'Answer to the XIX Propositions'*, Albana: Albana University Press, 1985.

3 Richard Tuck, *Natural Rights Theories: Their Origin and Development*, Cambridge: Cambridge University Press, 1979, pp. 101–42; Quentin Skinner, 'The context of Hobbes's theory of political obligation', in *Hobbes and Rousseau*, New York: Doubleday, Maurice Cranston and Richard S. Peters (eds), 1972, pp. 109–42; idem, 'Conquest and consent: Thomas Hobbes and the engagement controversy', in G. E. Aylmer (ed.), *The Interregnum: the Quest for Settlement 1646–1660*, London: Macmillan, 1974, pp. 79–98.

4 *A Letter from a Person of Quality to his Friend in the Country*, in *The Works of John Locke, in four volumes*, 7th edn, Vol. 4, London: H. Woodfall, 1768, pp. 539, 569–70.

5 Robert Willman, 'The origins of "Whig" and "Tory" in English political language', *Historical Journal*, Vol. 27, 1974, pp. 247–64.

6 See Gordon J. Schochet, *Patriarchalism in Political Thought: the Authoritarian Family and Political Speculation and Attitudes Especially in Seventeenth-Century England*, Oxford: Blackwell 1975; and James Daly, *Sir Robert Filmer and English Political Thought*, Toronto: University of Toronto Press, 1979, though Daly wrongly suggests that Filmer's absolutism was not characteristic of royalist political theory. An excellent attempt to set *Patriarcha* in the context of Restoration thought is Mark Goldie, 'John Locke and Anglican Royalism', *Political Studies*, Vol. 26, 1983, pp. 61–85.

7 John Locke, *Two Tracts on Government*, Philip Abrams (ed.), Cambridge: Cambridge University Press, 1967.

8 *Two Treatises of Government. In the former, the False Principles and Foundations of Sir Robert Filmer, and his Followers, Are Detected and Overthrown: The Latter, is an Essay Concerning the True Original, Extent, and End, of Civil Government*, in *The Works of John Locke, in four volumes*, 7th edn, Vol 2, London: H. Woodfall, 1768, p. 139.

9 Reliable accounts of political thought during and after the Glorious Revolution are Mark Goldie, 'The Revolution of 1689 and the structure of political argument: an essay and an annotated bibliography of pamphlets on the allegiance controversy', *Bulletin of Research in the Humanities*, 83, 1980, pp. 473–564; J. P. Kenyon, *Revolution Principles: the Politics of Party 1689–1720*, Cambridge: Cambridge University Press, 1977; H. T. Dickinson, *Liberty and Party: Political Ideology in*

Eighteenth-Century Britain, London: Weidenfeld & Nicolson, 1977.

10 Abednego Seller, *The History of Passive Obedience Since the Reformation*, Amsterdam: Theodore Johnson, 1689, 'Preface' and pp. 60–2.

11 *A Dialogue Betwixt Whig and Tory, Alias Williamite and Jacobite. Wherein the PRINCIPLES and PRACTICES of each Party are fairly and impartially stated; that thereby Mistakes and Prejudices may be removed from amongst us, and all those who prefer English Liberty, and Protestant Religion, to French Slavery and Popery, may be inform'd how to choose fit and proper Instruments for our Preservation in these Times of Danger*, 1693, p. iii.

12 Sir Humphrey Mackworth, *A Vindication of the Rights of the Commons of England*, in John, Lord Somers, *A Collection of Scarce and Valuable Tracts on the Most Interesting and Entertaining Subjects*, 2nd edn, Vol. II, London: T. Caddell & W. Davies , 1809–1815, pp. 282–7.

13 E.g. J. C. D. Clark, *English Society 1688–1832*, Cambridge: Cambridge University Press, 1985, pp. 216–35; J. A. W. Gunn, *Beyond Liberty and Property: The Process of Self-Recognition in Eighteenth-Century Political Thought*, Kingston and Montreal: McGill-Queen's University Press, 1983, ch.4.

14 Offspring Blackall, *The Divine Institution of Magistracy, and the gracious Design of its Institution. A Sermon Preach'd before the Queen At St. James's, On Tuesday, March 8, 1708. Being the Anniversary of Her Majesty's Happy Accession to the Throne*, London: H. Hills, 1709, p. 6.

15 Benjamin Hoadly, *Some Considerations Humbly Offered to the Right Reverend the Lord Bishop of Exeter. Occasioned by his Lordship's Sermon Preached before Her Majesty, March 8, 1708*, London: J. Morphew, 1709. Blackall reiterated his views in *The Lord Bishop of Exeter's Answer to Mr. Hoadly's Letter*, London, 1709, and Hoadly responded in *An Humble Reply to the Right Reverend the Lord Bishop of Exeter's Answer. In which the Considerations offered to his Lordship are vindicated. And an Apology is added for defending the Foundation of the Present Government*, London, 1709.

16 *Dr. Blackall's Offspring*, London, 1705, pp. 4, 7. See too *An Essay upon Government. Wherein the Republican Schemes Reviv'd by Mr. Lock, Dr. Blackal, etc. are Fairly Consider'd and Refuted*, London: G. Sawbridge, 1705.

17 William Oldisworth, *A Vindication of the Right Reverend the Lord Bishop of Exeter, Occasioned by Mr. Benjamin Hoadly's Reflections on His Lordships Two Sermons of Government*, London, 1709, p. 6. See too *The Revolution no Rebellion: Or, Serious Reflections Offered to the Reverend Mr. Benjamin Hoadly, Occasion'd by his Considerations on the Bishop of Exeter's Sermon, preach'd before Her Majesty, March the 8th, 1708*, London: Jonah Bowyer, 1709; *An Out of the Road Visit to the Lord Bishop of Exeter: Or, A Better Answer than the Best Answer ever was made, Wherein Not only Mr. Hoadly is reprimanded for his Rudeness to his Lordship; but also, his Lordship's Seconds are*

unmask'd, and severely lash'd for their Presumption and Treachery . . . by A.J.A.M. a true Son of the Church of England, London: John Baker, 1709; *A Submissive Answer to Mr Hoadly's Humble Reply, to my Lord Bishop of Exeter. By a Student at Oxford*, London, 1709; *A Letter to a Noble Lord, About his Dispensing Abroad Mr. Hoadly's Remarks upon the Bishop of Exeter's Sermon Before the Queen, Humbly Recommending to his Lordship's Perusal an Answer to it: Entitul'd, The Best Answer Ever was Made etc.*, London: John Baker, 1709; *Faith and Obedience: Or, A Letter to Mr Hoadly, Occasioned by his Doctrine of Resistance, and Dispute with the Bishop of Exeter*, Norwich, 1711.

18 Henry Sacheverell, *The Perils of False Brethren, both in Church, and State: Set Forth in a Sermon Preach'd before The Right Honourable, the Lord-Mayor, Aldermen, and Citizens of London, At The Cathedral-Church of St. Paul, On the 5th of November, 1709*, 2nd edn, London: Henry Clements, 1709, p. 11. See Geoffrey Holmes, *The Trial of Doctor Sacheverell*, London: Eyre Methuen, 1973.

19 *The Tryal of Dr. Henry Sacheverell, Before the House of Peers, for High Crimes and Misdemeanours; upon an Impeachment by the Knights, Citizens and Burgesses in Parliament, Assembled, in the Name of themselves, and of all the Commons of Great Britain: Begun in Westminster Hall on the 27th Day of February 1710; and from thence continu'd by several Ajournments until the 23rd Day of March following*, London: Jacob Tonson, 1710, pp. 125, 144, 161–2, 176, 261. Whigs were particularly agitated by the use made of Sanderson. His doctrine of passive obedience, according to Sir Joseph Jekyll for the prosecution, had been expressed in 'unlimited and bold Terms . . . I willingly admit he was a very learned, judicious and pious Prelate; and if so great and good a Man fell into such indiscreet, indecent and shocking Expressions on that Subject, as did visibly affect such an Assembly as this, one would think it should discourage others from delivering that Doctrine in such a Latitude'.

20 ibid., p. 118.

21 Reed Browning, *Political and Constitutional Ideas of the Court Whigs*, Baton Rouge and London: Louisiana State University Press, 1982.

22 Linda Colley, *In Defiance of Oligarchy: The Tory Party 1714–60*, Cambridge: Cambridge University Press, 1982.

23 For example, ibid.

24 J. C. D. Clark, *Revolution and Rebellion: State and Society in England in the seventeenth and eighteenth centuries*, Cambridge: Cambridge University Press, 1986, p. 125.

25 This is certainly true in Clark's case. A glimpse into his essentially ideological historiography is J. C. D. Clark, 'On moving the middle ground: the significance of Jacobitism in historical studies', in Eveline Cruickshanks and Jeremy Black (eds), *The Jacobite Challenge*, Edinburgh:John Donald, 1988, pp. 177–88.

26 D. Szechi, *Jacobitism and Tory Politics 1710–14*, Edinburgh: John

Donald, 1984, p. 52: 'The ideological mainspring of Parliamentary Jacobitism was zealous constitutionalism . . . The Parliamentary Jacobites were not archaic unreconstructed upholders of Divine Right, like the Nonjurors and Roman Catholics, they were very modern Tories in almost every sense.'

27 See H. T. Dickinson, *Bolingbroke*, London: Constable, 1970; Isaac Kramnick, *Bolingbroke and His Circle: the Politics of Nostalgia in the Age of Walpole*, Cambridge, Mass: Harvard University Press, 1968.

28 *Fragments or Minutes of Essays*, in *The works of the Late Right Honourable Henry St. John, Lord Viscount Bolingbroke . . . A New edition, in eight volumes*, Vol. 7, London: J. Johnson, 1809, pp. 419, 430–1; *The Idea of a Patriot King*, ibid., Vol. 4, p. 244.

29 Robert Eccleshall, 'Richard Hooker and the peculiarities of the English: the reception of the *Ecclesiastical Polity* in the seventeenth and eighteenth centuries', *History of Political Thought*, Vol. 2, 1981, pp. 63–117.

30 B. W. Hill, *British Parliamentary Parties 1742–1832: From the Fall of Walpole to the First Reform Act*, London: George Allen & Unwin, 1985, p. ix.

31 George Horne, 'The Origin of Civil Government', in *Discourses on Several Subjects and Occasions*, 4th edn, Vol. 2, Oxford: D. Prince 1793, pp. 305–29; 'Submission to government', ibid., Vol. 4, pp. 357–77; idem, 'Some considerations on Mr LOCKE's Scheme of Deriving Government from an *Original Compact*', in *The Scholar Armed Against the Errors of the Time, or, a Collection of tracts on the principles and evidences of Christianity*, Vol. 2, William Jones (ed.), London: F. & C. Rivington, 1795, pp. 342–52.

32 The point that Tories advocated non-resistance to the co-ordinate authority of the three estates is made by Paul Langford, 'Old Whigs, Old Tories, and the American Revolution', *Journal of Imperial and Commonwealth History*, Vol. 8, 1980, pp. 106–30.

33 Robert R. Dozier, *For King, Constitution, and Country*, Lexington, Kentucky: University Press of Kentucky, 1983; Eugene C. Black, *The Association: British Extra-Parliamentary Political Organization 1769–1793*, Cambridge, Mass: Harvard University Press, 1963, ch. 7; Donald E. Ginter, 'The Loyalist Association Movement of 1792–93 and British public opinion', *Historical Journal*, Vol. 9, 1966, pp. 179–90; Austin Mitchell, 'The Association Movement of 1792–93', *Historical Journal*, Vol. 4, 1961, pp. 56–77; 'Popular Conservatism and Militant Loyalism 1789–1815'; in H. T. Dickinson (ed.), *Britain and the French Revolution 1789–1815*, London: Macmillan, 1989, pp. 103–25.

34 Reeves does not feature, for example, in T. P. Schofield, 'Conservative political thought in Britain in response to the French Revolution', *Historical Journal*, Vol. 29, 1986, pp. 601–22, and receives scant attention in idem, 'English Conservatism: thought

and opinion in response to the French Revolution 1789–1796', PhD thesis, 1984, pp. 145–7.

35 John Reeves, *Thoughts on the English Government, Addressed to the Quiet Good Sense of the People of England. In a Series of Letters. Letter the Second. The Design of the first Letter Vindicated – Authorities from Records, Law Writers, and others, to support its Doctrines – Hale, Coke, Clarendon, Whitlock, Hooker, Mr. Burke, Mr. Pitt, Lord Thurlow, the present Attorney-General – The Expression of three Estates, three branches of the Legislature, and King, Lords, and Commons, considered – Censure of Opinions from Montesquieu, Locke, and other Philosophising Politicians – Criticism on Blackstone and Woddeson – Defence of the Paragraph prosecuted as libellous – The Author's Accusers proved guilty of Praemunire – The Author's Creed delivered in Nineteen Propositions – Expostulations on the Prosecution of Mr. Reeves*, London: J. Wright, 1799, p. 47.

36 'Mr. Fox's amendments to the address on the King's speech at the opening of the session', in Robert Eccleshall, *British Liberalism: Liberal Thought from the 1640s to the 1980s*, London: Longman, 1986, pp. 90–4.

37 Reeves later admitted that he had not read Filmer when writing the first *Letter*. Having read *Patriarcha*, however, he considered it to be a mixture of sound history and 'wild' speculation, *Letter the Second*, op.cit., pp. 161–2.

38 William Cobbett (ed.), *The Parliamentary History of England from the Earliest Period to the year 1803*, Vol. 32, London: Longman, 1806–20, cols. 608–87; 'Proceedings on the Trial of an Information exhibited Ex-Officio by his Majesty's Attorney General (in pursuance of an Address presented to his Majesty by the House of Commons) against JOHN REEVES, Esquire, for a Seditious Libel; tried at Guildhall, by a Special Jury, before the Right Hon. Lloyd Lord Kenyon, Lord Chief Justice of the Court of King's-Bench, May 20th: 36 George III 1796', in T. H. Howell (ed.), *A Complete Collection of State Trials*, Vol.26, London: Longman, 1811–26, cols. 529–96.

39 Joseph Cawthorne, *A Letter to the King, in Justification of a Pamphlet, Entitled 'Thoughts on the English Government'. With an Appendix in Answer to Mr. Fox's Declaration of the Whig Club*, London: J. Owen, 1796, p. 21.

40 William Cobbett (ed.), *The Parliamentary History of England from the Earliest Period to the year 1803*, Vol. 28, London: Longman, 1806–20, col. 361.

41 On the book's reception, see F. P. Lock, *Burke's Reflections on the Revolution in France*, London: George Allen & Unwin, 1985, ch. 5.

42 William Cobbett (ed.), *The Parliamentary History of England from the Earliest Period to the year 1803*, Vol. 29, London: Longman, 1806–20, cols. 364–426.

43 The same point was made by Joseph Moser, *An Examination of the Pamphlet Entitled Thoughts on the English Government, Addressed to*

the Quiet Good Sense of the People of England, London: J. Owen, 1796. Moser sent the manuscript of his pamphlet to Burke after his printer had advised against its publication. Burke declined to advise the author on the prudence of publication.

44 *The Correspondence of Edmund Burke*, Vol. 8, W. Copeland (ed.) Cambridge and Chicago: Cambridge University Press and University of Chicago Press, 1958–78, pp. 347, 349–51, 353–7, 369–73.

45 ibid., pp. 337–8, 343–4.

46 Donald Winch, 'The Burke-Smith problem and late eighteenth-century political and economic thought', *Historical Journal*, Vol. 28, 1985, pp. 231–47.

47 J. J. Sack, 'The memory of Burke and the memory of Pitt: English conservatism confronts its past, 1806–1829', *Historical Journal*, Vol. 30, 1987, pp. 623–40.

48 Boyd Hilton, *Corn, Cash, Commerce: the Economic Policies of the Tory Governments 1815–1830*, Oxford: Oxford University Press, 1977.

1. Robert Sanderson (1587–1663)

'The preface to the reader' in James Ussher, *The Power Communicated by God to the Prince, and the Obedience Required of the Subject. Briefly laid down, and Confirmed out of the Holy Scriptures, the Testimony of the Primitive Church, the Dictates of Right Reason, and the Opinion of the Wisest among the Heathen Writers*, 3rd edn, London: Charles Harper, 1688, no pagination

Sanderson was appointed a Fellow of Lincoln College, Oxford, in 1606 and Reader in Logic two years later. In 1619 he became rector of a Lincolnshire parish where he remained until the Restoration, apart from a brief return to Oxford as Regius Professor of Divinity from 1646 until his expulsion in 1648. In 1660 he was reinstated to the chair and also consecrated Bishop of Lincoln. Sanderson's reputation among his contemporaries, as perhaps the finest Anglican casuist and theologian of his generation, derived from the circulation of two sets of lectures delivered during the tenure of his professorship: *De Juramenti Promissorii*, published in Latin in 1647 and in English in 1655 in a translation by Charles I, and *De Obligatione Conscientiae*, published in 1660 in both Latin and English editions; and he was frequently cited against dissenters who rejected the discipline and worship of the Church of England. At the Restoration Sanderson was instrumental in modifying the liturgy, proscribed since 1644, and in 1662 he contributed the preface to the new Prayer Book, the jewel in the crown of the English language, where he depicted Anglican rites and ceremonies as decent and orderly practices to which nobody on grounds of conscience could legitimately object.

The Power Communicated by God to the Prince, which argued the familiar absolutist case that a king's limitations were imposed by himself rather than the community, was composed at the beginning of the Civil War at the request of Charles I. Ussher, Archbishop of Armagh, died in 1656 and the manuscript remained unpublished until 1661, when it was edited by his grandson, James Tyrrell. In castigating the principle of co-ordination and affirming that royal power originated from the paternal authority of Adam and Noah instead of the people's consent, Sanderson reiterated in the preface to the book some of the political themes outlined in his Latin lectures at Oxford. His denigration of contractualists as rationalists and atheists, for whom political allegiance was a matter of self-interest and mutual convenience rather than a divine injunction, was typical of the clerical response to theorists such as Thomas Hobbes. But the stridency with which he rebutted his ideological adversaries tends to belie the portrait drawn in Izaak Walton's *Life of Dr Robert Sanderson* (1678), of a humble, kindly and reserved parish priest whose exposition of Anglican doctrine was always conciliatory and temperate.

> That which some talk of, a mixt Monarchy, (which by the way is an arrant Bull, a contradiction *in adjecto*, and destroyeth itself), and others dream of such a Co-ordination in the Government, as was hatched amidst the heat of the late Troubles, but never before heard of in our Land; are in very Truth no better than senseless and ridiculous Fancies. Which although some Men have framed to themselves out of their own vain imaginations, made them as gay as they could, and then set them up as Idols to be adored by the Populacy, always apt to admire what they understand not; yet they are not able to stand up in the presence of that Oath, but must fall flat to the ground before it, as *Dagon* before the Ark, and be broken all to pieces. Are not the words of the Oath [*That the Kings Highness is the only Supreme Governor of this Realm*, etc.] as plain and obvious to every mans understanding, as the wit of Man can devise? . . .
>
> As for those in the next place that would derive the Original of all Government from the People by way of Pact of Contract: It may suffice to say that they take that for granted which never yet was proved, nor (I dare say) will ever be proved while the World standeth, either from Scripture, Reason or History. *Jus gladii*, the right and power of the Sword (which is really the

Sovereign Power) belongeth we know to Kings, but it is *by the Ordinance of God*, not the donation of the People: for *He beareth the Sword* (St *Paul* telleth us) as God's Minister, from whom he received it; and not as the Peoples Minister, who had no right to give it because they never had it themselves . . .

Besides, the supposed contract itself is encombred with so many doubts and difficulties, that it is not possible for the wit of man to devise *salvo's* or expedients sufficient to rescue it from infinite intanglements and irreconcileable contradictions. I believe it would trouble the ablest of them all that hold this opinion, to give a direct satisfactory answer (amongst a world of Queries more that might be tendered) to these following Interrogatories: First, for the Persons contracting; Of what sort of persons did the People, who are supposed to have made the first Contract in this kind, consist? Were all, without difference of Age, Sex, Condition, or other respect, promiscuously admitted to drive the bargain, or not? Had Women, and Children, and Servants, and Mad-men, and Fools, the freedom of suffrage, as well as Men of Age and Fortunes, and Understanding? Or were any of them excluded? If any excluded, who excluded them? by whose order, and by what Authority was it done? and who gave them that Authority? If all were admitted, whether with equal right to every one, or with some inequality? Was the Wives interest towards making up the bargain equal with that of her Husband? and the Childs with that of his Parents? and the servants (if there were or could be any such thing as Master and Servant) with that of his Master? If every one had not an equal share and interest in the business, whence did the Inequality arise? who made the difference between them? and what right had any Man, and how came he to have that right, to give more or less power to one than to another? If all were equal, who could summon the rest to convene together? or appoint the day and place of meeting? or when they were met, take upon him the Authority and Office of regulating their proceedings, or presiding or moderating in the Assembly, of determining such doubts and differences as might arise while matters were under debate, of calculating the voices, and drawing up the Articles of the Agreement in case they should agree?

But let us imagine all these could be declared, and the Contract made as they would have it; yet would the force and obligation of it remain questionable still: For it may be demanded, whether the majority of Votes shall conclude all that are present, Dissenters as well as others? And whether by virtue of an Act of those upon the place, an obligation shall lie upon such as are casually absent, or willingly absent themselves, when it was free for them so to do, no man having power to require their appearance? And whether a Contract made by such Persons as were at liberty before, can debar those that shall succeed them in the next Generation from the use of that Liberty their Ancestors had and enjoyed? . . .

Besides these and I know not how many more Difficulties no less insoluble, one thing there is which puzleth the men of this Opinion very much, and where with a man that were so disposed might make himself some sport: *to wit*, the Circle (between property and Government) which they have conjured themselves into, and wherein they run round even unto Giddiness, (like Men in a Maze or Labyrinth) not knowing which way to get out. That which some have said, because when they are put to it they must say something, *viz. That Dominion and Property is in order of Nature before Government*, be it true or be it false, as to their purpose signifieth nothing; unless it could be made out that they were before it in *order of Time* also . . . Whether were first the Hen or the Egg? We cannot imagine there could be a Hen, but we must suppose there must have been an Egg first, out of which that Hen must have been hatched: neither can we imagine there could be an Egg, but we must suppose there must have been a Hen first, to lay that Egg. Semblably here, We cannot imagine Property, but we must suppose some Government first; because the Right which any Man hath to that wherein he claimeth a Property must accrue to him by some Law, and that supposeth Government: Nor can we imagine a Government, one of the principal ends whereof is the preservation of mens Properties who live together in one Society, but we must suppose there were first such Properties to be so preserved. True it is, that a meer Rationalist, (that is to say in plain English, *an Atheist of the late Edition*) who giveth more faith to such Heathen Philosophy as affirmeth the World to have been *ab aeterno*, than to Divine Revelation which assureth us it had a beginning; (and some of the great Champions of the opinion we now speak of, have given cause enough of suspicion that they are little better): such a one I say cannot possibly get out of the Circle, or solve the difficulty in either of the aforesaid Instances: But to us, who believe the Scriptures and acknowledge a Creation, the solution of both is equally easie. If we will but follow the Clue of the Sacred History in the four first Chapters of *Genesis*, it will fairly lead us out of these Labyrinths in a plain way, and without any great trouble. It is certain that God in the first Creation made all living Creatures, each in their kind, in the full state and perfection of their Nature, and thence we may conclude, that undoubtedly the Hen was before the Egg. And it is no less certain, that as soon as *Adam* was created, God gave to him as an universal Monarch, not only Dominion over all his fellow Creatures that were upon the face of the Earth, but the Government also of all the inferior World, and of all the Men that after should be born into the World as long as he lived; so as whatsoever property any other Persons afterwards had or could have in anything in any part of the World, (as *Cain* and *Abel*, 'tis well known, had their properties in several, and distinct either from other) they held it all of him, and had it originally by his gift or assignment, either immediately or mediately. Whence we may also conclude, both in *Hypothesi*, that *Adam's* Government was before *Cain's* property; and in *Thesi*, that undoubtedly Government was before Property. And we have great reason to believe that after the Flood the sole Government was at first in *Noah*, and whatsoever either property in any thing they possessed in several, or share in the Government over any part of the World afterward any of his Sons had, they had it by his sole allotment and Authority, and transmitted the same to their Posterity meerly upon that account; without awaiting the Election or consent of, or entering into any Articles of Capitulations with the People that were to be governed by them. Those words in *Gen.* 10.32. seem to import as much, *These are the families of the sons of* Noah *in their generations after their Nations: and by them were the Nations divided in the Earth after the Flood.* And so this supposed Pact or Contract, which maketh such a noise in the World, proveth to be but a Squib, Powder without shot, that giveth a crack, but vanisheth into Air and doth no execution.

2. Sir Robert Filmer (1588–1653)

Patriarcha: or the Natural Power of Kings, London: 1680, pp. 2–3, 12–14, 70–3

Filmer was educated at Trinity College, Cambridge and at Lincoln's Inn. As the eldest son, he inherited his father's estates in 1629 to become patriarch of a wealthy family in Kent, where he participated in county administration and moved in a glittering intellectual circle. In 1643 he was imprisoned for at least two years because of his royalist sympathies. *Patriarcha* may have been written as early as 1628 (although there is a suggestion, somewhat implausible, that it was composed in the late 1640s) and was circulated in manuscript among the Kent gentry. *The Freeholders Grand Inquest Touching Our Sovereign Lord the King and His Parliament* (1648), which attacked the principle of three co-ordinate estates of King, Lords and Commons, was Filmer's first published work, although its authorship has been disputed. It was followed by several books, all of which were printed anonymously: *The Anarchy of a Limited or Mixed Monarchy* (1648), a concise exposition of partriarchal themes; *The Necessity of the Absolute Power of All Kings* (1648); *Observations Concerning the Originall of Government* (1652), a condemnation of Hobbes among others, and *Observations on Aristotle's Politiques Touching Forms of Government* (1652).

Filmer's works were issued after the onset of the Exclusion Crisis. The 1680 edition of *Patriarcha* was imperfect, and in 1685 a second edition was published from a more accurate copy owned by Archbishop Sancroft. In identifying through his opening comments a doctrinal conspiracy of Calvinists and Jesuits to subvert the authority of princes, Filmer had in mind radical Protestants such as George Buchanan, and writers such as Cardinal Bellarmine and the English Catholic, Robert Parsons; the latter, in *A Conference About the Next Succession to the Crown of England* (1594), had argued that the pope might act through the community to depose or exclude Protestant rulers. The link between Rome and populism, which Tories found so useful in their offensive against Whig exclusionists, was often made by absolutists before the Civil War. '*Adam* had *Dominion* setled in him', according to Roger Maynwaring in *Religion and Alegiance* (1627), 'before ever there was either *Pope*, or *People*: neither *Popes* nor *Populous Multitudes* have any right to giue, or take, in this case'.

> Since the time that School–Divinity began to flourish, there hath been a common Opinion maintained, as well by Divines, as by divers other Learned Men, which affirms,
>
> *Mankind is naturally endowed and born with Freedom from all Subjection, and at liberty to choose what Form of Government it please: And that the Power which any one Man hath over others, was at first bestowed according to the discretion of the Multitude.*
>
> This Tenent was first hatched in the Schools, and hath been fostered by all succeeding Papists for good Divinity. The Divines also of the Reformed Churches have entertained it, and the Common People every where tenderly embrace it, as being

the most plausible to Flesh and Blood, for that it prodigally destributes a Portion of Liberty to the meanest of the Multitude, who magnifie Liberty, as if the height of Humane Felicity were only to be found in it, never remembring That the desire of Liberty was the first Cause of the Fall of *Adam.*

But howsoever this Vulgar Opinion hath obtained a great Reputation, yet it is not to be found in the Ancient Fathers and Doctors of the Primitive Church: It contradicts the Doctrine and History of the Holy Scriptures, the constant Practice of all Ancient Monarchies, and the very Principles of the Law of Nature. It is hard to say whether it be more erroneous in Divinity, or dangerous in Policy.

Yet upon the ground of this Doctrine both *Jesuites*, and some other zealous favourers of the *Geneva* Discipline, have built a perillous Conclusion, which is, *That the People or Multitude have Power to punish, or deprive the Prince, if he transgress the Laws of the Kingdom* . . .

As *Adam* was Lord of his Children, so his Children under him, had a Command and Power over their own Children; but still with subordination to the First Parent, who is Lord-Paramount over his Childrens Children to all Generations, as being the *Grand-Father* of his People.

I see not then how the Children of *Adam*, or of any man else can be free from subjection to their *Parents*: And this subjection of Children being the Fountain of all *Regal Authority*, by the Ordination of God himself; It follows, that Civil Power not only in general is by Divine Institution, but even the Assignment of it Specifically to the Eldest Parents, which quite takes away that New and Common distinction which refers only Power Universal and Absolute to God; but Power Respective in regard of the Special Form of Government to the Choice of the people.

This Lordship which *Adam* by Command had over the whole World, and by Right descending from him the *Patriarchs* did enjoy, was as large and ample as the Absolutest Dominion of any *Monarch* which hath been since the Creation: For Dominion of Life and Death, we find that *Judah* the Father pronounced Sentence of Death against *Thamar his Daughter-in-law, for playing the Harlot; Bring her forth* (saith he) *that she may be burnt*. Touching War, we see that *Abram* commanded an Army of 318 Souldiers of his own Family. And *Esau* met his brother *Jacob* with 400 Men at Arms. For matter of Peace, *Abraham* made a League with *Abimelech*, and ratified the *Articles* with an Oath. These Acts of Judging in *Capital Crimes*, of making *War*, and concluding *Peace*, are the chiefest Marks of *Sovereignty* that are found in any *Monarch*.

Not only until the *Flood*, but after it, this *Patriarchal Power* did continue, as the very name *Patriarch* doth in part prove. The three Sons of *Noah* had the whole World divided amongst them by the Father . . .

Many men please themselves with an Opinion, that though the People may not Govern: yet they may partake and joyn with a King in the Government, and so make a State mixed of Popular and Regal power, which they take to be the best tempered and equallest Form of Government. But the vanity of this Fancy is too evident, it is a meer Impossibility or Contradiction, for if a King but once admit the People to be his Companions, he leaves to be a King, and the State becomes a Democracy; at least, he is but a Titular and no Real King, that hath not the Sovereignty to Himself; for the having of this alone, and nothing but this makes a King to be a King. As for that Shew of Popularity which is found in such Kingdoms as have General Assemblies for Consultation about making Publick Laws: It must be remembred that such Meetings do not Share or divide the Sovereignty with the Prince: but do only deliberate and advise their Supreme Head, who still reserves the Absolute power in himself; for if in such Assemblies, the King, the Nobility, and People have equal Shares in the Sovereignty, then the King hath but once Voice, the Nobility likewise one, and the People one, and then any two of these Voices should have power to over-rule the third; thus the Nobility and Commons together should have Power to make a Law to bind the King, which was never yet seen in any Kingdom, but if it could, the State must needs be Popular and not Regal.

If it be Unnatural for the Multitude to chuse their Governours, or to Govern, or to partake in the Government, what can be thought of that damnable Conclusion which is made by too many, that the Multitude may correct, or Depose their Prince, if need be? Surely the Unnaturalness, and Injustice of this Position cannot sufficiently be expressed: For admit that a King make a Contract or Paction with his people, either Originally in his Ancestors, or personally at his Coronation (for both these Pactions some dream of, but cannot offer any proof for either) yet by no Law of any Nation can a Contract be thought broken, except that first a Lawful Tryal be had by the Ordinary Judge of the Breakers thereof, or else every Man may be both party and

Judge in his own case, which is absur'd once to be thought, for then it will lye in the hands of the headless Multitude when they please to cast off the Yoke of Government (that God had laid upon them) to judge and Punish him by whom they should be Judged and punished themselves.

3. Offspring Blackall (1654–1716)

The Subjects Duty. A Sermon Preach'd at the Parish-Church of St. Dunstan in the West, on Thursday, March the 8th 1705. Being the Anniversary Day of Her Majesty's Happy Accession to the Throne, 2nd edn, London: H. Hills, 1708, pp. 2–4, 7, 9–10, 15

Appointed rector of St Mary's, Aldermary, London in 1694, Blackall first entered public controversy through a dispute with the free-thinking radical Whig, John Toland. In a sermon preached before the Commons in 1699 on the anniversary of the death of Charles I, he attacked Toland's *Life of Milton* (1698) which disputed the authenticity of the *Eikon Basilike* – revered by the High Church as the dying thoughts of the martyred king – and also of some early Christian writings. Blackall was rebuked by Toland for insinuating that he had doubted the validity of scripture itself. The following year Blackall gave the Robert Boyle Lectures on the theme of 'The Sufficiency of a Standing Revelation in general, and of the Scripture Revelation in particular', in which he castigated deists, atheists, papists and Jews. He featured in 'the bishoprics crisis of 1707' when Anne, impressed by his fine preaching, offered him the see of either Exeter or Chester. When Blackall chose the former, Chester was granted to another Tory cleric, Sir William Dawes, and the two appointments annoyed Low Churchmen and brought the Queen into conflict with Whig politicians.

The reference in *The Subjects Duty* to recent beneficial alterations to the succession was to the Act of Settlement (1701), which placed additional restrictions on the royal prerogative and stipulated 'that whosoever shall hereinafter come to the possession of the crown shall join in communion with the Church of England'. The sermon, which was republished three times, provoked only two replies. *The Divine Institution of Magistracy*, by contrast, aroused extensive controversy, largely because it was seized upon by the Anglican cleric and Whig polemicist, Benjamin Hoadly, as evidence that the High Church still promulgated a doctrine of passive obedience which provided no defence against tyranny and popery.

Prov. XXIV. 2I.
My Son, Fear thou the Lord and the King; and meddle not with them that are given to Change.

[O]ur next Care to that of keeping a good Conscience towards *God*, should be that of behaving our selves orderly and regularly in that Station which *God* has plac'd us in Subordination and Subjection to those Men that are set over *us* by *God* with a Power to order and enact such Constitutions (only not contrary to the Divine Laws), as are necessary to conserve Justice and Peace in that Society over which they preside . . .

[T]he Scripture only declares in general the Duties of Governors to their Subjects, and of Subjects to their Governors; but it does not expresley define or prescribe any one Form or Manner of Government as necessary to be set up and preserved in all Nations; but leaves every Country to it self to establish that Form of Government which is most suitable to its own particular Temper and Genius. Only when any sort of Government is set up and established (there being . . . in every Form of Government a Kingly, that is, an Absolute and Arbitrary Power lodg'd somewhere or other, either in one Hand or in more) it then commands Obedience, and forbids Resistance to this Sovereign Power; It commands Submission to this Power, as to *the Ordinance of* GOD, *(for there is no Power but of* GOD, *and the Powers that be are ordained of* GOD); and it declares, that they that being plac'd in Subjection to this Power do make Resistance to it, *resist the Ordinance of* GOD, *and shall receive to themselves Damnation* . . .

[T]here is no one particular Form of Government that can truly be said to be of Divine Institution and Appointment; and if there be not, then there is no one Form of Government but what may be chang'd and alter'd, provided that they who make the Change have sufficient Authority to make it; and sufficient Authority He or they must be allow'd to have to make any such change or Alteration in the Form and Manner of the Government, who has, or who have for the Time being the Supreme and Sovereign Authority in that Nation wherein such Change is made; For the Sovereign Authority of every State or Nation (whether it be lodg'd in One Hand, or in many) is, and in the Nature of the thing must needs be, Absolute, Unlimited, and Uncontroulable: That which is the Highest Authority in any Nation, may do what it pleases; and because it is the Highest upon Earth, can be accountable to none but *God* for what it does. This Sovereign Authority therefore, I say, may make what Changes and Alterations it self pleases in the Frame and Constitution of the Government; and whatever Changes it makes, they are Lawful and Valid, provided that no Natural Right of any other Man be thereby invaded and violated . . .

[Y]ou all know, (I shall not need to tell you that), that the Supreme Legislative Power of this Nation is by the Constitution lodg'd in the King or Queen for the time being, and in the Two Houses of Parliament; that what is Enacted by their joint Authority, is a Law of the Land, and that nothing is a Law of the Land to which they do not all Three give their Consent: And in this Essential and most Fundamental Constitution of the Government, there has not (*God* be thanked) been made, and I hope never will be made, any Change or Alteration. But as to the Succession to the Crown, there have been of late made some very considerable Limitations; and well had it been for the Nation if the same had been made an Hundred Years sooner. For whereas formerly the Crown descended of Course to the next in Blood, without any Exception, Condition or Limitation; it is now limited to descend to the next Heir that is a Protestant; and thereby not only One Person in particular who is of uncertain Birth, but likewise several others of the Popish Religion, of whose Legitimacy there has been no Doubt, are debarr'd and excluded from the Succession; and it is also declar'd to be a Forfeiture of the Crown, for any one that is posses'd of it to be reconcil'd to the Church of *Rome*, or to marry with a Papist . . .

That the Eldest Son should inherit all his Father's real Estate, is no Law of Nature, for by nature all his Children have Right alike; and even here with us, where this is the general Law of Inheritance, yet there are real Estates in some Places, that descend after another manner, all to the Younger Son, or to all Sons alike; and in some other Countries perhaps, the whole real Estate of every Person, after the Decease of the Possesor, may revert to the Crown from which it was granted, and the Exchequer or Public Treasury may be also the sole Heir to his Personal Estate. And if no Man has a Natural Right to an Estate much less can he have a Natural Right to Government, I mean, out of his own Family; 'tis the Supreme Power of every nation that gives this Right to whom it pleases, and in such Manner as it pleases: 'tis this Supreme Power of every Nation that establishes in several Nations a different sort of Government, and which in Monarchies makes the Crown of one Nation to be Elective, and of another Successive; and which in Hereditary Monarchies, excludes, in one Country, all the Females and their issue, and in another Country admits the next in Blood to inherit, whether Male or Female, and in the same proximity of Blood, prefers the Male before the Female. And I never yet heard it offer'd to be prov'd, that any of these Conditions or Limitations of Succession to a Crown, were Breaches of a Law of nature, or Violations of a natural Right . . .

As to the Constitution of our Government, that is certainly the best in the whole World: The *Utopians* would be hard put to it so much as to imagine a better: 'Tis a Constitution wherein the Power of the Sword is fully lodg'd in the Sovereign and yet with all the Security that can be that it shall never be Mis-us'd; whereby the Rights and Prerogatives of the Crown, and the Liberties and Properties of the People are with equal Care preserv'd; wherein the Sovereign has all the Power that can be to do Good, and none to do Hurt, In a word it is a Constitution, during the Continuance whereof, the People can never be Enslav'd and Ruin'd but with their own Consent, by Representatives of their own Choosing; and it may be reasonably hop'd, that they will never be so foolish as to give their Consent to their own Destruction.

4. Henry St John, Viscount Bolingbroke (1678–1751)

A Dissertation upon Parties, in *The Works of the Late Right Honourable Henry St. John, Lord Viscount Bolingbroke . . . A new edition, in eight volumes*, Vol. 3, London: J. Johnson, 1809, pp 10, 38–9, 44, 209–12, 214, 274, 304–5

An impulsive and ambitious man with an inordinate sexual appetite, St John succeeded his father in 1701 as a member for one of the family parliamentary seats at Wotton Bassett, Wiltshire. The following year he helped to prepare an Occasional Conformity Bill intended to prevent dissenters from holding public office. In the hope of joining the government, however, he soon distanced himself from the High Church wing of Toryism and in 1704 was appointed Secretary at War, a position he held until 1708. In the general election of that year St John lost his parliamentary seat, but he returned to the Commons in 1710 as Member for Berkshire, becoming Secretary of State for the North. Bolingbroke, raised to the peerage in 1712, again courted the right-wing parliamentary rank and file in a bid to wrest the party leadership from the moderate Tory, Robert Harley, Earl of Oxford. Their rivalry culminated with Bolingbroke's tentative approach in 1713 to the Pretender James, which weakened the chances of the Tories remaining in office once the Hanoverian succession had been secured. In 1714 George I dismissed Oxford and Bolingbroke, and the latter, fearing impeachment by the Whigs for intriguing with Jacobites, fled to France the following year where he became the Pretender's Secretary of State. His flight was a blunder which enabled Whigs to consolidate their ascendancy by smearing all Tories as Jacobites. Although Bolingbroke quickly severed his connection with James in order to gain pardon from the Whig Establishment, it was not until 1725 that his property rights were restored by parliamentary enactment. During these years in exile he moved in a circle of intellectuals and aristocrats, immersing himself in a study of history and philosophy.

Walpole had ensured that Bolingbroke's pardon did not extend to the right to hold public office again. On returning to England, therefore, Bolingbroke sought to lead the opposition from outside Parliament and in 1727 began writing for *The Craftsman*, a weekly newspaper which condemned every aspect of Walpolean corruption. His *Remarks on the History of England*, which documented efforts to preserve the balanced constitution from earliest times through to the Civil War, first appeared there. *A Dissertation upon Parties*, which took the story of constitutional struggle beyond the Glorious Revolution, was also initially printed as essays in *The Craftsman* between 1733 and 1734. Published as a whole in 1735, the *Dissertation* went through five editions in four years. In 1734 Bolingbroke was denounced by Walpole in Parliament and, fearing impeachment for treason if it became known that he had been financing the opposition from a French pension, he again fled to France, from where he did not finally return until 1744. During, or shortly after, a visit to England in 1738 he wrote *The Idea of a Patriot King*, tacitly admitting his failure to rally an effective opposition and appealing, in effect, to the heir to the throne to restore the ancient constitution. Bolingbroke spent his last years writing philosophy and occasionally indulging in political intrigue.

> I have endeavoured . . . to show how much our constitution hath been improved, how far our liberties have been better secured by the revolution, and how little is wanting to complete that glorious design, and to render the British constitution the most perfect system of a free government, that was ever established in the world . . .

The power and majesty of the people, an original contract, the authority and independency of parliament, liberty, resistance, exclusion, abdication, deposition; these were ideas associated, at that time, to the idea of a whig, and supposed by every whig to be incommunicable and inconsistent with the idea of a tory.

Divine, hereditary, indefeasible right, lineal succession, passive obedience, prerogative, nonresistance, slavery, nay, and sometimes popery too, were associated in many minds to the idea of a tory; and deemed incommunicable and inconsistent, in the same manner, with the idea of a whig.

But now that which neither side would have believed on the faith of any prediction, is come to pass;

—— quod divum promittere nemo
Auderet, volvenda dies, en! attulit ultro.

These associations are broken; these distinct sets of ideas are shuffled out of their order; new combinations force themselves upon us, and it would actually be as absurd to impute to the tories the principles, which were laid to their charge formerly, as it would be to ascribe to the projector and his faction the name of whigs, while they daily forfeit that character by their actions. The bulk of both parties are really united; united on principles of liberty, in opposition to an obscure remnant of one party, who disown those principles, and a mercenary detachment from the other, who betray them . . .

In short, the revolution is looked upon by all sides as a new aera; but the settlement then made is looked upon by the whole country-party as a new magna charta, from whence new interests, new principles of government, new measures of submission, and new obligations arise. From thence we must date both king and people. His majesty derives his title from acts, made in consequence of it. We likewise derive, not our privileges, for they were always ours, but a more full and explicit declaration, and a more solemn establishment of them, from the same period. On this foundation all the reasonable, independent whigs and tories unite . . .

'All publick regiment.' says Mr. Hooker, 'hath arisen from deliberate advice, consultation and composition between men.' The proposition is undoubtedly and universally true . . . Our original contract hath been recurred to often, and as many cavils as have been made, as many jests as have been broke about this expression, we might safely defy the assertors of absolute monarchy and arbitrary will, if there were any worth our regard, to produce any one point of time, since which we know any thing of our constitution, wherein the whole scheme of it would not have been one monstrous absurdity, unless an original contract had been supposed. They must have been blinded therefore by ignorance, or passion, or prejudice, who did not always see, that there is such a thing necessarily, and in the very nature of our constitution; and that they might as well doubt whether the foundations of an ancient, solid building were suited and proportioned to the elevation and form of it, as whether our constitution was established by composition and contract. Sure I am that they must be worse than blind, if any such there are, who do not confess at this time, and under the present settlement, that our constitution is in the strictest sense a bargain, a conditional contract between the prince and the people, as it always hath been, and still is, between the representative and collective bodies of the nation.

That this bargain may not be broken, on the part of the prince, with the people, (though the executive power be trusted to the prince, to be exercised according to such rules, and by the ministry of such officers, as are prescribed by the laws and customs of this kingdom) the legislative or supreme power is vested by our constitution in three estates, whereof the king is one. While the members of the other two preserve their private independency, and those estates are consequently under no dependency, except that which is in the scheme of our constitution, this control on the first will always be sufficient; and a bad king, let him be as bold as he may please to be thought, must stand in awe of an honest parliament.

That this bargain may not be broken, on the part of the representative body, with the collective body of the nation, it is not only a principal, declared right of the people of Britain, that the election of members to sit in parliament shall be free, but it hath been a principal part of the care and attention of parliaments, for more than three hundred years, to watch over this freedom, and to secure it, by removing all influence of the crown, and all other corrupt influence, from these elections. This care and this attention have gone still farther. They have provided, as far as they have been suffered to provide hitherto, by the constitutional dependency of one house on the other, and of both on the crown, that all such influence should be removed from the members after they are chosen . . .

It is by this mixture of monarchial, aristocratical, and democratical power, blended together in one system, and by these three estates balancing one another, that our free constitution of government hath been preserved so long inviolate, or hath been brought back, after having suffered violations, to it's original principles, and been renewed, and improved too, by frequent and salutary revolutions. It is by this that weak and wicked princes have been opposed, restrained, reformed, punished by parliaments; that the real, and perhaps the doubtful, exorbitancies of parliaments have been reduced by the crown; and that the heat of one house hath been moderated, or the spirit raised, by the proceedings of the other. Parliaments have had a good effect on the people, by keeping them quiet; and the people on parliaments, by keeping them within bounds, which they were tempted to transgress . . .

In short, nothing can destroy the constitution of Britain, but the people of Britain: and whenever the people of Britain become so degenerate and base, as to be induced by corruption, for they are no longer in danger of being awed by prerogative, to choose persons to represent them in parliament, whom they have found by experience to be under an influence, arising from private interest, dependents on a court, and the creatures of a minister; or others, who are unknown to the people that elect them, and bring no recommendation but that which they carry in their purses; then may the enemies of our constitution boast, that they have got the better of it, and that it is no longer able to preserve itself, nor to defend liberty . . .

[A] Dissertation upon Parties could not wind itself up more properly, we think, than by showing that the British constitution of government deserves, above all others, the constant attention, and care to maintain it, of the people who are so happy as to live under it; that it may be weakened for want of attention, which is a degree of danger; but that it cannot be destroyed, unless the peers and the commons, that is, the whole body of the people, unite to destroy it, which is a degree of madness, and such a monstrous iniquity, as nothing but confirmed and universal corruption can produce; that since the time, when all our dangers from prerogative ceased, new dangers to this constitution, more silent and less observed are arisen; and finally, that as nothing can be more ridiculous than to preserve the nominal division of whig and tory parties, which subsisted before the revolution, when the difference of principles, that could alone make the distinction real, exists no longer; so nothing can be more reasonable than to admit the nominal division of constitutionists and anticonstitutionists, or of a court and a country-party, at this time, when an avowed difference of principles makes this distinction real. That this distinction is real cannot be denied, as long as there are men among us, who argue for, and who promote even a corrupt dependency of the members of the two houses of parliament on the crown; and others who maintain that such a dependency of the members takes away the constitutional independency of the two houses, and that this independency lost, our constitution is a dead letter, and we shall be only in a worse condition by preserving the forms of it.

5. John Reeves(1752?–1829)

Thoughts on the English Government. Addressed to the Quiet Good Sense of the People of England. In a Series of Letters. Letter the First. On the National Character of Englishmen – The Nature of the English Government – The Corruptions caused in both by the Introduction of French Principles – The Effects produced by the Reformation and the Revolution upon Political Principles – The Conduct of the Whig Party – The Character of the modern Democrats, London: J. Owen, 1795, pp. 12–13, 20–2, 38, 44–7, 57–8, 67–8, 70, 72, 77–8

A tight-fisted bachelor with a talent for acquiring lucrative government posts, Reeves was educated at Eton and Merton College, Oxford. Elected a Fellow of Queen's College, Oxford in 1778 and called to the bar the following year, he entered public service in 1780 as a commissioner of bankruptcy, and later became counsel to the Mint, clerk and secretary to the Board of Trade, and superintendent of Aliens. After serving for a year as a stern Chief Justice of Newfoundland, he returned to England in 1792 as Receiver of Public Offices (paymaster of the metropolitan police) and founded his Association for the Preservation of Liberty and Property against Republicans and Levellers on 20 November of that year in the Crown and Anchor tavern. He was amply rewarded for his efforts on behalf of law and order by appointment in 1793 to the high stewardship of the Manor and Liberty of Savoy and, notwithstanding his embarrassing libel trial, to the post of King's printer in 1800.

A distinguished classical scholar and legal historian, Reeves was elected a Fellow of the Society of Antiquaries in 1789 and Fellow of the Royal Society the following year. His five volumes of *A History of English Law*, from the time of the Saxons to the reign of Elizabeth, were published between 1783 and 1829. Other works written by him included *An Enquiry into the Nature of Property and Estates as defined by the Laws of England* (1779), *A Chart of Penal Laws, exhibiting by lines and colours an historical view of crimes and punishments, according to the law of England* (1792), *History of the Government of the Island of Newfoundland* (1793), *A Collection of the Hebrew and Greek Texts of the Psalms* (1800), *Considerations on the Coronation Oath to maintain the Protestant Reformed Religion, and the Settlement of the Church of England* (1801), and he also published several editions of the Bible and Book of Common Prayer in his capacity as King's printer. In 1799 and 1800, undaunted by his trial, Reeves added three more *Letters* to *Thoughts on the English Government.*

> With the exception . . . of the advice and consent of the Two Houses of Parliament, and the interposition of Juries; the Government, and the administration of it in all its parts, may be said to rest wholly and solely on the King, and those appointed by him. Those two adjuncts of *Parliament* and *Juries* are subsidiary and occasional; but the King's Power is a substantive one, always visible and active. By his Officers, and in his name, every thing is transacted that relates to the peace of the Realm and the protection of the Subject. The Subject feels this, and acknowledges with thankfulness a superintending sovereignty, which alone is congenial with the sentiments and temper of Englishmen. In fine, the Government of England is a *Monarchy*; the Monarch is the antient stock from which have sprung those goodly branches of the Legislature, the Lords and Commons, that at the same time give ornament to the Tree, and afford shelter to those who seek protection under it. But these are still only branches, and derive their origin and their nutriment from their common parent; they may be lopped off, and the Tree is a Tree still; shorn indeed of its honours, but not, like them, cast into the fire. The Kingly Government may go on, in all its functions, without Lords or Commons: it has heretofore done so for years together, and in our times it does so during every recess of Parliament; but without the King *his* Parliament is no more. The King, therefore, alone it is who necessarily subsists, without change or diminution; and from *him* alone we unceasingly derive the protection of Law and Government . . .
>
> We all know the destructive doctrines upon which the French Liberty of the present day is founded; and we see, with uneasiness, the pains and the success in propagating them in this Country . . .

Such is the *present* novelty from France! We may learn from History what was the nature of the principles which *Calvin* and *Beza*, and their followers at Geneva, instilled into the *Puritans*, who infested our Government in the reign of Queen Elizabeth; and who, under the name of *Presbyterians*, *Commonwealth's-men*, *Independents*, and other factions and sects without number, at length overturned first the Government of Scotland, and afterwards the Government of England. Upon examination we shall find a similar spirit prevailing in the French principles of those days, and of the present times.

It would be curious to pursue the comparison that sometimes makes a contrast, and sometimes a parallel, between the character and designs of the French Reformers of old time in the Church, and those of the present day in the State; the Religious and the Civil *Jacobins*; the *Puritans*, and the *Democrats*. It is wonderful how similar they all are in their doctrines, and how they agree in the system and the instruments they use for disseminating their principles, for gaining proselytes, and for *carrying on* the unhallowed *work* of setting the populace against the established Government. How analogous was the machinery of their party; the cant and imposture of their pretences! – The unalienable rights of the People to form the Government of the Church, taught by *Calvin* and the *Puritans*; and the unalienable right of the People to form the Government of the State, taught by the *French Democrats*: – The pretended commands of God for the one; and that omnipotent power upon earth, the Sovereign Will of the people commanding the other . . .

The abdication of King James the Second, and the transactions that ensued upon the vacancy thereby made in the Throne, compose a very important and curious passage in the History of our Government and Laws. It has been vulgarly called, *The Revolution*; upon what authority I know not; it was not so named by Parliament; nor is it a term known to our Laws . . .

Whatever were their motives for joining in the new settlement, the *Republicans*, *Presbyterians*, and *Sectaries* . . . took their stand among *The Whigs*: under the pretence of that way of thinking, they began to vent their political opinions; which, however, they now so tempered and turned as to adapt them to the Government established by Law. As they sacrificed the rigour of their own notions, they did not fail to take a similar liberty with the principles of the Government; and so they have gone on, from those times to our own, corrupting the genuine principles of the English Laws and Government, in order to suit them to their own theories and systems, till they have filled the whole with uncertainty; and *The Constitution*, of which they are so incessantly debating, is made one of the most doubtful and difficult things to comprehend.

To these men, and to this sinister design, we are indebted for the jargon of which I have just complained. *They* invented the term *Revolution*, to blind and mislead; and they have never ceased repeating it, that they may put the People in mind of making another. This mystery they have couched under the still more loose metaphysical idea of *Revolution principles*; and by the glorious spell of – *The Constitution* – they can conjure up any form, fashion, modification, reform, change, or innovation in Government they please, and it shall still be nothing more, as they pretend, than the genuine true English Constitution . . .

I always thought, that it was the disposition of Englishmen to require plain and defined sentences for the Charter of their Rights and Liberties; that they claimed to have known, written, and express Laws to govern them; and that they regarded high pretensions founded on visionary and refined theories, as the air in which they were built: and I thought, that *the divine indefeasible Right of Kings* with other fancies of former times, were exploded principally, because they were positions that had no warrant from the known express Laws of the Land, but rested on general reasoning, from topics not known to the usage and laws of the country: and I always believed, that the set of men who most clamoured against those pretensions, upon the very grounds here alledged, were those who afterwards set up this new system.

But it seems to me, that this new system, giving origin to positions like that above mentioned, and so carrying the mind beyond the bounds of law equally with the other, is quite as absurd as the former, and differs from it only in being much more mischievous. For whereas the former attempted to raise the imagination to something above us, which might sooth and elevate the senses; the latter opens to us no space wherein the imagination can exercise itself, but the very gulph of Democracy, there to toil and turmoil, without hope of rest or consolation . . .

The *Government* we know – and the *Laws* we know – but the *Constitution* we know not. – It is an unknown region, that has never been visited but by dreamers, and men who see visions; and the reports they make are so contradictory, that no one relies upon them. Yet we can manage to spell out of them, that there is resident there a great deal of faction and sedition; envy and ambition; and something that looks like eternal warfare of Party. But the English Government is real and substantial; we see and feel it; we can take its height and its depth; and we know its movements, because they are regulated by established and known Laws. This is the only Constitution ever supposed or named by men of sober minds and sound understanding; that is, *the Constitution of our Government*, or *the Constitution established by Law* . . .

[T]he principles of the Whigs were never so much put to the test as when they came into the Administration of the Government. It is a well-known complaint of them, that 'the Whigs in place always acted like Tories'. This is certainly a just remark, and in the nature of things it could not be otherwise; nothing can better shew than this comparison, how unjustly the Party of Tories have been run down and exploded; and, on the other hand, that the pretensions of the Whigs were founded in nothing but their own imaginations, and were totally incompatible with our Government and Laws.

For when the Whigs came into office, they found at Whitehall nothing of the *Constitution*, and the *Revolution principles*, with which they had been used to amuse themselves. They were to conduct a Government that had been formed long before their party or notions were heard of; and they were to conduct it by the Laws of the Land, and the rules of office, that had long been the guides of practice, and could not safely be changed or abandoned. For it is a sad truth to be told to those Gentlemen who are running the career of Opposition with great eminence of talent and display of ability, that the object they propose to themselves, as the reward of all their toil, is one of the dullest affairs in the world. When they are in office they must have done with mere words, and must come to things; they must set down to work by line and rule; must search Laws, hunt precedents, examine minutes of proceedings, consult and discuss, and pursue a detail; often submitting themselves to the advice of subordinate persons, who, though never heard of, do more perhaps to keep the machine a-going than their Principals . . .

[T]he finishing blow to all Party distinctions, and to the credit of all political principles that had no reference but to Party distinctions, seems to me to have been struck in the latter end of the year 1792. At that time an alarm for the safety of the Constitution as established by Law, which seemed to be threatened by the Republican party from within, assisted by the French Republic from abroad, roused the Nation as one man. All Party considerations immediately vanished before that of the common interest of us all. From that time the attention of all sober men has been fixed on the preservation of the Government and Laws; all former distinctions of Party are thrown aside, and the illusion of their principles is forgotten. There are now no divisions in the Nation, but that of the Friends to the Constitution as established by Law, and that of the Republicans, who are laying by for an opportunity to level everything to the Equality of a French Democracy; and there are no political opinions by which men are distinguished, but those that are in favour of the Constitution as established by Law, and those who are against it . . .

But though Party is destroyed, Faction will remain; and Whiggism is not of a nature to lie quietly in its grave; its ghost still haunts us, hovering round the scenes of its former exhibition, and attempting, as well as it can in its present unembodied state, to act over again those parts in which it so much delighted when in life and vigour . . .

To tell men, that they are by nature equal to their superiors, and that the present inequality between them is brought about by oppression and tyranny; – to lay down, that the people may make and unmake the Government, and to tell the populace that *they* are the People; – in the hearing of the poor and necessitous, to censure and vilify the rich and opulent; – to disparage those put in authority in the presence of the evil doers, to whom they should be a terror; – to make sport of the person and office of the King himself; and train the minds of men to a contempt of his authority and the Government they live under; – these are topics that are too congenial with the self-love, the malice, and lightness of some minds, not to be heard with approbation and applause; and they cannot long and repeatedly be declaimed on, sometimes in Political Clubs, and sometimes in Public Lectures, to a numerous auditory, without warping the best disposed to an habitual dislike for the Government, and a disposition to attempt, or concur in any change that shall be proposed; more especially if the change is to place them, as they believe, in a situation to become their own Legislators and Governors.

Such is the description of the new *Democrats* who at present infest the Country; a set, who in the meanness of their personal character, in the danger of their principles, and in the open profession of them, exceed everything we have yet had in the nature of Party; a set, that are not a Party, but a Conspiracy; a band of Catilinarians, that look only for plunder and bloodshed, general confusion and anarchy.

And these are the men with whom the *Refuse* of the *Whig Club* have fraternized to make a common cause! the dregs of the upper classes of society mingled with the dregs of the lower.

6. Edmund Burke (1729–97)

An Appeal from the New to the Old Whigs, in Consequence of Some Late Discussions in Parliament, Relative to the Reflections on the French Revolution, 2nd edn, 1791, in *The Works of the Right Honourable Edmund Burke. A New Edition*, Vol. 6, London: C. & J. Rivington, 1826–7, pp. 147–8, 216–19

Born in Dublin to a Catholic mother and Protestant father, Burke was educated at a Quaker boarding school and Trinity College, Dublin, where he helped to produce a weekly newspaper, *The Reformer*, which campaigned against the evils of absentee landlordism. Although Burke enrolled at the Middle Temple, London in 1750, he did not follow his father into the legal profession. Instead he turned to the study of literature and in 1756 published *A Vindication of Natural Society* (a parody of the deism of Bolingbroke among others), which was followed by *A Philosophical Inquiry into the Origins of Our Ideas of the Sublime and the Beautiful*. In 1758, now married, Burke began to edit the *Annual Register*, a review of literature, politics and history, which provided him with a decent income for about twenty years. The following year he became private secretary to William Hamilton and, on the latter's appointment as chief secretary to the Lord Lieutenant of Ireland, spent four years immersed in Irish affairs. In 1761 he drafted, but did not publish, a *Tract on the Popery Laws*, which condemned the penal legislation against Irish Catholics.

Appointed private secretary in 1765 to the second Marquis of Rockingham, First Lord of the Treasury, Burke entered Parliament the following year as Member for Wendover. He was to remain in the Commons until 1794, later as Member for Bristol and then Malton. But, apart from two brief periods in 1782 and 1783 as Paymaster-General of the Forces, he did not attain ministerial office. For most of these years Burke was in opposition and made his mark through fine oratory and brilliant writings. His first substantial pamphlet as a politician was *Observations on a Late Publication Intituled the Present State of the Nation* (1769), a defence of the Rockingham government of 1765–6, which was followed in 1770 by *Thoughts on the Cause of the Present Discontents*, advocating a revival of party politics to prevent the court undermining Parliament's independence. During the 1770s he spoke and wrote against Britain's rapacious colonial policies in America, and in the next decade devoted his energy to exposing the activities of the East India Company and persuading Parliament to impeach Warren Hastings for the maladministration of India. Burke's enlightened attitude on such issues as Catholic rights and colonialism explains why Fox, a friend and ally from 1774, accused him of departing from Whig principles in so vehemently denouncing the French Revolution. After reviewing his political career in the *Appeal* in order to establish its consistency, Burke concluded with the remark that he would rather be the last and least of the old Whigs 'than the first and greatest of those who have coined to themselves whig principles from a French die, unknown to the impress of our fathers in the constitution'.

> These new whigs hold, that the sovereignty, whether exercised by one or many, did not only originate *from* the people (a position not denied nor worth denying or assenting to) but that, in the people the same sovereignty constantly and unalienably resides; that the people may lawfully depose kings, not only for misconduct, but without any misconduct at all; that they may set up any new fashion of government for themselves, or continue without any government at their pleasure; that the people are essentially their own rule, and their will the measure of their conduct; that the tenure of magistracy is not a proper subject of contract; because magistrates have duties, but no rights; and that if a contract *de facto* is made with them in one age, allowing that it binds at all, it only binds those who are immediately concerned in it, but does not pass to posterity. These doctrines concerning the *people* (a term which they are far from accurately defining, but by which, from many circumstances, it is plain enough they mean their own faction, if they should grow by early arming, by treachery, or violence, into the prevailing force) tend, in my opinion, to utter subversion, not only of all government, in all modes, and to all stable securities to rational freedom, but to all the rules and principles of morality itself.
>
> I assert, that the ancient whigs held doctrines, totally different from those I have last mentioned. I assert, that the foundations laid down by the commons, on the trial of Dr. Sacheverel, for justifying the Revolution of 1688, are the very same laid down in Mr. Burke's Reflections; that is to say, – a breach of

the *original contract*, implied and expressed in the constitution of this country, as a scheme of government fundamentally and inviolably fixed in king, lords, and commons. – That the fundamental subversion of this ancient constitution, by one of its parts, having been attempted, and in effect accomplished, justified the Revolution. That it was justified *only* upon the *necessity* of the case; as the *only* means left for the recovery of that *ancient* constitution, formed by the *original contract* of the British state; as well as for the future preservation of the *same* government . . .

To enable men to act with the weight and character of a people, and to answer the ends for which they are incorporated into that capacity, we must suppose them (by means immediate or consequential) to be in that state of habitual social discipline, in which the wiser, the more expert, and the more opulent conduct, and by conducting enlighten and protect the weaker, the less knowing, and the less provided with the goods of fortune. When the multitude are not under this discipline, they can scarcely be said to be in civil society . . .

A true natural aristocracy is not a separate interest in the state, or separable from it. It is an essential integrant part of any large body rightly constituted. It is formed out of a class of legitimate presumptions, which, taken as generalities, must be admitted for actual truths. To be bred in a place of estimation; To see nothing low and sordid from one's infancy; To be taught to respect one's self; To be habituated to the censorial inspection of the publick eye; To look early to publick opinion; To stand upon such elevated ground as to be enabled to take a large view of the wide spread and infinitely diversified combinations of men and affairs in a large society; To have leisure to read, to reflect, to converse; To be enabled to draw the court and attention of the wise and learned whereever they are to be found; – To be habituated in armies to command and to obey; To be taught to despise danger in the pursuit of honour and duty; To be formed to the greatest degree of vigilance, foresight, and circumspection, in a state of things in which no fault is committed with impunity, and the slightest mistakes draw on the most ruinous consequences – To be led to a guarded and regulated conduct, from a sense that you are considered as an instructor of your fellow-citizens in their highest concerns, and that you act as a reconciler between God and man – To be employed as an administrator of law and justice, and to be thereby amongst the first benefactors to mankind – To be a professor of high science, or of liberal and ingenuous art – To be amongst rich traders, who from their success are presumed to have sharp and vigorous understandings, and to possess the virtues of diligence, order, constancy, and regularity, and to have cultivated an habitual regard to commutative justice – These are the circumstances of men, that form what I should call a *natural* aristocracy, without which there is no nation.

The state of civil society, which necessarily generates this aristocracy, is a state of nature; and much more truly so than a savage and incoherent mode of life. For man is by nature reasonable; and he is never perfectly in his natural state, but when he is placed where reason may be best cultivated, and most predominates. Art is man's nature. We are as much, at least, in a state of nature in formed manhood, as in an immature and helpless infancy. Men, qualified in the manner I have just described, form in nature, as she operates in the common modification of society, the leading, guiding, and governing part. It is the soul to the body, without which the man does not exist. To give therefore no more importance, in the social order, to such descriptions of men, than that of so many units, is a horrible usurpation.

When great multitudes act together, under that discipline of nature, I recognise the PEOPLE. I acknowledge something that perhaps equals, and ought always to guide the sovereignty of convention. In all things the voice of this grand chorus of national harmony ought to have a mighty and decisive influence. But when you disturb this harmony; when you break up this beautiful order, this array of truth and nature, as well as of habit and prejudice; when you separate the common sort of men from their proper chieftains so as to form them into an adverse army, I no longer know that venerable object called the people in such a disbanded race of deserters and vagabonds.

7. Edmund Burke

Thoughts and Details on Scarcity, Originally Presented to the Right Hon. William Pitt, in the month of November, 1795, London: F. & C. Rivington, 1800, pp. 2–4, 6, 17–18, 32, 45–6, 48

Burke's strident advocacy of a policy of non-intervention in the market and condemnation of cant about the labouring poor were, in large measure, a continuation of his feud with Fox. 'It is, indeed, a melancholy and alarming fact, that the great majority of the people of England – an enormous and dreadful majority – are no longer in a situation in which they can boast that they live by the produce of their labour', Fox lamented during the parliamentary debate of 3 November 1795 on the high price of corn,

> and that it does regularly happen, during the pressure of every inclement season, that the industrious poor are obliged to depend for subsistence on the supplies afforded by the charity of the rich. I agree in opinion with those who think the price of labour ought to be advanced, and the great majority of the people of England freed from a precarious and degrading dependence.

At this stage, however, even Fox was opposed to legislation for improving wages, and on 17 November Burke wrote to Windham that the report of the parliamentary select committee on grain prices 'is all that it can be. The danger is their going further. What folly it is to recommend Potatoes to the People.'

On 9 December Samuel Whitbread introduced a bill empowering magistrates to fix minimum wages. After repeating his earlier arguments about the unfortunate dependence of the poor upon private charity, Fox announced on this occasion that he would support legislation 'to afford relief and protection to the poor'. The debate probably persuaded Burke to reshape and expand his memorandum to Pitt, because the *Oracle* reported on 17 December: 'Speedily will be published A Letter from the Right Honourable Edmund Burke to Arthur Young, Esq. Secretary to the Board of Agriculture, on the projects talked of in Parliament for an increase of Wages to Day Labourers in Husbandry and other topics of rural oeconomy.' Burke failed to complete the letter, however, and fragments found among his papers after his death were inserted into the memorandum, which was then published as *Thoughts and Details on Scarcity*.

> To provide for us in our necessities is not in the power of Government. It would be a vain presumption in statesmen to think they can do it . . .
>
> The labouring people are only poor, because they are numerous. Numbers in their nature imply poverty. In a fair distribution among the vast multitude, none can have much. That class of dependant pensioners called the rich, is so extremely small, that if all their throats were cut, and a distribution made of all they consume in a year, it would not give a bit of bread and cheese for one night's supper to those who

labour, and who in reality feed both the pensioners and themselves.

But the throats of the rich ought not to be cut, nor their magazines plundered; because, in their persons they are trustees for those who labour, and their hoards are the banking-houses of these latter. Whether they mean it or not, they do, in effect, execute their trust – some with more, some with less fidelity and judgement. But on the whole, the duty is performed, and every thing returns, deducting some very trifling commission and discount, to the place from whence it arose. When the poor rise to destroy the rich, they act as wisely for their own purposes as when they burn mills, and throw corn into the river, to make bread cheap . . .

Nothing can be so base and so wicked as the political canting language, 'The Labouring *Poor*'. Let compassion be shewn in action, the more the better, according to every man's ability, but let there be no lamentation of their condition. It is no relief to their miserable circumstances; it is only an insult to their miserable understandings. It arises from a total want of charity, or a total want of thought. Want of one kind was never relieved by want of any other kind. Patience, labour, sobriety, frugality, and religion, should be recommended to them; all the rest is downright *fraud*. It is horrible to call them 'The *once happy* labourer' . . .

Labour is a commodity like every other, and rises or falls according to the demand. This is in the nature of things; however, the nature of things has provided for their necessities. Wages have been twice raised in my time, and they bear a full proportion, or even a greater than formerly, to the medium of provision during the last bad cycle of twenty years. They bear a full proportion to the result of their labour. If we were wildly to attempt to force them beyond it, the stone which we had forced up the hill would only fall back upon them in a diminished demand, or, what indeed is the far lesser evil, an aggravated price of all the provisions, which are the result of their manual toil.

But what if the rate of hire to the labourer comes far short of his necessary subsistence, and the calamity of the time is so great as to threaten actual famine? Is the poor labourer to be abandoned to the flinty heart and griping hand of base self-interest, supported by the sword of law, especially when there is reason to suppose that the very avarice of farmers themselves has concurred with the errors of Government to bring famine on the land.

In that case, my opinion is this. Whenever it happens that a man can claim nothing according to the rules of commerce, and the principles of justice, he passes out of that department, and comes within the jurisdiction of mercy. In that province the magistrate has nothing at all to do: his interference is a violation of the property which it is his office to protect. Without all doubt, charity to the poor is a direct and obligatory duty upon all Christians, next in order after the payment of debts, full as strong, and by nature made infinitely more delightful to us. Puffendorf, and other casuists do not, I think, denominate it quite properly, when they call it a duty of imperfect obligation. But the manner, mode, time, choice of objects, and proportion, are left to private discretion; and perhaps, for that very reason it is performed with the greater satisfaction, because the discharge of it has more the appearance of freedom; recommending us besides very specially to the divine favour, as the exercise of a virtue most suitable to a being sensible of it's own infirmity . . .

I beseech the Government . . . manfully to resist the very first idea, speculative or practical, that it is within the competence of Government, taken as Government, or even of the rich, to supply to the poor, those necessaries which it has pleased the Divine Providence for a while to with-hold from them. We, the people, ought to be made sensible, that it is not in breaking the laws of commerce, which are the laws of nature, and consequently the laws of God, that we are to place our hope of softening the divine displeasure to remove any calamity under which we suffer, or which hangs over us . . .

It is one of the finest problems in legislation, and what has often engaged my thoughts whilst I followed that profession, 'What the State ought to take upon itself to direct by the public wisdom, and what it ought to leave, with as little interference as possible, to individual discretion'. Nothing, certainly, can be laid down on the subject that will not admit of exceptions, many permanent, some occasional. But the clearest line of distinction which I could draw, whilst I had my chalk to draw any line, was this: That the State ought to confine itself to what regards the State, or the creatures of the State, namely, the exterior establishment of its religion; its magistracy; its revenue; its military force by sea and land; and corporations that owe their existence to its flat; in a word, to every thing that is *truly and properly* public, to the public peace, to the public safety, to the public order, to the public prosperity . . .

Tyranny and cruelty may make men justly wish the downfall of abused powers, but I believe that no government ever yet perished from any other direct cause than it's own weakness. My opinion is against an over-doing of any sort of administration, and more especially against this most momentous of all meddling on the part of authority; the meddling with the subsistence of the people.

3 *Peel, paternalism and political economy 1827–46*

Liverpool's resignation in 1827, after a stroke, inaugurated a period of intra-party strife and shifting alliances. Within a few years, however, Tories had largely submerged their differences so as to oppose a Whig measure to abolish rotten boroughs and enfranchise the middle classes. Robert Peel, who became leader of the Conservative Party (the epithet had been acquired by Tories during the parliamentary reform debates) after the enactment of the Reform Bill, sought to unite the enlarged political nation around a conception of the state inherited from the Liverpool era: a strong framework of law and order capable of sustaining market forces. But Peel's attachment to the science of political economy horrified some of his party who feared the dissolution of traditional social bonds by the cash nexus. Whereas he intended to forge an alliance of the landed and middle classes, Tory paternalists wanted to curb entrepreneurial greed by cultivating an affinity between the aristocracy and the unenfranchised masses. Their image of beneficent hierarchy was refined in the quarrelsome years preceding the Reform Act, and by the 1840s it had become the focus of mounting opposition to Peel's economic libertarianism.

Whig arguments for parliamentary reform were not radical. There was no appeal to natural rights or the attendant doctrine of popular sovereignty. Instead the Reform Bill was defended as a cautious expedient to strengthen the constitution by harmonizing the interests of different types of property.[1] The proposal to eliminate pocket boroughs and increase the urban electorate was nevertheless condemned by Tories as an assault upon constitutional equipoise and inherited wealth, and a preliminary step towards revolution. The measure 'destroys the balance of opposing, but not hostile, powers', Peel informed Parliament in 1831, and did so by depriving the Crown and Lords of the co-ordinate authority they shared with the Commons. Once aristocratic influence had been undermined, moreover, the tendency 'to substitute for a mixed form of government, a pure unmitigated democracy' would be reinforced by the incessant agitation of a multitude no longer subdued by habits of deference and of respect for property rights.[2] Practically every Tory prophesied the collapse of ordered hierarchy, and their comments echoed Burke's response to the spectre of Jacobinism. 'The people without hereditary leaders are like an army without officers' who after a period of mob rule, wrote the historian Archibald Alison, usually settled for 'the tranquillity of undisturbed despotism'.[3] The British, on this account, were poised for the kind of upheaval suffered by their ancestors in the middle of the seventeenth century and more recently by the French.

There was no anarchical whirlwind in the wake of the Reform Act, and Tories soon acknowledged that the broadened electorate provided an opportunity to postpone catastrophe indefinitely. For Alison, who in January 1834 detected a drift back to 'Conservative principles', 'the door to the Demon of Revolution' might remain permanently shut if efforts were made to secure a 'cordial co-operation of all the respectable classes'.[4] By the end of the year the Conservative Party had an unexpected chance to consolidate 'the bonds of mutual interest' between the old squirearchy and the new urban electorate, when William IV dismissed the Whigs and invited Peel to become head of a minority government. After the announcement of a general election Peel issued an address to his Tamworth constituents in which he conceded the irreversibility of the Reform Act, and also affirmed his willingness to govern in its spirit by implementing further reforms – so long as they did not erode the great institutions of church and state. Although the Tamworth Manifesto is regarded by historians as the ideological flagship of the new Conservative Party, it is a rather dull document which hardly amounts to the 'frank and explicit declaration of principle' Peel claimed it to be. The kind of conservatism it outlined, a determination to maintain the framework of the constitution without inhibiting organic change, had already been elaborated with greater cogency by writers such as Burke and Reeves.

More revealing than the manifesto is an address which Peel gave to a group of London merchants and financiers in May 1835, shortly after his resignation as Prime Minister when the government was defeated. Peel reaffirmed his conviction that post-Reform conservatism should steer a middle course between preservation and renewal. But on this occasion he appealed directly to the middle classes to join with other men of property in safeguarding the *ancien régime* against further democratic pressures, and so was more careful to indicate the kind of abuses which should be remedied.[1] What was inviolable was strong executive government, buttressed by the constitution and the Anglican establishment, and so thereby capable of suppressing popular agitation in 'the interests of order and property'. Amenable to reform, on the other hand, were obstacles to 'real economy', meaning restrictions upon *laissez-faire*, for which Peel displayed a 'fixation' throughout his career.[5] Peel is often depicted as a conciliator anxious to occupy a halfway house between the extremes of reaction and radicalism for the sake of national unity: a pragmatist who eschewed dogma for 'the concept of moderate, rational, objective reform'.[6] This assessment is misleading in so far as it obscures his mission to rally the propertied classes around the ideal of a disciplinary state that accommodated a free-market economy. Peel's formula for sound polity, in fact, was not dissimilar to that devised by Burke when he confronted Jacobinism.

On returning to office in 1841 Peel again revealed his penchant for a market economy. While inclined to free trade from political constraints, he was not disposed in his words 'to relax the strict rules of political economy' by extending government regulation of the hours and conditions of work. Compulsory reduction of the hours of labour, he told the Commons in an unsuccessful attempt to block Lord Ashley's amendment to the Factory Bill of 1844, would diminish productivity and squeeze profits. The working classes themselves would suffer when manufacturers cut wages to ensure that prices remained competitive in the world market. To suggest otherwise from misguided philanthropic motives was to ignore 'the doctrines which have prevailed on foreign trade from the days of Adam Smith to the present moment'.[7]

If Peel's adherence to the laws of supply and demand reassured commercial and manufacturing interests, his free-trade policies aroused suspicion among Tory stalwarts. Many rural Conservatives wished to retain protective tariffs on the import of grain; this was partly out of self-interest, but also because the Corn Laws symbolized a network of traditional relationships based upon the ownership of land. Protectionism was opposed by Richard Cobden and other members of the Anti-Corn Law League on the ground that the commercial privileges of farmers inflated bread prices, and were in consequence a form of indirect taxation on the poor for the benefit of an affluent minority. Once the price of corn was fixed by market forces instead of government, according to the league, there would ensue industrial expansion and a consumer boom. More domestic commodities, especially textiles, would be needed to exchange for imported grain, resulting in higher wages and increased purchasing power for the mass of people. Peel – who shared the league's distaste for economic monopolies, while detesting its agitation of the masses 'to a frenzy' – reduced the tariffs on imported corn by half in his 1842 budget. For a period, however, he conceded the protectionist case that unrestrained market forces were inappropriate for agriculture, because of the 'social and moral . . . relation between landlord, tenant, and labourer, which does not rest merely on pecuniary considerations'.[8] What finally convinced Peel of the desirability of repeal was the potato famine in Ireland, because he judged that Parliament would resent granting taxation to feed the Irish peasantry if the Corn Laws were retained.

Whereas protectionists believed that abolition of the Corn Laws would disturb the balanced constitution by undermining the power of inherited wealth, Peel insisted that repeal would guarantee the continuing influence of the landed classes. Citing Burke, he claimed that the English aristocracy had previously secured the framework of the constitution by initiating the remedy of abuses and the removal of outmoded privileges. By now resisting a widespread demand for greater economic competition, the 'territorial aristocracy' would jeopardize the system of mixed government by diminishing its own authority. With the general prosperity resulting from a 'continued relaxation of commercial restrictions', however, political stability would be anchored in an even closer liaison between agricultural and manufacturing interests.[2] Although Peel had persistently used these kinds of argument in favour of an anti-radical alliance of the propertied classes, he failed on this occasion to convince the bulk of Conservatives. The repeal of the Corn Laws in 1846 split the Conservative Party, leaving Peel in charge of a loyalist rump which eventually merged with the new Liberal Party.

Prior to the débâcle of 1846 Peel was not wholly unsuccessful in uniting divergent interests. He was nevertheless plagued throughout his party leadership – as he had been in the 1820s when Home Secretary – by dissidents who feared the consequences of industrialization and resisted many of his reforms, especially those intended to woo the middle classes.[9] For paternalists the best way of tending 'the anti-democratic powers of the constitution', as Thomas De Quincey characterized the task of Toryism,[10] was by cultivating anew the hierarchical values which had emerged in a predominantly rural society. Patrician Tories reiterated the aristocratic ideal of a chain of social discipline through which the wealthy and powerful performed their custodial functions with regard to the lower orders – responsibilities discharged primarily through a network of localized communities in which each squire, with the assistance of an Anglican parson, was 'exercising faithfully, and earnestly, and affectionately, the duties of a little monarch, and so carrying into the minutest details, from day to day, the principles of a paternal government'.[11] These standard-bearers of old Toryism were as committed as their eighteenth-century predecessors to the ancient constitution and established church, though benevolent paternalism was now finally freed from its earlier moorings in a patriarchal account of the source of political authority. But whereas writers such as Burke and Reeves had extolled the social and political functions of 'chieftains' as a means of rallying the propertied classes against the threat of radical populism, Tory paternalists now accused one section of the governing élite of abdicating its responsibilities for the common people. The social fabric was threatened less by the potentially unruly masses, they supposed, than by the devotees of political economy intent on displacing the affective ties associated with landed proprietorship by the harsh, impersonal relations of the capitalist market. Hence their desire for a concordat between rich and poor in opposition to the industrial middle classes and their allies, including the Peelite wing of the Conservative Party.

Tory paternalism was foreshadowed by the apostasy of some of the literati who in their youth had been captivated by the ideals of the French Revolution. In middle age these disillusioned romantics lamented the disappearance of a pastoral world, in which an ethos of *noblesse oblige* among the wealthy evoked filial respect from those socially dependent upon them. Their nostalgia for a vanishing past intensified in the years of economic depression from 1815, when urban and rural unrest was vigorously repressed by the Liverpool administration. The poets William Wordsworth, Robert Southey and Samuel Taylor Coleridge attributed popular distress and agitation to what Coleridge called '*an overbalance of the commercial spirit in consequence of the absence or weakness of the counter-weights*'. These counter-weights consisted of inherited wealth and a Church of England which, neglecting its pastoral duties, had as Wordsworth put it, failed to 'embrace an ever-growing and ever-shifting population of mechanics and artisans'.[12] For Southey, the closest of the three to Tory paternalists in his analysis of social dislocation and remedies for restoring a measure of symmetry, the apotheosis of this commercial spirit was political economy, and Smith's 'hard-hearted' *Wealth of Nations* was its creed. In this 'colliquative diarrhoea of the intellect' were dissolved the values which had sustained the protection of the poor, leaving the labourer exposed as a manufacturing animal perceived solely as a source of profit.[13] The ethos of the old order could be partially restored, according to Southey, if the urban poor were provided with decent conditions at home and at work, as well as edifying religious and moral instruction.

Coleridge, more inclined than his fellow romantics to abstract speculation, eventually conceived a grand scheme for reconstructing an organic society. In his last work, *On the Constitution of the Church and State*, published in 1830, Coleridge argued that a balance could be achieved between stability and progress if the landed and middle classes were enabled to perform their complementary functions within the constitution. More radically, he advocated the formation of a new national church in which moral and spiritual leadership would be the prerogative of lay intellectuals. But few patrician Tories were willing to make this kind of *rapprochement* with the commercial classes; and none wished to supplant Anglican clergy with a secular 'clerisy'.

Patrician Toryism developed into a parliamentary faction around 1824, in opposition to the Liverpool administration's free-trade budgets as well as to mounting pressure to remove Catholic disabilities. Ultras (the epithet acquired by members of the faction) believed that Roman Catholics were legitimately excluded from political power because of their intolerant theology and ultimate loyalty to a supra-national pope. Catholic emancipation, according to Ultras, would breach that partnership between church and state which had been sealed by the Glorious Revolution: a settlement made necessary by the despotism of the non-Anglican James II who, once in exile, had gathered around him traitors unwilling to take the oath of allegiance to a firmly Protestant and constitutional monarch. In 1828 the principle of a confessional state was breached when the Tory government, now led by Wellington, admitted nonconformists to public office by repealing the Test and Corporation Acts. A few months later Daniel O'Connell, leader of the Catholic Association, won an election for County Clare, and the government considered that civil war would erupt in Ireland if he were prevented from taking his seat at Westminster. The Bill for Catholic Relief was guided through the Commons in March 1829 by Peel, Leader of the House and Home Secretary, until then regarded as a champion of the Protestant constitution. Ultras were infuriated by 'the great betrayal' and began to act as a breakaway party. They created mass organizations in the country, plotted unsuccessfully to form their own ministry, voted with Whigs in November 1830 to defeat Wellington, and only settled their differences with erstwhile Tory colleagues when parliamentary reform became the dominant political issue.[14]

Ultra ideals were expressed in *Blackwood's Edinburgh Magazine*, founded in 1817 to counter the opinions of the Whig *Edinburgh Review*. *Blackwood's* authors persistently denounced free-traders for discarding experience in favour of dogma, and they refuted the 'sophistries of the economists' with arguments not unlike those later used by patrician Tories against Thatcherism. *Laissez-faire* was derided as little else than a fanciful pretext for mercenary capitalists to treat labourers as 'beasts of burden',[15] and they condemned lower tariffs and tight currency control as means of increasing profits for a few at the cost of economic instability and mass unemployment. Contributors to *Blackwood's* confronted the austere logic of political economy from the perspective of those benign principles

> which, while they maintain the due order and proportion of each separate rank in the state, maintain also that protection and support are the right of all . . . As Tories, we maintain that it is the duty of the people to pay obedience to those set in authority over them: but it is also the duty of those in authority to protect the people who are placed below them. They are not to sit in stately grandeur, and see the people perish, nor, indeed, are they ever to forget that they hold their power and their possessions upon the understanding that they administer both more for the good of the people at large, than the people would do, if they had the administration of both themselves.[16]

After Catholic emancipation *Blackwood's* launched a bitter attack upon Peel, accusing him of infidelity, hypocrisy and sycophancy, and of opportunism in stealing Whig clothes.[17] Samuel O'Sullivan, reviewing the parliamentary session in which Catholic disabilities were removed, deplored the mischief that had been done and predicted Peel's political demise. He nevertheless took comfort from the arrival at Westminster of one who, besides defending the Protestant constitution, had for the first time 'stripped the Economists of the attribute of infallibility' through a mixture of eloquence, arithmetical dexterity, and historical and philosophical perception – one who thereby bid them 'turn their eyes from the capitalist to the labourer; and who had the spirit and feeling to ask them . . . whether that could be a good system . . . where . . . national prosperity is made to take the resemblance "of Moloch, horrid god, besmeared with gore", and to proceed upon its course amidst the sweat, and the blood, and the groans of its victims'.[18] He had in mind Michael Sadler, who had won a by-election earlier in the year on a wave of anti-Catholic sentiment.

Sadler is entitled to a prominent place in the pantheon of Tory social reformers, and deserves more than the scant attention he usually receives in Conservative Party chronicles, where the tendency is to depict him as a decent old fogy who, in contrast to Peel, was out of touch with the spirit of the age.[19] He passionately championed the poor in his speeches and writings, and, eventually, through his chairmanship of a parliamentary committee on factory labour. Although Sadler was a public figure for a relatively brief period – remaining in the Commons for less than four years and dying within another three – he played a decisive role in shaping Tory paternalism into a denunciation of possessive individualism.

Arriving at Westminster in time to oppose the Catholic Relief Bill on its second reading, Sadler condemned the measure (in a speech which sold half a million copies when printed) as an attempt to subvert the constitutional settlement of 1688, which had been made by people who not unreasonably identified popery with 'cruelty, tyranny, and arbitrary power . . . having had full experience as to its tendency greatly to weaken, if not to withdraw, that allegiance which is due to the sovereign power of this Protestant empire'.[20] He also spoke against parliamentary reform, and in April 1831 seconded a motion which led to the fall of the Whig ministry. Whereas the balanced constitution had been refined by the wisdom of centuries, Sadler argued in common with other Tories, Whigs viewed it as 'another Bastille – a dungeon of slavery instead of the temple of freedom'. In the flood unleashed by reform, he said, not only the privileges of property, but the barriers protecting the poor would be swept away.[21]

Before entering Parliament Sadler had become known for his refutation of T. R. Malthus, the man reviled by the Ultras, who in *An Essay on the Principle of Population*, published in 1798 and frequently reprinted, contended that there was a natural tendency for population growth to outstrip the means of subsistence. Malthus concluded, as Burke had done by a different line of argument, that neither artificially increased wages nor public charity were appropriate means of alleviating economic hardship. Instead the labouring classes might rescue themselves from pauperism by exercising foresight and moral restraint, postponing marriage until they could afford to support a family. '*Noblesse-obligers*' were appalled by this message of self-help to the poor, because it absolved the rich of their paternal responsibilities. In particular, they were affronted by the attack upon the old poor laws, inherited from the sixteenth century and administered by local property-owners, which Malthus and other economists denounced as a ramshackle and expensive system, discouraging self-reliance and making recipients of charity dependent upon the benevolence of the higher orders. Sadler's repudiation of Malthus was prompted by a desire, shared with other Ultras, to implement an amended version of the English poor laws in Ireland; this was a country providing prima-facie evidence of the principle of population, in that the fecundity of its people was matched by their indigence. An extension of public relief to that part of the British Isles, Malthus told a Select Committee on Emigration in 1827, would only aggravate the distress of its inhabitants.[22]

In *Ireland; its Evils, and their Remedies*, published in the year preceding his election to Parliament, Sadler stood Malthus on his head, arguing that rates of fertility are regulated by rising living standards, not by the fear of starvation. The truth of this contrary principle was obscured by political economy which, masquerading as scientific certainty, sanctioned 'the misrule of those whose elevated duty it is to mitigate or remove human miseries, by attributing those miseries to the laws of nature and of God'.[23] Ireland's problems, according to Sadler, derived from this selfish misrule rather than overbreeding by its population. Much of the ample prosperity produced by the Irish was appropriated by absentee landlords, who suppressed peasant proprietorship through a combination of exorbitant rents and the clearing of smallholdings. One consequence was the flooding of the English labour market with Irish emigrants, driven from their homeland by destitution. The solution was to treat the Irish peasantry as

> they ought to be: let their natural patrons and protectors return to them, not 'for a short time', as exactors and 'drivers', but, permanently, as kind and resident landlords; let labour be fostered and encouraged; let want be relieved, and life preserved, by a moderated system of poor-laws, which shall concede those humble claims to all, which GOD and Nature have immutably established, and which policy itself has long sanctioned: in a word, let the different ranks resume their equally essential stations, each performing their several duties; and the social edifice, thus 'compact together and at unity in itself', shall never again be shaken. These are the means, simple and obvious, though deprecated by inveterate selfishness, and ridiculed by theoretic folly, which would, and in no long time, renovate

> Ireland, and repay the wrongs of many generations . . . The benevolence of the great would then be reflected in the thankful and gratified demeanour of their inferiors . . . Then, indeed, the different ranks of society, instead of so many steps of a dungeon, descending down to lower and still lower depths of misery and degradation, would, like Jacob's ladder, seem reaching up to Heaven, and the Angels of Mercy and Gratitude would be seen ascending and descending thereon, for ever.[24]

Here was a vivid picture of beneficent hierarchy. William Johnstone, writing in *Blackwood's Magazine*, where the plight of Ireland was a recurrent topic, welcomed the book because the conclusions of the Select Committee on Emigration regarding the alleged evils of over-population 'have been shattered to pieces by the battery of Mr. Sadler's erudition'.[25] But *Ireland* was ridiculed in the *Edinburgh Review* by the economist J. R. McCulloch, who had given evidence before the committee and, contrary to Sadler, had attributed the country's misfortunes to excessive fertility coupled with small-scale proprietorship.[26] McCulloch, in turn, was rebuked by Johnstone for his rudeness to Sadler and ignorance about Ireland.[27]

Ireland was intended as a supplement to a projected three-volume work, *The Law of Population: A Treatise in Six Books In Disproof of the Superfecundity of Human Beings and Developing the Real Principle of their Increase*. Only the first four books were eventually published, in 1830, though the two volumes ran to over six hundred pages each. Sadler assembled a mass of evidence from the ancient and modern worlds to verify his benevolent principle and discredit its 'darker' rival. Reviewing the book in the *Edinburgh Review*, T. B. Macaulay, the great Whig historian, denigrated Sadler as a bombastic windbag who confounded statistical incompetence with 'blundering piety'. Sadler wrote a rejoinder which provoked Macaulay to refute him again.[28] John Wilson, the editor of *Blackwood's* also joined the fray, describing as 'paper pellets' all the missiles which Whigs and economists hurled at someone who, besides having written a 'stupendous work', was a champion of the ancient constitution.[29]

Ireland featured in Sadler's speeches as well as his writings. Opposing Catholic relief in his first address to the Commons, he attributed the country's unrest to economic rather than religious grievances. On several occasions he tried, unsuccessfully, to persuade Parliament to extend the poor laws to that part of the British Isles, arguing that the Union would remain perilous while the Irish peasantry were crushed between the greed of absentee landlords and the dogma of political economy. Irish nationalism would triumph, he warned Parliament in 1831, unless the wealthy, closing their ears to the 'cuckoo note' of economists who endorsed the Malthusian population principle, realized that property was held in trust for the welfare of the people.[3] Poor relief was extended to Ireland in 1838, but it incorporated the workhouse structure, approved by economists as a means of encouraging thrift and self-reliance, that had been established by the new English Poor Law of 1834.

Sadler was also anxious for the wealthy to resume their protective responsibilities in rural England, where the elimination of smallholdings had given rise to 'a system of cruelty, oppression and extortion' almost as bad as that prevailing across the Irish Sea. He wanted parish authorities to build cottages for letting at low rents, and also to provide the rural poor with gardens and allotments.[30] Towards the end of 1831, moreover, he became involved in the factory reform movement, and his parliamentary leadership of the campaign for a shorter working day triggered an alliance between Tory paternalists and working-class radicals. Earlier that year Sir John Cam Hobhouse had introduced a Bill to restrict child labour. Faced with strong opposition Hobhouse modified his proposal, and the Act merely limited the hours of children working in cotton mills to twelve a day. Richard Oastler, a Huddersfield Tory who persuaded operatives in Yorkshire to form 'Short-Time Committees' against 'industrial slavery', now asked Sadler – an old friend and political ally – to take parliamentary responsibility for a Bill limiting the daily hours of young people in mills and factories to ten. On agreeing to the request, Sadler received an address from the Huddersfield committee expressing their gratitude to 'a *father* who is ever wishful to promote the welfare and happiness of his children'.[31]

The Short-Time Committees and their sympathizers mounted a massive propaganda campaign between the introduction of the Bill in December 1831 and its second reading the following March. They organized rallies, and, in numerous leaflets, tracts, pamphlets and broadsheets, countered the charge of Whigs and economists that fewer working hours would lead to a spiral of diminished production, higher prices, lower wages and mass unemployment. Sadler presented petitions to Parliament from workers throughout England and Scotland, and his speech on the second reading of the Bill was packed with evidence of the cruelty, degradation and ill health suffered by children in factories. His opening remarks were judged by the editor of *Blackwood's* to be worthy of being 'written in letters of gold'.[32] In them Sadler dwelt on the increasingly exploitative nature of free-market capitalism in order to ridicule the notion that government regulation of the conditions of labour constituted unwarranted interference with the laws of supply and demand.[4] The Whig government had agreed to the second reading of the Bill on condition that it was referred to a select committee. This was chaired by Sadler and called 87 witnesses between April and August 1832. But Parliament was dissolved before employers could give evidence, and the committee decided to publish its minutes without commentary. Robert Southey told Lord Ashley that the shocking revelations of the 700-page report had caused him several restless nights.[33]

Sadler was not elected to the new Parliament, and Ashley (later to become seventh Earl of Shaftesbury) now succeeded 'that great and good man' as sponsor of the Ten Hours Bill.[34] Ashley's involvement in factory reform marked the start of his long career as perhaps the most renowned of Victorian Tory philanthropists.[35] Combining a patrician sense of *noblesse oblige* with the moral fervour of a staunch Low Churchman, Ashley believed that he had a mission to descend into the 'gutter' to promote the moral and material improvement of 'beings created, as ourselves, by the same Maker, redeemed by the same Saviour, and destined to the same immortality'.[36] His reforming zeal was boundless. He worked tirelessly on behalf of the Ten Hours Bill, which met persistent opposition from government and was not enacted until 1847; introduced a Mines Bill to exclude women and children from collieries; sought for years to improve the treatment of the insane; spoke often for a better system of public health; became involved in the Society for Improving the Condition of the Labouring Classes, which attempted to remove the 'festering mischief' of squalid lodging houses by building decent accommodation for the urban poor;[37] and in 1844 was elected President of the Ragged School Union which provided a 'wild and lawless race' of destitute children with religious and moral instruction.[38]

Ashley, unlike Sadler, had neither the inclination nor the ability to vindicate Tory paternalism through a sustained analysis of the 'theoretic folly' of political economy. He nevertheless became increasingly impatient with the cold logic of a doctrine which appeared to absolve its adherents of their protective responsibilities for the poor. Peel, who was unsympathetic to the Ten Hours movement, distrusted Ashley's evangelical earnestness, and declined to appoint him to a senior post in the administration of 1841–6. Ashley, in turn, described Peel as an 'iceberg' obsessed by free-trade dogma. His vision was of a benevolent hierarchy in which each enjoyed 'full, fair, and free opportunity so to exercise all his moral, intellectual, physical, and spiritual energies, that he may, without let or hindrance, be able to do his duty in that state of life to which it has pleased God to call him'.[39] And, like other patrician Tories, he used a mixture of moral and practical arguments to appeal to the wealthy to cultivate afresh the affection and deference of the unenfranchised masses. Unless church and state restored the custodial functions of rank and property, he warned in an essay entitled 'Infant labour', the poor would be driven into the arms of radicals and democrats. The potential fragility of the chain of social discipline was demonstrated by the growing popularity of 'the two great demons [of] Socialism and Chartism'.[5]

Ashley's campaign for a Ten Hours Bill was supported by a handful of youthful MPs who acted as a Tory ginger group for much of Peel's second administration. The contrast between Ashley and Young England, as this coterie of Eton- and Cambridge-educated aristocrats was known, was marked. Whereas he was dour and fervently evangelical, they were romantic and exuberantly High Church; and while Ashley busied himself with philanthropy, Young Englanders dreamed of a lost golden age in which altar and throne had been exalted, and the higher ranks were respected for their generosity and chivalry. What Young England shared with Ashley was a conviction that the custodial responsibilities of the propertied classes were being lost in a 'whirl of money-making', distaste for Peel's complicity with the spirit of commerce, and the fear that failure to restore harmony between social ranks would drive the poor towards Chartism and socialism.

The charms of 'Merrie England' were embellished in the prose and verse of Lord John Manners, second son of the Duke of Rutland, who yearned for a time when:

> Each knew his place – king, peasant, peer or priest,
> The greatest owned connexion with the least;
> From rank to rank the generous feeling ran,
> And linked society as man to man.[40]

His proposals for retrieving an idyllic past included the provision of allotments and smallholdings for the English and Irish peasantry, measures previously advocated by Michael Sadler, who had been Member of Parliament for Newark, the constituency now represented by Manners. Another of Manner's recommendations was for the revival of holy days, to relieve the monotony of the labouring poor by returning them to the fold of a beneficent church:

> From year to year, as wealth has been accumulating and simplicity dying away – as new habits have come in and old ones gone out – as traditional holy-days have been disregarded and fresh hours and days of work obtained; so, in proportion, have dissent and discontent, anarchy and infidelity advanced; until now, when scarce a Maypole is left in England, or a holy-day observed, the banks of the mighty river of pent-up sin and misery are beginning to give way, and men shrink from contemplating the impending deluge.[41]

A deal of youthful naïvety was needed to imagine that the erection of maypoles throughout England might arrest the spread of bourgeois values and avert revolution. Sadler's analysis of political economy and Ashley's passion for good works were attempts, however flawed, to confront the unsavoury realities of an expanding industrial society. The nostalgia of Young England for a mythical yesteryear, in contrast, was little else than what the *Morning Herald* termed 'mental dandyism'.[42] Young England dilettantes were but a small thorn in Peel's side. They articulated a growing dissatisfaction with his free-market policies without formulating a plausible alternative programme, and as a parliamentary faction they began to fragment in the year preceding the repeal of the Corn Laws. As exotic publicists of the ideals of *noblesse oblige*, however, they did provide a platform for someone who was profoundly to influence the future course of the Conservative Party.

The target of Benjamin Disraeli's literary salvoes in the 1830s had been Whiggism rather than Peelite conservatism. He depicted Whigs, rather as John Reeves had done forty years earlier, as an oligarchy who in pursuit of their selfish ambitions were ever willing to undermine national institutions by allying themselves with radicals. Factional Whiggism had been opposed, sometimes effectively, by a national party largely because of Bolingbroke who

> eradicated from Toryism all those absurd and odious doctrines which Toryism had adventitiously adopted, clearly developed its essential and permanent character, discarded *jure divino*, demolished passive obedience, threw to the winds the doctrine of non-resistance . . . and in the complete reorganisation of the public mind laid the foundation for the future accession of the Tory party to power.[43]

By 1845, however, Disraeli was claiming that the Conservative Party had abandoned the principles of Bolingbroke's Toryism, and was in consequence itself a faction. Annoyed by Peel's refusal to grant his request for office in the new administration, he had assumed the leadership of Young England in 1842, and during the next three years gradually distanced himself from government policies. Initially his contempt was reserved for those outside the Conservative Party who wished to drown 'the territorial and feudal system' in a sea of market economics. In a speech of 1843 to his Shrewsbury constituents he extolled aristocratic values, and also defended Peel for resisting mounting pressure from liberals, economists and the Anti-Corn Law League to abolish tariffs on imported grain. Disraeli endorsed the *ancien régime*, acclaimed the protective responsibilities associated with landed proprietorship, and regretted that the spirit of the age had nourished a selfish millocracy. The speech is an eloquent statement of the ideals of Young England and other paternalists.[6]

Disraeli hoped in 1843 that Peel would refuse to repeal the Corn Laws, in spite of having already halved tariffs. But his relations with the government rapidly deteriorated, and in *Coningsby*, published in 1844 as the first of a trilogy of novels embodying the ethos of Young England, he denounced the conservatism of the Tamworth Manifesto as a concoction of policies 'without a guide and without an aim'. *Coningsby* was followed the next year by *Sybil*, which portrayed an England torn apart by 'the selfish strife' of two factions, Whig and Conservative, neither of whom cared for the welfare of the people. Rich and poor were consequently divided into 'Two Nations, governed by different laws, influenced by different manners, with no thoughts or sympathies in common; with an innate inability of mutual comprehension'. National unity would not be restored until the propertied classes again viewed their wealth as a trust for the common benefit. Disraeli's opposition to Peel reached a climax in 1846, and within three years of the fracturing of the Conservative Party he headed the protectionists in the Commons. Two decades later, as Conservative leader, Disraeli was to fashion the patrician Toryism with which he had accused Peel of 'political infidelity' into an appeal to the working class – now partially enfranchised – to support the programme of a reconstituted national party.

NOTES

1 See the arguments of Macaulay and Russell in Robert Eccleshall, *British Liberalism: Liberal Thought form the 1640s to the 1980s*, London: Longman, 1986, pp. 94–8.

2 *The Speeches of the late Right Honourable Sir Robert Peel, Bart. Delivered in the House of Commons . . . in four volumes*, Vol. 2, London: George Routledge, 1853, pp. 391–2.

3 Archibald Alison, 'The British peerage', *Blackwood's Edinburgh Magazine*, Vol. XXX, 1831, pp. 86, 88.

4 Archibald Alison, 'Hints to the Aristocracy', *Blackwood's Edinburgh Magazine*, Vol. XXXV, 1834, pp. 68–80.

5 Boyd Hilton, 'Peel: a reappraisal', *Historical Journal*, Vol. 22, 1979, pp. 585–614.

6 Norman Gash, 'Wellington and Peel 1832–1846', in Donald Southgate (ed.), *The Conservative Leadership 1832–1932*, London: Macmillan, 1974, p. 42.

7 *The Speeches of the late Right Honourable Sir Robert Peel, Bart. Delivered in the House of Commons . . . in four volumes*, Vol. 4, London: George Routledge, 1853, pp. 344, 371.

8 ibid., p. 531.

9 See Ian Newbould, 'Sir Robert Peel and the Conservative Party, 1832–1841: a study in failure?' *English Historical Review*, Vol. 98, 1983, pp. 529–57.

10 'A Tory's account of Toryism, Whiggism, and Radicalism in a letter to a friend in Bengal', in David Masson (ed.), *The Collected Writings of Thomas De Quincey*, Vol. IX, London: A. & C. Black, 1897, p. 337.

11 William Sewell, 'Carlyle's *Works*', *Quarterly Review*, Vol. LXVI, 1840, p. 501.

12 Samuel Taylor Coleridge, 'Blessed are ye that sow beside all Waters', in Derwent Coleridge (ed.), *Lay Sermons*, 3rd edn. London: Edward Moxon, 1852, pp. 188–9; William Wordsworth, 'Postcript', in *The Poetical Works*, Vol. VI, London: Edward Moxon, 1857, p. 413.

13 Robert Southey, 'On the State of the Poor, the principle of Mr. Malthus's Essay on Population, and the Manufacturing System', in *Essays, Moral and Political . . . in two volumes*, Vol. I, London: John Murray, 1832, p. 111; 'On the state of the Poor, and the means pursued by the Society for bettering their condition, ibid., p. 246. The best short account of the benevolent Toryism of the period is Iain Robertson Scott, '"Things as they are": the literary response to the French Revolution, 1789–1815', in H. T. Dickinson (ed.), *Britain and the French Revolution 1789–1815*, London: Macmillan, 1989, pp. 229–49.

14 D. G. S. Simes, *The Ultra Tories in British Politics*, D. Phil. thesis, Oxford University, 1974; G. I. T. Machin, *The Catholic Question in English Politics 1820 to 1830*, Oxford: Clarendon Press, 1964.

15 Edward Edwards, 'The Influence of Free Trade upon the Condition of the Labouring Classes', *Blackwood's Edinburgh Magazine*, Vol. XXVII, 1830, pp. 553–68. See F. W. Fetter, 'The economic articles in *Blackwood's Edinburgh Magazine*, and their authors, 1817–1853', *Scottish Journal of Political Economy*, Vol. 7, 1960, pp. 85–107, 213–31; and Harold Perkin, *The Origins of Modern English Society 1780–1830*, London: Routledge & Kegan Paul, 1969, pp. 237–52.

16 William Johnstone, 'Our Domestic Policy No. I', *Blackwood's Edinburgh Magazine*, Vol. XXVI, 1829, p. 768.

17 E.g. David Robinson, 'Political Economy. No. IV', ibid., Vol. XXVII, 1830, p. 41.

18 Samuel O'Sullivan, 'Review of the Last Session of Parliament', ibid., Vol. XXVI, 1829, pp. 224–37.

19 E.g. Robert Blake, *The Conservative Party from Peel to Thatcher*, London: Fontana, 1985, pp. 21–2. Blake describes Sadler as a 'High Tory paternalist' who did not belong to the Ultras; this is odd because he became the leading parliamentary spokesman of the group. The phrase 'High Tory' is probably best avoided in case it is taken to imply a religious, as well as political, standpoint. Although most Tory paternalists were firm Anglicans, some of them – Sadler and Ashley, for example – were staunch Low Churchmen. There is no biography of Sadler apart from the hagiographical R. B. Seeley, *Memoirs of the Life and Writings of Michael Thomas Sadler, Esq., M.P. F.R.S.*, London: R. B. Seeley & W. Burnside, 1842.

20 Hansard, *Parliamentary Debates*, 2nd series, Vol. XX (Feb.–Mar. 1829), cols 1156, 1170.

21 ibid., 3rd series, Vol. III, 1831, cols 1530–67; 3rd series IX (Dec.–1831–Feb. 1832), cols 1220–1.

22 On the debate about Irish poor relief, see R. D. C. Black, *Economic Thought and the Irish Question 1817–1870*, Cambridge: Cambridge University Press, 1960, ch. IV.

23 Michael Sadler, *Ireland; its Evils, and their Remedies: Being a Refutation of the Errors of the Emigration Committee and Others, Touching that Country. To which is Prefixed, a Synopsis of an Original Treatise, about to be Published, on the Law of Population; Developing the Real Principle on Which it is Universally Regulated*, London: John Murray, 1828, p. xlvi.

24 ibid., pp. 407–12.

25 William Johnstone, 'Ireland as it is; in 1828', *Blackwood's Edinburgh Magazine*, Vol. XXIV, 1828, pp. 753–4.

26 J. R. McCulloch, 'Sadler on Ireland', *Edinburgh Review*, Vol. 49, 1829, pp. 300–17.

27 William Johnstone, 'Mr Sadler, and the Edinburgh Review', *Blackwood's Edinburgh Magazine*, Vol. XXVI, 1829, pp. 825–8.

28 'Sadler's Law of Population' and 'Sadler's Refutation', in *The Miscellaneous Writings of Lord Macaulay*, popular edn, London: Longmans, Green, 1900, pp. 226–66; Sadler, *A Refutation of an Article in the*

'Edinburgh Review' (No. CII) entitled, 'Sadler's Law of Population, and Disproof of Human Superfecundity'; containing also Additional Proofs of the Principle enunciated in that Treatise, founded on the Census of different Countries recently published, London, 1832.

29 ['Christopher North'], 'Mr Sadler and the Edinburgh Reviewer. A Prolusion, in three Chapters', *Blackwood's Edinburgh Magazine*, Vol. XXIX, 1831, pp. 392–428.

30 Hansard, *Parliamentary Debates*, 3rd series, Vol. VIII, 1831, cols, 498–536.

31 Cited in Cecil Driver, *Tory Radical: the Life of Richard Oastler*, New York: Oxford University Press 1946, p. 114.

32 John Wilson, 'The Factory System', *Blackwood's Edinburgh Magazine*, Vol. XXXIII, 1833, p. 424.

33 Geoffrey Carnall, *Robert Southey and his Age: the Development of a Conservative Mind*, Oxford: Clarendon Press, 1960, p. 190.

34 'Legislation for the Labouring Classes', in *Speeches of the Earl of Shaftesbury upon Subjects Relating to the Claims and Interests of the Labouring Class*, London: Chapman & Hall, 1868, p. 146.

35 He has attracted much more attention than Sadler: Edwin Hodder, *The Life and Work of the Seventh Earl of Shaftesbury*, London: Cassell, 1887; J. L. and Barbara Hammond, *Lord Shaftesbury*, London: Constable, 1925; Georgina Battiscombe, *Shaftesbury: a Biography of the Seventh Earl 1801–1885*, London: Constable, 1974; Geoffrey B. A. M. Finlayson, *The Seventh Earl of Shaftesbury 1801–1885*, London: Eyre Methuen, 1981.

36 'Children not protected by the Factory Acts', in *Speeches of the Earl of Shaftesbury*, op. cit., p. 28.

37 Lord Ashley, 'Lodging-Houses', *Quarterly Review*, Vol. LXXXII, 1847, p. 142.

38 Lord Ashley, 'The Ragged Schools', *Quarterly Review*, Vol. LXXIX, 1846, p. 139.

39 'Sanitary Legislation', in *Speeches of the Earl of Shaftesbury*, op. cit., p. 308.

40 'England's Trust', cited in Richard Faber, *Young England*, London: Faber, 1987, p. 61. On Young England see too Charles Whibley, *Lord John Manners and His Friends*, London: William Blackwood, 1925; and W. F. Monypenny and G. F. Buckle, *The Life of Benjamin Disraeli, Earl of Beaconsfield, Vol. II 1837–1846*, London: John Murray, 1912, ch. VIII.

41 Lord John Manners, *A Plea for National Holy-Days*, London: Painter, 1843, pp. 19–20.

42 Cited in Faber, *Young England*, op. cit., p. 125.

43 *Vindication of the English Constitution in a Letter to a Noble and Learned Lord*, in William Hutcheson (ed.), *Whigs and Whiggism: Political Writings by Benjamin Disraeli*, London: John Murray, 1913, p. 219.

1. Sir Robert Peel (1788–1850)

'At Merchant Tailors' Hall. May 11th, 1835.' In *Speeches by the Right Honourable Sir Robert Peel, Bart. During his Administration, 1834–1835* . . . , 2nd edn, London: Roake & Varty, 1835, pp. 291–7

Peel's father symbolized that fusion of land and industry which his son considered to be a principal source of political stability and economic expansion. He was a Lancashire cotton manufacturer, who in 1790 became parliamentary representative for Tamworth, a borough in Staffordshire where he bought estates and eventually settled. The elder Robert supported the efforts of the Pitt administration to stifle Jacobinism. His son was educated at Harrow and Christ Church, Oxford, from where he graduated in 1808 with a double first in classics and mathematics. He entered Parliament the next year as member for Cashel, County Tipperary, transferring to a seat at Chippenham in 1812 and one at Oxford University in 1817. After two years as Under-Secretary at the Department of War and Colonies Peel was appointed chief secretary to the Lord Lieutenant of Ireland in 1812 and, during his six years in the post, strengthened the Irish system of law and order and opposed moves to abolish Catholic disabilities. Peel was Home Secretary from 1822 until Liverpool's resignation in 1827, and again between 1828 and 1830, when he reformed the criminal law, established a metropolitan police force and, to the disgust of Ultras who had formerly regarded him as the champion of the Anglican establishment, removed the prohibitions on Roman Catholics from holding public office, by steering the Catholic Relief Bill through Parliament. After losing his seat at Oxford University Peel became Member of Parliament for Westbury in 1829, transferring to Tamworth on the death of his father in the following year. In November 1834 he was recalled by William IV from holiday in Italy to 'put himself at the head of the administration of the country'. After a general election, Peel led a minority government for three months, until it was defeated in April 1835 by a Whig/Radical motion to use the revenues of the established church in Ireland for the benefit of the whole community.

Peel gave the following speech at a dinner hosted by London bankers and traders in appreciation of the principles by which he had governed.

On taking office, I avowed my determination to abide by the Reform Bill. I trust I have redeemed that pledge. On this broad constitutional principle my friends and I acted. We acted in the spirit of the Reform Bill, not niggardly, not merely content with a cold assent and submission to its details, but with an honest and generous deference to its spirit and to the authority which it established . . . Let us then declare our readiness to accept in good faith, as a constitutional settlement, the provisions of the Reform Bill, and let us by that declaration fortify ourselves in the resistance to new agitations of the public mind on questions of government, to new innovations on what was called but yesterday, by its friends, the second charter of our liberties . . .

[W]e disclaim any separation from the middling classes of society in this country. O no, we are bound to them by a thousand ramifications of direct personal connexion, and common interests, and common feelings. If circumstances may appear to have elevated some of us above the rest, to what, I venture to ask, is that elevation owing? It is owing to nothing else but to the exercise, either on our own part or on the part of our immediate forefathers, of those qualities of diligence, of the love of order, of industry, of integrity in commercial dealings, which have hitherto secured to every member of every middle class of society the opportunities of elevation and distinction in this great community; and it is because we stand in our present situation – it is because we owe our elevation in society to the exercise of those qualities, and because we feel that so long as this ancient form of government, and the institutions connected with it, and the principles and feelings which they engender, shall endure, the same elevation will be secured by the same means, that we are resolved, with the blessing of God, to keep clear for others those same avenues that were opened to ourselves, that we will not allow their course to be obstructed by men who want to secure the same advantages by dishonest means – to reach by some shorter cut, that goal, which can be surely attained, but can be attained, only through industry, patient perseverance, and strict integrity. Gentlemen, what was the charge against myself? It was this, that the king had sent to Rome for the son of a cotton-spinner, in order to make him prime minister of England. Did I feel that a reflection? Did it make me discontented with the state of the laws and institutions of the country? No; but does it not make me, and ought it not to make you, Gentlemen, anxious to preserve that happy order of things under which the same opportunities of distinction may be ensured to other sons of other cotton-spinners, provided they can establish a legitimate claim on the confidence of their King and Country? We are charged with having some interest in the perpetuation of abuses. Why, can there be any one with a greater interest than we have, that the public burdens should be as much lightened as they can possibly be, consistently with the maintenance of the public engagements? We are represented as fattening on the public income. Looking to this company, and to those associated with it in feeling, is there any gain, I ask, connected with the increase of the public burdens that can countervail the interest we have in their reduction? We have a direct, a superior interest to any others in the correction of every abuse and the application of every just principle of just and wise economy.

At the same time, consistently with these feelings, consistently with the determination to correct real abuses, and to promote real economy, we do not disguise that it is our firm resolution to maintain to the utmost of our power, the limited monarchy of this country, to respect the rights of every branch of the legislature, to maintain inviolate the united Church of England and Ireland, to maintain it as a predominant establishment, meaning by predominance, not the denial of any civil right to other classes of the community, but maintaining the Church in the possession of its property and of all its just privileges. Such is our firm resolution; we will submit to no compromise, and we will exercise every privilege which the constitution has intrusted to us for the legitimate maintenance and support of the constitution in Church and State. This is the appeal we make to the middle classes of the community – to those who are mainly the depositaries of the elective franchise. We tell them that it is not only our determination to resist any direct attack on our institutions, but that we are also resolved that we will not permit the ancient prescriptive Government of this country – the mitigated monarchy, consisting of three branches of the legislature – we are determined that we will not allow it to be changed, by plausible and specious propositions of reform, into a democratic republic. We will not allow, if we can prevent it – we will not allow that, through plausible and popular pretexts of improvement and reform, there shall gradually take place such an infusion of democracy into the institutions of this country as shall essentially change their theory and practical character, and shall by slow degrees rob us of the blessings we have so long enjoyed under our limited monarchy and popular but balanced constitution.

Now, Gentlemen, that is what I apprehend we mean by – this is the construction we put upon – the term 'Conservative principles'; and such is the ground on which we make an appeal to the country at large for the maintenance of those principles. We tell all, in whatever class of life they may be, that they ought to feel as deep an interest in the maintenance of those principles as any of the politicians or men of property who are now within my hearing. The preservation of order depends on them, the maintenance of that security, which has hitherto led men through honest industry to accumulate property in this country, depends upon them.

My advice to you is, not to permit past differences on political subjects now to prevent a cordial union with those who take a similar view with yourselves on matters of immediately pressing importance. There are many questions on which you formerly differed from others, that are now settled. There are many public men from whose views you formerly dissented, who agree with you that the Reform Bill is not to be made a platform from which a new battery is to be directed against the remaining institutions of this country. If they agree with you in this, the essential practical point; if, wishing with you to correct real abuses, they are still determined to maintain the ancient principles on which the constitution of the country is founded, to protect the interests of order and property, it would be madness to revive old and extinguished differences, and to allow the remembrance of such shadows to obstruct an harmonious and cordial union for the defence and preservation of all that remains.

2. Sir Robert Peel

'Corn Importation Bill. May 4 1846.' In *The Speeches of the late Right Honourable Sir Robert Peel, Bart. Delivered in the House of Commons . . . in four volumes*, Vol. 4, London: George Routledge, 1853, pp. 681–2, 684–5

Peel may have judged as early as the 1820s that the Corn Laws could not survive permanently, but his policy on returning to office in 1841 was steadily to reduce the tariffs on imported grain rather than instantly to abolish them. Faced with the activities of the Anti-Corn Law League, poor harvests, high prices and an economic depression, however, he probably decided in 1843 that repeal could not be postponed for long. In the early months of 1846 protectionists formed themselves into a group led by Lord George

Bentinck, who vilified Peel for his alleged treachery in advocating abolition, and two-thirds of Conservative MPs voted against the final reading of the Corn Importation Bill on 15 May 1846. The Bill, which was carried with Whig/Radical support, received its third reading in the Lords on 25 June, and a few hours later Peel was defeated in the Commons because Whigs and Radicals now joined protectionists in opposing a request for additional coercive powers to quell unrest in Ireland. In 1847 the protectionist wing of the shattered party decided to retain the name Conservative, leaving Peel in charge of an independent group which supported the Whig administration on many issues. Peel died in 1850 after falling from his horse, and within three years Peelites had entered a formal coalition with Liberals.

> I do not think that you can defend any restrictions upon the importation of food, that is, to increase the natural price of food by legislative intervention, except on some great public reasons connected with the public good. I think, Sir, the presumption is against those restrictions. The natural presumption, I think, particularly in the House of Commons, which has already adopted the principle of freedom from restriction in respect to almost all other articles of importation, is in favour of the unrestricted importation of food. Consistency on the part of the House requires that the same principle that has been applied to almost all other articles of foreign produce shall be applied in like manner to food, unless you can, for some reason connected with the general and the permanent welfare of the country, establish a distinction between food and all other articles of produce. You must, in fact, show that it is for the general interest of the country that these restrictions would continue. Sir, it is because I cannot with truth allege that if you establish free trade in corn, you will probably become dependent upon foreign nations for your supply of the necessaries of life – it is because I do not believe that the rate of wages varies directly with the price of food – it is because I cannot persuade myself that with respect to the intelligent farmers, it can be considered that this protection is necessary to agricultural prosperity – it is because I cannot establish these facts, I have come to the conclusion that the natural presumption in favour of unrestricted importation ought to prevail, and therefore that it is unjust to continue these legislative restrictions upon food . . . I believe . . . that the great mass of the manufacturing population will be doubly benefited by the removal of these restrictions;

first, by increasing the demand for those manufacturing articles upon which their labour is expended; and, in the next place, by giving them, from the wages which they receive, a greater command over the necessaries and comforts of life. I think that will be the double operation of this repeal in the Corn-laws; and, therefore, as far as that part of the population is concerned, I cannot maintain the continuance of restrictions on the ground of benefit to them . . . I believe it to be of the utmost importance that a territorial aristocracy should be maintained. I believe that in no country is it of more importance than in this, with its ancient constitution, ancient habits, and mixed form of government . . .

My firm belief is, that you will more increase the just influence and authority of that body by now foregoing this protection than by continuing it. No author or statesman has dealt more fully and forcibly on this subject than Burke. And what does he say? Mr. Burke says, that it is absolutely essential that a territorial aristocracy should be maintained in this country; that it has taken the lead in all great measures of reform; and that, on the other hand, it has been the great strength and stay of a conservative government. He says, how is it that the territorial aristocracy of England has maintained this influence? Because, he answers, it has always identified itself with the people; it has never pertinaciously insisted on the maintenance of a privilege when the time for foregoing that privilege has arrived. He draws the contrast between the aristocracy of England, wisely consulting public opinion, relinquishing privilege when the time for exercise of privilege had gone, and the territorial aristocracy of France, insisting upon the maintenance of privilege long after that period . . . I infer that the privileges of a territorial aristocracy will not be diminished or its influence destroyed by consenting to a free trade in corn, because I firmly believe, speaking generally, that the aristocracy will sustain no injury from it whatever. I do not believe, as I said before, generally speaking, that the value of land, or the privileges of land, or the influence of land, will be diminished. Of this I am sure, that if it will not, you are establishing for the aristocracy a new claim upon the affection and sympathies of the people by making a sacrifice of your prejudices . . . I said long ago, that I thought agricultural prosperity was interwoven with manufacturing prosperity; and depended more on it than on the Corn-laws. Continued reflection has confirmed me in that opinion. I believe that it is for the interest of the agriculturist that you should lay a permanent foundation of manufacturing prosperity; and as your land is necessarily limited in quantity, as your population is increasing, as your wealth is increasing, that the true interests of land are co-existent with the manufacturing and commercial prosperity. I see in the continued relaxation of commercial restrictions a new foundation laid for manufacturing and commercial prosperity; and therefore, I look forward to their indirect operation, and I believe you will find the value of land increased with the removal of these restrictions, and with additional opportunities for carrying on extended commerce.

3. Michael Thomas Sadler (1780–1835)

'*Aug*. 29. Poor Laws (Ireland) – Motion by Mr. Sadler, that it is expedient and necessary to constitute a Legal Provision for the Poor (Ireland).' In *Hansard's Parliamentary Debates . . . comprising the period from the fifteenth day of August, to the thirteenth day of September, 1831*, 3rd series, Vol. VI, London: Baldwin & Cradock, 1832, cols 791–2, 800–1, 814–15

Sadler was born at Snelston, Derbyshire, into an Anglican family with evangelical sympathies, and at the age of 18 wrote a pamphlet defending itinerant Methodist preachers against persecution. In 1800 he joined his brother's flax business in Leeds, and ten years later the Sadlers entered into partnership with a firm which imported Irish linens. Michael became a Sunday school superintendent and an administrator of poor relief, joined a 'Church and King' group, commanded a volunteer company, contributed to the Tory *Leeds Intelligencer*, spoke against parliamentary reform and Catholic emancipation, and was a founder member of the Leeds Literary and Philosophical Society.

Sadler was returned to Parliament as a Tory at a by-election held in March 1829 after Sir William Clinton, Lieutenant-General of the Ordnance, resigned his seat at Newark-upon-Trent in protest against the Catholic Relief Bill. It was alleged that Sadler won because supporters of his opponent, Serjeant Wilde, had been intimidated by the borough's patron, the Ultra Duke of Newcastle. The following year Parliament voted against referring to a select committee a petition from the inhabitants of Newark, who complained about the election and demanded action to curtail the duke's corrupt practices. In April 1831 Sadler seconded a successful anti-government motion to retain the existing number of parliamentary members for England and Wales, and at the ensuing general election was returned for the safer seat of Aldborough, Yorkshire, for which he had been nominated by Newcastle.

> The marks and badges of poverty remain just the same in Ireland as they were centuries ago, when Spencer, and after him Petty, Swift, and a whole host of political writers, described the miserable clothing, the wretched habitations, sties, as such writers have constantly denominated them, in which an Englishman would scruple to house for a single night his pampered brute – food, in quality and quantity inadequate to the preservation of health, being then as now, principally vegetable, and of an inferior kind than even to that consumed at present; a state, in short, always pushed to the utmost extremity of endurance, and to which the common misfortunes incident to humanity, such as the failure of a single crop, the loss of cattle, the illness of a family, the death of a parent, bring irretrievable ruin, when the wretched sufferers have to swell that general mass of mendicity, which is constantly inundating Ireland with misery and pollution. But if the evils to which poverty is subject every where, are thus fearfully increased in Ireland, there are others peculiar to that country, which still heighten the general misery. The constant and vast confiscations in that country, which has been too often parcelled out in immense portions, among the selfish instruments of power, have had the effect of transferring much of the property of Ireland to absentees, the number of whom has been also increased by a variety of other causes. These, as Coke argues, have broken the legal condition on which such property was bestowed; they have, at all events, violated the moral duties which its possession imposed. Evils of the most frightful nature, and of the greatest magnitude, especially bearing upon the poorer classes, have resulted from this cause. It has given rise to that race of Irish oppressors (for such, with some honourable exceptions, they may be regarded) – the middlemen. It has, on the one hand, mainly occasioned the exaction of those exorbitant rents, to which the wretched peasantry of Ireland have been long subject, and, on the other, it has deprived them of that labour by which alone those rents could, in many instances, be perfectly discharged. It has been the means of constantly exhibiting the horrible spectacle of a people starving in a land of plenty, and a country exporting its produce in the very moment of famine. It muzzles the mouth of the ox that treadeth out the corn, which it goads on by privation and insult, to desperation. Above all, it sets the example, and

is itself the principal instrument in those sudden and extensive clearances, which if perpetrated in this country, where the poverty so created would have to be sustained, would not be very popular; but in Ireland, where there is no such provision, amount to the height of cruelty. The want of a law in favour of the oppressed there, amounts to a direct encouragement to and premium upon such a course, instead of repressing it, and thus shares the crime of such proceedings. It is idle and false to assert, that these drivings are the necessary consequence of surplus numbers, as some ignorantly allege . . .

It is notoriously otherwise. There is no one who has the slightest knowledge of the subject that is not perfectly aware of the utter fallacy, the extravagant folly of such a supposition. Let those who, on the subject of the extreme poverty and degradation of Ireland, repeat the cuckoo note of the economists 'surplus population', and suppose they have solved the fearful political enigma which the condition of Ireland propounds, stand forth and say whether they do or do not know, that the misery of the Irish, arising either from the nature and insufficiency of their food, their clothing, and their habitations; from the dearths and famines, and the epidemics, which they periodically endure, more fatal often than the plague; from the constant want of labour, and its inadequate remuneration – were evils which did not exist, to a still greater degree, when the population was notoriously scanty, not a third nor a fourth of its present amount, and when the political economists of those days attributed these sufferings to a paucity of population, and busied themselves about the task of replenishing it; always busied, therefore, in attempts beyond their reach, and neglecting the obvious duties dictated alike by policy and humanity, and easy to perform . . .

At this moment the distresses the people suffer, the tolerated desertion of so large a portion of the wealthier classes, and the absence of all legal provision for the poverty thus occasioned, are loosening the attachments which many of the inhabitants of that island had cherished for an intimate connection with this; and the Anti-unionists, it must be confessed, are hourly gaining strength, and their triumph would be the downfall of this great and ancient empire. A dark cloud of suffering has long hung over the west, where the angry elements are again heard from afar, and threatening that storm which may again shake the empire to its very foundations. The time is come when property must be taught that it has duties to perform as strictly and righteously due, as those it exacts from poverty. Politicians and economists may agree as they please, but their palliations and apologies will not much longer avail.

4. Michael Thomas Sadler

'*Mar.* 16. Factories Regulation Bill – read a second time, and referred to a Select Committee.' In *Hansard's Parliamentary Debates . . . comprising the period from the ninth day of March, to the sixth day of April, 1832*, 3rd series, Vol. XI, London: Baldwin & Cradock, 1832, cols 342–4, 375

Sadler became prospective candidate for Leeds shortly after assuming parliamentary leadership of the factory reform movement; his Aldborough constituency having been abolished by the Reform Bill. In the months preceding the general election of December 1832, Leeds was the focus of a dramatic and virulent contest between a Tory-Radical alliance and Whigs. The Yorkshire Short-Time Committees fought a vigorous campaign on behalf of Sadler, who received messages of support from operatives throughout the country. His Whig opponents were John Marshall, a wealthy manufacturer, and T. B. Macaulay – scornful reviewer of *The Law of Population* – who called Sadler 'a *convenient philanthropist*' and beat him into third place in the election.

When Lord Ashley re-introduced the Ten Hours Bill in the new session of Parliament, the government set up a Royal Commission and Sadler wrote a couple of pamphlets condemning the secrecy with which the commissioners conducted their inquiry. In 1833 he contested a by-election at Huddersfield, but a split within the Tory-Radical alliance secured victory for the Whig candidate. Meanwhile Macaulay had resigned from Leeds to join the new Legislative Council of India, but Sadler was too ill to contest the seat. In 1834 he moved to Belfast, where the family firm had links with the linen industry, and died there on 29 July the following year. The 'heaven-born man', as Oastler described him, was buried at Ballylesson.

Sir, the Bill which I now proceed to implore the House to sanction by its authority, has, for its purpose, to liberate children and other young persons employed in the mills and factories of the kingdom, from that over exertion and confinement which common sense, as well as long experience has shown to be utterly inconsistent with the improvement of their minds, the preservation of their morals, or the protection of their health: in a word, to rescue them from a state of suffering and degradation which, it is conceived, the children of the industrious classes in hardly any other country endure, or ever have experienced, and which cannot be much longer tolerated . . . But, I apprehend, the strongest objection that will be offered on this occasion will be grounded upon the pretence that the very principle of the Bill is an improper interference between the employer and the employed, and an attempt to regulate by law the market of labour. Were that market supplied by free agents, properly so denominated, I should fully participate in those objections. Theoretically, indeed, such is the case, but practically, I fear the fact is far otherwise, even regarding those who are of mature age; and the boasted freedom of our labourers in many pursuits will, on a just view of their condition, be found little more than nominal. Those who argue the question upon mere abstract principles seem, in my apprehension, too much to forget the condition of society, the unequal division of property, or rather its total monopoly by the few, leaving the many nothing whatever but what they can obtain from their daily labour; which very labour cannot become available for the purpose of daily subsistence, without the consent of those who own the property of the community, all the materials, elements, call them what you please, on which labour is to be bestowed, being in their possession. Hence it is clear that, excepting in a state of things where the demand for labour fully equals the supply (which it would be absurdly false to say exists in this country), the employer and the employed do not meet on equal terms in the market of labour; on the contrary, the latter, whatever be his age, and call him as free as you please, is often almost entirely at the mercy of the former: he would be wholly so were it not for the operation of the Poor-laws, which are a palpable interference with the market of labour, and condemned as such by their opponents. Hence it is, that labour is so imperfectly distributed, and so inadequately remunerated, that one part of the community is over-worked, while another is wholly without employment; evils which operate reciprocally upon each other, till a country which might afford a sufficiency of moderate employment for all, exhibits at one and the same time part of its inhabitants reduced to the condition of slaves by over exertion, and another to that of paupers by involuntary idleness. In a word, wealth, still more than knowledge, is power, and power, liable to abuse whenever vested, is least of all free from tyrannical exercise, when it owes its existence to a sordid source. Hence have all laws, human or divine, attempted to protect the labourer from the injustice and cruelty which are too often practised upon him. Our Statute-book contains many proofs of this, and especially in its provision for the poor . . .

The principle features, then, of this Bill for regulating the labour of children and other persons in mills and factories, are these: First, the inhibiting of the labour of infants therein under the age of nine; the limitation of the hours of actual work of children from nine to eighteen years of age to ten hours, exclusively of time allowed for meals and refreshment, with an abatement of hours on the Saturday as a necessary preparation for the Sabbath; and the forbidding of all night work under the age of twenty-one.

5. Anthony Ashley Cooper, seventh Earl of Shaftesbury (1801–85)

'Infant Labour', *Quarterly Review*, Vol. LXVII, December 1840, pp. 173–5, 180–1.

Ashley's ancestor, the first Earl, was John Locke's patron and fellow conspirator against Restoration absolutism, and his own father became an important figure in the Lords after succeeding to the title in 1811. Ashley was educated at Harrow and Christ Church, Oxford, graduating with a first in classics. He entered Parliament in 1826 as Member for Woodstock, the pocket borough of his uncle, the Duke of Marlborough, and in 1828 accepted Wellington's offer of a Commissionership at the India Board of Control. During the same year he helped to frame two Bills intended to improve the treatment of lunatics and, after his appointment as one of the Commissioners responsible for inspecting asylums, began a lifetime's work on behalf of the insane. Although Ashley had been elected to Parliament on a 'no popery' platform, he eventually supported Catholic Relief as a means of subduing unrest in Ireland. In 1830 he became Member of Parliament for Dorchester, and in the following year was returned as an anti-reform candidate for one of the county seats of Dorset, claiming in usual Tory fashion that the Whig Reform Bill would subvert the balanced constitution.

Ashley's patrician sensibilities were sharpened by his friendship and correspondence with Robert Southey. Writing to Ashley in January 1833, Southey lamented Sadler's defeat at Leeds in the general election of the previous December: 'Sadler too is a loss;

he might not be popular in the House or in London society, but his speeches did much good in the country, and he is a singularly able, right-minded, religious man. Who is there that will take up the question of our white slave trade with equal feeling?' Within a few weeks Ashley had agreed to become the new parliamentary champion of industrial 'slaves'. He had served in 1832 on a select committee investigating Sunday observance, and another member of the committee, a leading Scottish evangelical, introduced him to the Reverend George Bull, who had been sent to London by the Short-Time Committees to find a replacement for Sadler. Bull asked Ashley to take responsibility for the Ten Hours Bill after unsuccessfully approaching a number of other people. Ashley steered the Bill through its first and second readings but was outmanoeuvred by the Whig administration, which established a Royal Commission to gather evidence from the manufacturers, who had not been given the opportunity of appearing before Sadler's select committee. The outcome was the Factory Act of 1833 which met only some of the demands of the Ten Hours movement.

Ashley reluctantly accepted the minor post of Civil Lord of the Admiralty in Peel's brief government of 1835. His evangelical beliefs intensified at this time and in 1836 he became lifelong President of the Church Pastoral Aid Society, founded in that year to extend the ministry of the Anglican Church in densely populated urban parishes. Later he became President of the British and Foreign Bible Society and of the London Society for Promoting Christianity among the Jews, Vice-President of the Church Missionary Society and of the Colonial and Continental Church Society, Chairman of the Church of England's Young Men's Society for Aiding Missions at Home and Abroad; he also engaged in endless battles to combat the spread of Romish influences within the church. He resumed parliamentary leadership of the Ten Hours movement in 1836 and tried on several occasions to widen the scope of the 1833 Act. In 1840 the Commons agreed to Ashley's motion to set up a Children's Employment Commission to examine mines and branches of trade and industry not covered by legislation, and, after its initial report, he proposed a Mines Bill which was enacted in 1842 with some modifications. After the Commission's second report the government introduced a new Factory Bill and Ashley, who in 1841 had refused Peel's offer of a post in the Queen's Household so as to remain free to pursue the Ten Hours cause, moved an amendment against opposition from his party leader. The House accepted the amendment, but the subsequent Act still failed to incorporate a ten-hours clause. In 1845 Ashley was more successful in piloting a Bill to restrict the employment of women and children in cotton printworks, and also in persuading Parliament to strengthen legislation governing the supervision of lunatics.

Unlike most Tory paternalists Ashley ceased to be a protectionist, partly in the belief that repeal of the Corn Laws was inevitable and also on the ground that their continuation gave industrialists a pretext for opposing factory reform. In January 1846, therefore, he resigned from his agricultural constituency of Dorset. By the time he returned to Parliament in July 1847 as Member for Bath, a Ten Hours Bill had been enacted. Ashley, who remained aloof from the Peelite and protectionist wings of the broken Conservative Party, now became even more involved in philanthropy. He encouraged the erection of Ragged Schools, and on being appointed to the Board of Health campaigned for sanitary reforms. His patrician views are revealed in a note written at this time, after Prince Albert had agreed to accompany him on a tour of London slums and to preside at the annual meeting of the Society for Improving the Condition of the Labouring Classes: 'Aye, truly this is the way to stifle Chartism . . . Rank, leisure, station are gifts of God, for which man must give an account. Here is a full proof, a glowing instance! The aristocracy, after a long separation, are re-approaching the people; and the people the aristocracy.' Shaftesbury, who succeeded to the title in 1851, continued with his philanthropic and religious endeavours until his death. In 1864, for instance, he successfully moved a Bill in the Lords to curtail the employment by chimney sweeps of climbing boys, and he attempted on numerous occasions to secure the appointment of evangelicals to bishoprics. At his funeral, members of the societies with which he had been associated carried banners inscribed with such texts as 'Naked and ye clothed me'.

> It is a monstrous thing to behold the condition, moral and physical, of the juvenile portion of our operative classes, more especially that which is found in the crowded lanes and courts of the larger towns, the charnel-houses of our race. Covetousness presided at their construction, and she still governs their economy; that 'covetousness which is idolatry'. Damp and unhealthy substrata, left altogether without drainage; frail tenements, low and confined, without conveniences or ventilation; close alleys, and no supply of water: all these things overtopped by the *ne plus ultra* of rent, reward the contractor,

and devour the inhabitants. Emerging from these lairs of filth and disorder, the young workers, 'rising early, and late taking rest', go forth that they may toil through fifteen, sixteen, nay, seventeen relentless hours, in sinks and abysses, oftentimes more offensive and pernicious than the holes they have quitted. Enfeebled in health, and exasperated in spirit, having neither that repose which is restorative to the body, nor that precious medicine which alone can tranquillise the soul, they are forced to live and die as though it were the interest of the state to make them pigmies in strength, and heathens in religion. Much are we often tempted to imprecate on these cities the curse of Jericho; but far better is it for us, at most humble distance, to imitate those gracious and holy tears which fell over the pride, the covetousness, and ignorance of Jerusalem. . .

The question is not whether the children of the poor may not with perfect propriety, with advantage to their parents and themselves, be employed to a certain extent in the labour of looms and shops. No doubt they may – But can it be pronounced necessary to our social welfare, or national prosperity, that children of the tenderest years should toil, amid every discomfort and agony of posture, and foul atmosphere, for fifteen or sixteen successive hours, oftentimes for a long consecutive period, tuurning night into day, without the compensating enjoyment in fashionable life, of turning day into night? Can it be for our honour, or our safety, that their young hearts, instead of being trained in tttthe ways of temperance and virtue, should be acquiring knowledge of those vices which they will afterwards practise as adults? . . .

Is the government of this kingdom as tranquil as it was before? Will discontent be frowned down, or rebellion always be checked with equal facility? The two great demons in morals and politics, Socialism and Chartism, are stalking through the land; yet they are but symptoms of an universal disease, spread throughout vast masses of the people, who, so far from concurring in the *status quo*, suppose that anything must be better than their present condition. It is useless to reply to us, as our antagonists often do, that many of the prime movers in these conspiracies against God and good order are men who have never suffered any of the evils to which we ascribe so mighty an influence. We know it well; but we know also that our system begets the vast and inflammable mass which lies waiting, day by day, for the spark to explode it into mischief. We cover the land with spectacles of misery; wealth is felt only by its oppressions;

few, very few, remain in those trading districts to spend liberally the riches they have acquired; the successful leave the field to be ploughed afresh by new aspirants after gain, who, in turn, count their periodical profits, and exact the maximum of toil for the minimum of wages. No wonder that thousands of hearts should be against a system which establishes the relations, without calling forth the mutual sympathies, of master and servant, landlord and tenant, employer and employed . . .

But here comes the worst of all – these vast multitudes, ignorant and excitable in themselves, and rendered still more so by oppression or neglect, are surrendered, almost without a struggle, to the experimental philosophy of infidels and democrats. When called upon to suggest our remedy of the evil, we reply by an exhibition of the cause of it; the very statement involves an argument, and contains its own answer within itself. Let your laws, we say to the Parliament, assume the proper functions of law, protect those for whom neither wealth, nor station, nor age, have raised a bulwark against tyranny; but, above all, open your treasury, erect churches, send forth the ministers of religion; reverse the conduct of the enemy of mankind, and sow wheat among the tares – all hopes are groundless, all legislation weak, all conservatism nonsense, without this alpha and omega of policy; it will give content instead of bitterness, engraft obedience on rebellion, raise purity from corruption, and 'life from the dead' – but there is no time to be lost.

6. Benjamin Disraeli, first Earl of Beaconsfield (1804–81)

'Explanation to constituents of his votes in parliament, Shrewsbury, May 9, 1843.' In *Selected Speeches of the late Right Honourable the Earl of Beaconsfield . . . in two volumes*, Vol. I, T. E. Kebbel (ed.), London: Longmans, Green, 1882, pp. 47–52, 57

Disraeli's father was a London Jew with Tory sympathies who prospered by writing novels, anthologies and history. Benjamin, the second child, was baptized an Anglican and educated at minor boarding-schools where he was romantically involved with several boys. In 1821 he became an articled clerk and spent three boring years with a firm of London solicitors. During the next two years he wrote pamphlets about foreign mining companies, ran up debts by speculating on the stock exchange, and became assistant to John

Murray, a publisher, with whom he collaborated in launching a short-lived and financially ruinous Tory newspaper, the *Representative*. His finances improved with the publication in 1826 of *Vivian Grey*, a somewhat scandalous 'society novel' which *Blackwood's Magazine* denounced as 'shameless puffery'. It was followed in 1828 by *The Voyage of Captain Popanilla*, by *The Young Duke* in 1831, and *Contarini Fleming* the year after. Meanwhile Disraeli was playing the dandy on the London scene, partly shielded from its anti-Semitic darts by his arrogance and flamboyance.

After two abortive attempts in June and December 1832 to become Radical Member of Parliament for High Wycombe, Disraeli published a pamphlet, *What is He?*, advocating a Tory-Radical merger into a 'national' party. He was beaten for the third time at High Wycombe in January 1835 and, now standing as a Tory, at Taunton in April of the same year. During this period Disraeli continued to write. His anti-Whig *Vindication of the English Constitution* was followed in 1836 by an abbreviated version, *The Spirit of Whiggism*, and by articles in *The Times* and *Morning Post*. There was also *The Revolutionary Epick* (1834), and three more novels: *The Wondrous Tale of Alroy* (1833), *Henrietta Temple* (1827) and *Venetia* (1837). Eventually returned to Parliament in 1837 as member for Maidstone, he married a wealthy widow the following year.

In 1841 Disraeli was elected for Shrewsbury and, bitterly disappointed by Peel's refusal to appoint him to the new administration, soon found himself, as he wrote to his wife, 'without effort the leader of a party chiefly of the youth and new members'. The Young England coterie first revolted against Peel in the latter part of 1843 on the issue of Irish policy, and next year most of them supported Ashley's amendment to the Factory Bill. By 1845, the year in which *Sybil* was published, Disraeli was a persistent rebel, accusing the government of 'cunning' and 'habitual perfidy'. Fiercely opposing the decision to repeal the Corn Laws, he later recounted the struggle against Peel in *Lord George Bentinck* (1851), the subject of the book being Disraeli's principal ally in the protectionist cause.

In 1847 Disraeli was elected for Buckinghamshire and published the last of his trilogy of Young England novels, *Tancred*, which depicted Christianity as the completion of Judaism. The support which he and Bentinck gave to a Whig proposal for removing Jewish disabilities resulted in the latter's resignation as leader of the protectionists, most of whom resisted a further erosion of Anglican privileges, and in Disraeli's failure to succeed him. By 1849, however, Disraeli was second-in-command to Lord Derby and *de facto* head of the protectionists in the Commons. During the next few years he attempted to persuade his colleagues to refurbish the Conservative Party by discarding protectionism, which he now judged a 'hopeless question'. He was Chancellor of the Exchequer in 1852 and again in 1858/9, on each occasion under the premiership of Derby. The second Reform Bill, which established household suffrage, was piloted through the Commons by Disraeli in 1867, the year after he had become Chancellor for the third time. Disraeli succeeded Derby as Prime Minister in 1868.

The Shrewsbury address in 1843 was the last occasion on which Disraeli heartily endorsed Peel's conduct. Richard Cobden, the principal target of the speech, was a Radical Member of Parliament and leader of the Anti-Corn Law League. Protectionism, according to Cobden, buttressed an unjust system of hereditary privilege which had been established at the Norman Conquest and reinforced by the Glorious Revolution. The Anti-Corn Law League wished to destroy the ascendancy of the aristocracy, which they regarded as an idle and parasitic class who treated the poor as feudal serfs, by forging an alliance between middle and working classes. Hence Disraeli's concern to defend the beneficent hierarchy of landed proprietorship.

> Sir Robert Peel, I believe, is influenced by a desire of practically mediating between great contending parties. I believe he has adopted opinions which are just and right, and that he is anxious to support native industry; but, at the same time, if native industry will not support Sir Robert Peel, how is he to go on?
>
> I do not care whether your corn sells for this sum or that, or whether it is under a sliding scale or a fixed duty; but what I want, and what I wish to secure, and what, as far as my energies go, I will secure, is, the preponderance of the landed interest. Gentlemen, when I talk of the preponderance of the landed interest, do not for a moment suppose that I mean merely the preponderance of 'squires of high degree', that, in fact, I am thinking only of justices of the peace. My thought wanders farther than a lordly tower or a manorial hall. I am looking in that phrase, in using that very phrase, to what I consider the vast majority of the English nation. I do not undervalue the mere superiority of the landed classes; on the contrary, I think it a most necessary element of political power and national civilisation; but I am looking to the population of our innumerable villages, to the crowds in our rural towns: aye, and I mean even something more than that by the landed interest

– I mean that estate of the poor which, in my opinion, has been already tampered with, dangerously tampered with . . .

I mean by the estate of the poor, the great estate of the Church, which has, before this time, secured our liberty, and may, for aught I know, still secure our civilisation. I mean, also, by the landed interest, that great judicial fabric, that great building up of our laws and manners which is, in fact, the ancient polity of the realm, and the ancient constitution of the realm – those ancient institutions which we Conservatives are bound to uphold – which you sent us to Parliament to uphold; for there is not a greater, or a more general, there is not a more prevalent or a more superficial error of misconception, than to suppose that the English constitution only consists of Queen, Lords, and Commons. Why, gentlemen, that is only a part, and not even the most important part, of the constitution of England. Your trial by jury is as important a part, and it is also an institution of England. Your institution of trial by jury arises out of your landed tenure of property. And if you, because commerce is declining, forsooth, because gentlemen hire theatres, make tawdry speeches in tawdry places, and say that the spirit of the age is against the territorial and feudal system, and declare that it is all the consequence of the remains of that old system – if you, upon this account, uproot that tenure of property; if you destroy all those institutions; if you destroy all those manners and duties which only are supported by this species of property – which you will do if you have a great territorial revolution in this country (for I will show you that if you have any change it will soon lead to much change) – I want to know what will become of your institutions? . . .

[W]e have all heard how Mr. Cobden, who is a very eminent person, has said, in a very memorable speech, that England was the victim of the feudal system, and we have all heard how he has spoken of the barbarism of the feudal system, and of the barbarous relics of the feudal system. Now, if we have any relics of the feudal system, I regret that not more of it is remaining. Think one moment – and it is well you should be reminded of what this is, because there is no phrase more glibly used in the present day than 'the barbarism of the feudal system'. Now, what is the fundamental principle of the feudal system, gentlemen? It is that the tenure of all property shall be the performance of its duties. Why, when the Conqueror carved out parts of the land, and introduced the feudal system, he said to the recipient, 'You shall have that estate, but you shall do something for it: you shall feed the poor; you shall endow the Church; you shall defend the land in case of war; and you shall execute justice and maintain truth to the poor for nothing.'

It is all very well to talk of the barbarities of the feudal system, and to tell us that in those days when it flourished a great variety of gross and grotesque circumstances and great miseries occurred; but these were not the result of the feudal system: they were the result of the barbarism of the age. They existed not from the feudal system but in spite of the feudal system. The principle of the feudal system, the principle which was practically operated upon, was the noblest principle, the grandest, the most magnificent and benevolent that was ever conceived by sage, or ever practised by patriot. Why, when I hear a political economist, or an Anti-Corn-Law Leaguer, or some conceited Liberal reviewer come forward and tell us, as a grand discovery of modern science, twitting and taunting, perhaps, some unhappy squire who cannot respond to the alleged discovery – when I hear them say, as the great discovery of modern science, that 'Property has its duties as well as its rights', my answer is that that is but a feeble plagiarism of the very principle of that feudal system which you are always reviling. Let me next tell those gentlemen who are so fond of telling us that property has its duties as well as its rights, that labour also has its rights as well as its duties: and when I see masses of property raised in this country which do not recognise that principle; when I find men making fortunes by a method which permits them (very often in a very few years) to purchase the lands of the old territorial aristocracy of the country, I cannot help remembering that those millions are accumulated by a mode which does not recognise it as a duty 'to endow the Church, to feed the poor, to guard the land, and to execute justice for nothing'. And I cannot help asking myself, when I hear of all this misery, and of all this suffering; when I know that evidence exists in our Parliament of a state of demoralisation in the once happy population of this land, which is not equalled in the most barbarous countries, which we suppose the more rude and uncivilised in Asia are – I cannot help suspecting that this has arisen because property has been permitted to be created and held without the performance of its duties . . .

Your Corn Laws are merely the outwork of a great system fixed and established upon you territorial property, and the only object the Leaguers have in making themselves masters of the outwork is that they may easily overcome the citadel.

4 *Tory Democracy 1867–1918*

Although the Conservative Party occasionally formed brief minority administrations in the twenty years after the repeal of the Corn Laws, it had neither distinctive policies nor a clear sense of direction. The second Reform Bill, enacted in 1867 under a Conservative ministry, inaugurated a period of rehabilitation in which Disraeli sought to adapt the party he now led to an enlarged electorate. This he did by using the language of nation rather than class, arguing as he had done in his Young England phase that the wealthy and powerful had a responsibility to cultivate an affinity between themselves and the masses. In a letter to *The Times* in 1907 J. E. Gorst, whom Disraeli had appointed party organizer, characterized Tory paternalism for a democratic age as the conviction

> that all government exists solely for the good of the governed; that Church and King, Lords and Commons, and all other public institutions are to be maintained so far, and so far only, as they promote the happiness and welfare of the common people; that all who are entrusted with any public function are trustees, not for their own class, but for the nation at large; and that the mass of the people may be trusted so to use electoral power, which should be freely conceded to them, as to support those who are promoting their interests. It is democratic because the welfare of the people is its supreme end; it is Tory because the institutions of the country are the means by which the end is to be attained.[1]

Disraeli intended to broaden the appeal of the party of property and privilege by providing it with imagery more potent than that of liberalism. Yet 'Tory Democracy' – as patrician conservatism became known shortly after his death – was an elastic concept, amenable to a variety of purposes. It appealed to political adventurers as well as to genuine social reformers, and, like old-style paternalism, featured at least as much in internal party disputes as in the ideological warfare between Conservatives and their opponents.

The rhetoric of class reconciliation served several purposes: for some it was a device for advocating a programme of social welfare; for others a stick with which to beat the leadership for lack of flair; for aristocratic Tories a means of lamenting the decline of *noblesse oblige* in a party allegedly hijacked by the 'moneyed interests'; while, in the early years of the twentieth century, it was used to urge a pragmatic yet progressive conservatism capable of steering a middle course between *laissez-faire* and doctrinaire radicalism.

Parliamentary reform became an issue again after 1851, and in 1866 the Liberal government introduced a moderate Bill for extending the franchise. Conservatives responded in familiar manner by predicting the destruction of hierarchy and constitutional balance in a democratic deluge. For Robert Cecil, who later became Lord Salisbury and eventually Tory Prime Minister, the measure was a decisive phase in 'the struggle between property, be its amount small or great, and mere numbers'.[2] Disraeli, echoing Peel's assault in 1831 upon the Whig Reform Bill, contended that the Liberal scheme would demolish 'the ordered state of free England' by unhinging the 'co-ordinate estates of the realm'.[3] The Liberal initiative failed, and in 1867 Disraeli, Chancellor of the Exchequer in a new minority government, successfully steered another Reform Bill through the Commons. Although the initial proposals were modest, the Act which eventually emerged established household suffrage in the boroughs. Maybe Disraeli was persuaded to embrace this radical measure by a belief that it would strengthen the natural alliance of higher and lower classes. Certainly he was soon telling an Edinburgh audience, in language reminiscent of his youth, that the Bill had been introduced by a national party in touch with its past – a party which, eschewing the abstract principles of a selfish oligarchy, favoured the kind of evolutionary change periodically needed to ensure that 'institutions . . . fulfil their original intention [and that] the people are led by their natural leaders'.[4] But the Act was probably the outcome less of a consistent philosophy than of opportunism. By outmanoeuvring the opposition, Conservatives hoped to remain in office long enough to establish their credibility as a governing party. They also anticipated electoral advantages from a redistribution of seats in the counties where the vote was restricted to twelve-pound householders.

Disraeli succeeded Derby as Prime Minister in 1868, but within a few months the government was defeated. For a while, in opposition, he did little to improve the party's image. In 1870, however, Disraeli appointed Gorst to streamline party machinery, and a couple of years later, with Gladstone's administration crumbling, began the task of appealing to a mass electorate. This he did in two famous speeches of 1872, the first delivered at Manchester and the other at Crystal Palace.

The latter address was a counter-revolutionary manifesto in which Disraeli promised that a revitalized Conservative Party would undo the damage of Liberal governments during the previous forty years – rather as Margaret Thatcher, a little over a century later, was to declare her intention of putting back the Great into Great Britain by turning the tide of postwar collectivism. Earlier in the century, according to Disraeli, the Conservative Party had been severed from its philosophical roots and withered. Successive Liberal ministries, exploiting the weakness of their opponents, had borrowed 'cosmopolitan' principles to justify an assault upon venerable institutions. Now, however, the people were weary of alien doctrines and reckless legislation, and Conservatives were poised to embark upon restoration, because they had reconstituted themselves as a national party able to nourish the patriotic sentiments of propertied and working classes alike. To the former he pledged, as Peel had done forty years earlier, that a Conservative government would secure order and stability by preserving the ancient institutions of church and state. Appealing to the new electorate, on the other hand, he outlined the Tory record on issues like factory legislation, and announced that the dogmas of political economy which made liberals reluctant social reformers would not deflect his party from improving the condition of the people. The sanctity of traditional institutions and the welfare of the lower classes were familiar themes, which Disraeli had outlined, for example, in the Shrewsbury speech of 1843. To them Disraeli now added a vision, calculated to appeal to all classes, of a Britain sitting astride an empire, which, though threatened by the anti-colonial policies of Liberal governments, might become an even richer source of national pride and greatness.[1]

In office from 1874 to 1880, the Disraeli government introduced various measures to elevate the condition of the people. According to historiographical wisdom, however, these reforms were not the eventual implementation of that ideal of Tory paternalism stretching back through the Crystal Palace speech to the days of Young England and beyond, but the product of 'confused and nervous empiricism'.[5] Perhaps the case is overstated, for of what government, even those as ideologically zealous as the post–1979 Thatcher administrations, can it be said that each item of policy represents a firm step towards a chosen destination? In politics accident – the *ad hoc* response to unforeseen circumstances – is at least as important as design. Disraeli's failure to pursue a systematic programme of social reform does not necessarily signify indifference to policies for binding the masses to their natural leaders.[6] There were nevertheless several factors inhibiting a coherent legislative scheme of popular Toryism: Disraeli himself, always better at creating romantic images than formulating concrete proposals, was by now old and sick; the patrician sense of responsibility towards the poor, rooted as it was in the localized ties of rural communities, did not readily embrace the concept of a centralized state bureaucratically confronting the problems of a complex industrial society; finally, in the 1870s, the fear of Gladstonian radicalism drove increasing numbers of the urban bourgeoisie into the Conservative Party. Few of its members wished to arrest the growing unity of the propertied classes by energetically promoting the welfare of the propertyless.

Disraeli bequeathed a rich if uncertain legacy of benevolent paternalism. Believing that social reform would secure working-class deference in a democratic age, he included the condition of the people in his picture of the Conservative nation, alongside loyalty to the throne, reverence for a national church, the magic of empire, and the beneficence of social hierarchy. On the details of popular legislation, however, he was usually vague. By exploiting this imprecision, a variety of later Conservatives were able to lay claim to the Disraelian inheritance.

Within a few years of Disraeli's death in 1881 the ambivalence of his legacy became evident. The phrase 'Tory Democracy' entered public discourse after the press had used it as a pejorative description of Arthur Forwood, unsuccessful Conservative candidate at the Liverpool by-election of December 1882. Forwood was not unhappy to accept the tag as an indication of his commitment to 'active and enlightened Conservatism'. His depiction of democratic Toryism was characteristically Disraelian: a determination to maintain national institutions and uphold the empire allied with a 'safely progressive policy' intended to fortify instinctive working-class aversion from 'Revolutionary or Socialistic ideas'. Moreover, in listing the kind of progressive measures the Conservative Party should adopt to retain the people's trust: extension of the Employers' Liability Act, household suffrage in the counties, redistribution of the endowments of the established church for the benefit of poor parishes, reform of Irish land laws, and so forth, Forwood went into rather more detail than Disraeli was apt to do.[7]

But it was Lord Randolph Churchill, rather than the relatively insignificant Forwood, who came to be regarded in late nineteenth-century Conservative mythology as the one 'who, more than any other man, had taught Toryism to the democracy, and explained democracy to the Tories'.[8] Churchill and three other Conservative MPs grouped themselves into the Fourth Party, as it was known, which badgered the Liberal government, and, after Disraeli's death, inveighed against the dual Tory leadership of Sir Stafford Northcote and Lord Salisbury, censuring the former for his weak performance in the Commons. From 1883 Churchill attempted to gain control of the National Union of Conservative and Constitutional Associations in order to run a grass-roots campaign against Northcote.

The rhetoric of Tory Democracy featured in this crusade to improve the party's electoral chances. Yet Churchill, unlike Gorst (another member of the gang of four) gave little sign of what he meant by the expression, beyond the need to win popular support for traditional institutions. He wanted 'the mantle of Elijah' to descend upon someone capable of bringing 'to perfection those schemes of imperial rule, of social reform which Lord Beaconsfield had only time to dream of, to hint at, and to sketch'. Having reproved Forwood for using the phrase Tory Democracy 'without knowing what he was talking about', however, he himself failed to provide even a rudimentary prospectus of progressive legislation.[9] On some issues, indeed, Churchill was palpably unenlightened, and he used Tory Democracy, not to advocate extensive legislation in the interests of the working class, but principally as an oratorical device for persuading the electorate to cherish old-style conservatism.[10] Perhaps Gladstone had a point when, writing to Lord Acton in 1885, he described Tory Democracy as 'a demogagism . . . as obstinately attached as ever to the evil principle of class interests'.[11]

There was further evidence that some Conservatives who claimed the Disraelian inheritance in the 1880s were more concerned to tame democratic impulses than to improve the lot of the poor. The Primrose Tory League, named after Disraeli's allegedly favourite flower, was launched by Churchill and others in 1883 as 'an extra-parliamentary Fourth Party',[12] though it soon received the seal of approval from the party leadership. In both ideology and structure the league embodied an ethos of *noblesse oblige*. It claimed to represent 'the alliance between the noble and the worker foreshadowed forty years ago in *Coningsby* and *Sybil*,'[13] and its founders shared with Lord John Manners, the last surviving member of Young England and himself associated with the league, nostalgia for a romantic past. Its stratified organization, pageantry and quaint 'titles that had been banished from real life to the regions of Opéra Bouffe'[14] all symbolized the ideal of an organic community, bounded on one side by paternal responsibility and on the other by grateful deference. Unlike Young England, however, the league attracted a mass membership, reaching about one million in 1890, by enabling social classes to mingle in a merry-go-round of teas, fêtes, musical events and the like. Yet the Primrose League did not entice its working-class members with the promise of progressive legislation towards a better tomorrow. Instead the virtues of empire, monarchy, religion and the estates of the realm were proclaimed in the hope of widening the basis of support for the established order.

In October 1886 Churchill, now in the cabinet, did flesh out Tory Democracy with a programme including free elementary education, provision of smallholdings for agricultural labourers, changes in local government, and land reforms for Ireland.[15] Within a couple of months, however, he resigned his ministerial post and entered the political wilderness. For the remainder of the century there was little evidence to substantiate George Curzon's claim of 1887 'that the party as a whole can be said to have been impregnated with [a Disraelian] enthusiasm for reform'.[16] Salisbury, who headed three administrations between 1885 and 1902, disapproved of Disraeli's mission to attach the people to their natural leaders. Suspicious of big government and determined to preserve the rights of property owners, he was disinclined to jeopardize the interests of the 'classes' by legislating on behalf of the 'masses'. Although he was flexible in accepting some demands for social improvement, the relatively meagre reforms of the Salisbury era were prompted, not by an ideal of Tory paternalism, but by a willingness to make piecemeal concessions in order to preclude pressure for more radical innovation.[17] Not that there was much pressure to improve the condition of the people. The steady absorption of the propertied middle classes into the party continued to erode its landed ethos, leaving a dwindling number ready to carry the banner of benevolent paternalism. Conservatives, moreover, were able to draw electoral capital from the weakness of their Liberal opponents by depicting themselves as a patriotic party firmly resolved to avoid costly and injudicious reforms. As the Victorian age drew to a close, in consequence, the Conservative government lacked imaginative policies to deal with pressing fiscal and social problems. The party was shaken from its lethargy by Joseph Chamberlain's campaign for tariff reform.

'Radical Joe' claimed much of the credit – probably too much – for whatever social legislation had been enacted during the various Salisbury administrations. After several energetic years as 'King of Birmingham' he had become Liberal MP for the city in 1876, and within four years held cabinet office. But he soon grew impatient with Gladstone's reluctance to engage in comprehensive social reconstruction, and in 1886 joined with other Liberal Unionists who seceded from the party on the issue of Irish Home Rule. Although Chamberlain's roots in middle-class nonconformity made him suspicious of the paternalism of the landed Anglican establishment, he had long believed that social improvement was a means of subduing popular discontent. So, having realized that there was no going back to the Liberal Party, he set about inserting the kernel of radical liberalism into a Tory paternalist shell. Contending that on factory reform and other 'social questions the Tories have almost always been more progressive than the Liberals', he urged his new allies to ward off the menace of socialism by accepting 'all practicable proposals for still further ameliorating the condition of the great masses of the population'.[18] Among the proposals he had in mind were shorter working hours for shop assistants and railway workers, an eight-hour day for miners, extension of the Employers' Liability Act, old-age pensions, arbitration tribunals to settle industrial disputes, control of immigration to reduce unemployment, labour exchanges, and the empowering of local authorities to provide cheap transport and grant loans to workers for the purchase of houses.

Chamberlain probably exerted his greatest influence upon Conservative social policy from 1886 to 1892, when Salisbury's government tolerated his 'dynamic bustle' for the sake of Liberal Unionist support.[19] He bore some responsibility, for example, for the overhaul of local government in 1888 and for the extension of free elementary education three years later. Salisbury adopted an eclectic approach to the reform proposals with which Chamberlain bombarded him, modifying the more palatable ones and rejecting those offensive to the *laissez-faire* wing of the party. In 1891 Chamberlain became leader of the Liberal Unionists in the Commons, and after the fall of the Liberal government in 1895 was made Colonial Secretary in a Conservative and Unionist administration. Although Chamberlain had pressed for a programme of social reform as a condition for joining the administration, for a while ministerial responsibilities deflected his energies towards imperial matters. By 1902, however, he was frustrated by the government's threadbare domestic policies, as well as by its sluggishness in strengthening the ties of empire. The following year he launched a crusade intended to secure imperial economic links and also to improve living standards at home.

Since leaving the Liberal Party Chamberlain had condemned its 'Little Englandism' and dreamed of an imperial federation with a strong Britain at its centre. Commercial unification of the empire was the objective of his tariff-reform campaign, conducted from the middle of 1903 by means of endless speech-making throughout the country. Challenging free-trade orthodoxy, he advocated a system of tariff reciprocity whereby Britain would give fiscal preference to colonial imports of raw materials and food in return for similar treatment of its manufactured exports. There was an electoral snag in this scheme of imperial protectionism. Requiring Britain to erect tariff barriers against the influx of cheap food from countries outside the empire, it exposed Chamberlain and his allies to the charge made against defenders of the Corn Laws sixty years earlier – of wanting the poor to pay higher prices to line the pockets of a section of the propertied classes. Chamberlain tackled this unattractive aspect of protective tariffs by stressing their economic benefits for the people. The nation could not continue to compete successfully in an unfettered world market, he argued, because of its progressive legislation on behalf of the working class. Compensation for accidents at work, for example, added to the cost of production, giving an unfair advantage to foreign competitors employing cheap labour. Without restrictions upon imports from less humanitarian countries, in consequence, British workers must either accept lower wages to keep prices competitive or else suffer unemployment. Dearer food, for which, in any case, compensation could be made by adjustments to taxation, was a small sacrifice to make for security of employment, decent living standards, and provision against life's vicissitudes.

Dealing with these at Limehouse in December 1904, Chamberlain broadened his attack upon free trade into a condemnation of the legislative record of dogmatic individualism since the 1840s. Richard Cobden, the Anti-Corn Law League leader whom Disraeli had decried in his Shrewsbury speech of 1843, was identified as the arch-exponent of a doctrine which had saddled the nation with its defective fiscal policy. Free-market ideology, he reminded his audience, had been formulated in a pre-democratic age, and still predisposed its Liberal Party adherents against action in the interests of the people. Tories had a more laudable record of social reform because they refrained from genuflecting to the laws of political economy. This tactic of evoking the mythology of Tory paternalism – one used to underpin his campaigns since he had left the Liberal Party – involved Chamberlain in a selective account of nineteenth-century history, which glossed over the doctrinal squabbles and Peelite practices of the Conservative Party and ignored the radical measures of previous Liberal governments. By the turn of the century, moreover, progressive Liberals were busy providing their party with collectivist principles.[20] Chamberlain resorted to another well-tried tactic in the hope of gaining working-class support for more state intervention on fiscal issues. Linking the case for protective tariffs with the need for tighter immigration controls, he pandered to popular fears that the country was being swamped by aliens who threatened the livelihood and cultural identity of the native population.[2] This denunciation of free trade in people was calculated to stir the xenophobia of his Limehouse listeners because East London, a stronghold of working-class conservatism, contained large numbers of immigrants from Eastern Europe.

Chamberlain's brand of radical Unionism brought to the surface tensions within the Conservative Party regarding fiscal and social matters. A. J. Balfour, leader of the party since 1902, was initially non-committal about tariff reform in the hope of preventing his government's disintegration. But the rival factions fought strenuous campaigns, and by the end of 1903 Chamberlain and his free-trade opponents had left the cabinet. Conservatives were hopelessly divided, as they had been over the Corn Laws, and lost the general election of 1906 in a Liberal landslide. Having weakened the Liberal Party by his departure twenty years earlier, Chamberlain had now split another party – a distinction shared with David Owen (another politician combining a determined stance on external affairs with a willingness to use the state to improve domestic living standards) who undermined the Labour Party by his defection in 1981, and six years later divided Social Democrats by refusing to lead them into a merger with Liberals.

Chamberlain's crusade had torn the Conservative Party apart and enabled the Liberal Party to become more united than it had been for twenty years. Paradoxically, however, the defeat of 1906 led to the temporary adoption of tariff-financed social reform as official Unionist strategy. It was not merely that the election had reduced free-traders in Parliament to a handful. Other factors persuaded a growing number of Conservatives that food taxes should be used to promote social improvement.[21] One was the Lib-Lab electoral pact of 1906 which ushered in the Labour Party as a third force in British politics. Some Unionists claimed that a constructive policy on issues such as old-age pensions was necessary to inhibit the otherwise inexorable spread of predatory socialism. The party could not 'win back the ear of *industrial* democracy', according to J. L Garvin, 'by telling the British masses that the Socialist theory is a sort of iridescent insanity and that Socialist practice means plunder'.[22] The working class had to be persuaded that their lot could be bettered without the destruction of property. Collectivism was inevitable on this assessment, and the choice lay between financing it through confiscatory taxation or by preferential tariffs which secured the interests of capital and labour alike.

Belief in tariff reform as an antidote to revolutionary socialism was reinforced by anxieties about 'national efficiency', which Unionists shared with members of the Liberal Party and Fabian socialists such as Beatrice and Sidney Webb.[23] Britain could not continue to maintain its economic and military ascendancy in an increasingly competitive world, many argued, without policies for creating a healthy, skilled, properly housed and docile workforce. The concept of national fitness had a particular attraction for those Unionists who wanted Britain to sustain its empire by becoming more integrated and disciplined. Not unnaturally they assumed Disraelian garb when urging greater national cohesion. Lord Milner, an ardent imperialist and a leading tariff-reform campaigner, warned Unionists not to neglect 'those social evils, of which honest Socialism is striving, often, no doubt, by unwise means, to effect a cure. If the Unionist party did that, it would be unfaithful to its own best traditions from the days of *Sybil* and *Coningsby* to the present time.'[24] Instead the party should endorse imperial protectionism as a means of improving the condition of the people without plundering the rich. Disraeli's ideal of class harmony would then be realized in a nation of patriotic citizens proud to be at the heart of a glittering empire.

What eventually swung most Unionists behind tariff reform was the Liberal government's plan to finance social legislation by income tax and death duties. Even erstwhile free-traders, condemning Lloyd George's 'People's Budget' of 1909 as a socialist assault upon property, conceded that food taxes were less disagreeable than redistributive taxation as a source of revenue for welfare purposes. The general election of January 1910, called after the Lords had rejected the budget, was fought by Unionists on a tariff-reform platform.

After losing the election, however, Unionists began to retreat from protectionism, in part because their 'anti-budget crusade had tarred tariff reform irretrievably as the rich man's method of avoiding taxation'.[25] Fiscal controversies, moreover, were soon eclipsed by a constitutional crisis. In 1911, after another election the previous December, a Parliament Bill to remove the absolute legislative veto of the Lords was enacted, against 'die-hard' opposition from some Unionists. Chamberlain had grafted his social radicalism on to Tory paternalism while remaining detached from the usual veneration for the institutions of church and state. The emasculation of the Lords, coupled with a threat to disestablish the church in Wales, now prompted Unionists to rally in defence of the established order. Still more decisive in persuading them to turn aside from social issues was the determination of the Liberal government, which depended upon the support of Irish MPs, to press ahead with Home Rule. Unionists, now led by Bonar Law, were resolved to resist the dislocation of the empire at its centre, and some of them supported Sir Edward Carson's Ulster resistance movement.

Not all Unionists were happy that the condition of the people had become obscured by their party's frenzy over the Lords and Ireland. Sir Geoffrey Butler, prefacing his little book on great Conservatives of the past, regretted that recent events had 'concentrated the attention of the man in the street upon the negative rather than the constructive side of Toryism'.[26] Some – their sense of impending catastrophe heightened by a wave of labour unrest after 1910 and by the widespread syndicalist belief that capitalism could be destroyed by industrial class struggle – feared that the siege mentality of militant Unionism would tilt the nation towards revolution. Towards the end of 1913 Professor W. A. S. Hewins, who had been secretary of Chamberlain's Tariff Commission, noted in his diary:

> We had Sidney and Beatrice Webb to lunch and talked over the Labour question, particularly the decline of constitutional and parliamentary socialism and the spread of syndicalism. The spread of the latter has been much fostered by the reactionary conduct of the Unionist party and Carsonism, 'which is only syndicalism in another form'. Unless we rapidly reorganise on the lines of Disraelian Toryism, adapted of course to modern conditions, we cannot now stop revolution.[27]

There were nevertheless some Unionists, even among those castigated by Hewins as 'reactionary' for their stance on constitutional issues, who had not abandoned the search for a coherent social policy. Hewins omitted on this occasion to mention his association with a group of Unionists already formulating a programme of Tory Democracy adapted 'to modern conditions' – to the extent, at least, that its implementation did not hinge upon preferential tariffs.

What induced these Unionists to detach social reform from protectionism was the general election defeat of December 1910. A few months later a number of MPs, most of them young, became involved in the Unionist Social Reform Committee, an unofficial 'think-tank' which in the next three years produced reports on issues such as health, education and the poor law.[28] Aiming to upstage the Liberal government on collectivist proposals the committee, unlike the tariff-reform movement, wanted social welfare to be financed by direct taxation. Its members advocated the extension of government by recalling the record of protective legislation on behalf of the weak. In recommending the establishment of arbitration tribunals and a minimum wage for certain industries, for example, the sub-committee on industrial unrest invoked the authority of Southey, Sadler, Shaftesbury and other Tory paternalist heroes. F. E. Smith introduced the sub-committee's report by portraying the Conservative Party as a persistent ally of the working class 'against the oppressions of the Manchester school of Liberalism, which cared nothing for the interests of the State, and regarded men as brute beasts whose labour could be bought and sold at the cheapest price irrespective of all other considerations'.[29] Smith, who was chairman of the Social Reform Committee, provided a theoretical justification for its proposals in an essay entitled 'State Toryism and social reform'.[30]

Smith countered the charge that the committee's proposals were a pale imitation of progressive Liberal legislation by distinguishing Tory reformism from the 'Radical-Socialism' of Lloyd George and the Labour Party, as well as from the 'Individualist-Whig' principles of free-marketeers in the Liberal and Conservative Parties. Whereas egalitarian radicalism undermined private enterprise, individualism allowed the strong to trample on the weak in an unbridled struggle for riches. Each was a recipe for class conflict. The alternative was to foster social harmony by securing the welfare of those in need without curbing the ambition of energetic and talented individuals. And this required Tories to act in the spirit of Disraeli, Churchill and Chamberlain by prudently using the power of the state to sustain the organic unity of the nation. Smith gave a romantic account of the efforts of Tory Democrats, especially Disraeli, to elevate the condition of the people.[3] In so far as he acknowledged tensions in the Conservative Party between paternalists and libertarians, however, it was at least an improvement on Chamberlain's lopsided conception of the nineteenth century as a battleground between humanitarian Tories and heartless Liberals.

The Social Reform Committee had some impact on party policy before disbanding at the outbreak of the First World War. Meanwhile another impetus to the revival of Tory Democracy was a growing resentment of the *nouveaux riches*. Anxieties had been expressed since the 1870s that the influence of landed proprietorship was being eroded by a sinister plutocracy of self-made financiers and industrialists. Condemnation of cowboy capitalism reached a peak in the Edwardian period, and initially focused on the government's sale of honours in return for financial support.[31] Unionists were quick to emphasize the hypocrisy of a Liberal administration which dipped into the coffers of big business, while at the same time purporting to side with the people through its taxation of inherited wealth and its assault on the Lords. Soon, however, Unionists were berating their own leaders for indifference to the corruption of the political system by parvenus, many of them Jewish, who allegedly placed self-interest before the common good. Some die-hard opponents of the Parliament Bill and Irish Home Rule, for example, urged the party to stem national degeneration with a legislative programme intended to restore a sense of patrician responsibility among the wealthy. Recent scholarship has focused on the social attitudes of these ultra-right Unionists who were ready to defend the constitution by extra-parliamentary methods.[32] Yet the desire to retrieve the beneficent hierarchy of traditional society spread beyond these 'die-hards'.

For some Tories the Unionist obsession with constitutional issues was itself symptomatic of the negative attitude of a party which had lost its philosophical bearings in a plutocratic sea. Commitment to tariff reform as a solution to every social problem was taken to be a further sign that Unionists had drifted from their ideological moorings and were, in consequence, in danger of being 'shipwrecked' on a narrow reef of economic doctrine.[33] Pierse Loftus attributed the disappearance of genuine Toryism to the merger of Liberal Unionists with the Conservative Party:

> Every one with a genuine feeling for Toryism – with the Conservative love of continuity, must bitterly regret that the fusion ever took place; and above all that of late it has been officially recognized by the amalgamation of both parties under the ephemeral name of Unionists. To-day, it

> seems, we are no longer permitted to be Tories. The great traditions of Bolingbroke and Burke are to be blended with the discarded remnants of Whig Liberalism. What yet remains of the Aristocratic and Feudal ideal is to be subordinated to the hard plutocratic philosophy of Birmingham and Belfast.

National disintegration could be averted only if Tories cultivated anew the alliance of upper and lower classes, thereby reviving 'the great tradition of aristocratic service against all the snares of Plutocracy'.[34] This required a programme of Tory Democracy which, in addition to tariff reform, included industrial profit sharing and co-partnership schemes, poor-law reform, and government loans to encourage peasant proprietorship.

Hostility towards buccaneering capitalists increased with wartime profiteering, especially after Lloyd George appointed businessmen to run some ministries in the coalition government which he headed from December 1916. In 1917 Lord Henry Bentinck, the Conservative MP for South Nottingham, accused him of running a 'directorate' and warned the Commons of a mounting suspicion that 'the people are being asked to fight, not in order to make the world safe for democracy . . . but in order that our captains of industry and our great commercial men may get a monopoly when this War is over'. Bentinck, an aristocrat who was a stout-hearted Tory Democrat, condemned the exploitation of the masses with the same passion as had Michael Sadler. Infuriated by Unionist complicity with political corruption, he depicted Disraeli as a scourge of the plutocracy who had reminded Conservatives that their objective

> should not be to multiply the number of peerages, baronetcies, and under-secretaryships, but to promote the welfare and happiness of the people, and that the best way of defending property was for property to realise that labour is its twin brother, and that the essence of all tenure is the performance of duty.[35]

The spirit of Young England was alive once again.

The following year Bentinck dealt with these themes in *Tory Democracy*. Much of the book consists of a eulogy to philanthropists such as Sadler and Shaftesbury. It also contains a comprehensive account of the activities of the Unionist Social Reform Committee, with which Bentinck had been associated, and of its struggle 'to keep alight the Disraelian tradition' at a time when the party was full of people 'whose faith in the ability of Tariff Reform to produce a Utopia was so robust that they felt there was little need to trouble about other matters'.[36] He wanted the 'excavation work' of its various sub-committees to provide the foundations for a wide-ranging programme including adequate social security, an enlightened penal policy, a public health system guaranteeing a decent environment at home and work, wider provision of agricultural smallholdings, and state supervision of industry to enforce a minimum wage, shorter hours and workers' participation in managerial decisions.[37] The Conservative Party was in poor shape to implement such a programme, according to Bentinck, because it had declined from a national party, becoming a selfish faction which had opposed the 'People's Budget' and endangered the constitution, and was now conniving with the plutocracy. His message was that the party could allay fears of being 'engaged in a capitalist conspiracy' only by shunning rapacious individualism in order to retrieve the ideal of an organic community – an ideal that since the Tudor age had inspired genuine Tories to view wealth as a trust for the common benefit.[4]

Bentinck, nostalgic for a seemingly irrecoverable world, was regarded by his contemporaries as an amiable 'crank' playing 'rather a lone hand' against the irresponsible rich.[38] Yet many Conservatives returned from the war with a fresh sense of *noblesse oblige* which heightened their concern for the men alongside whom they had fought. In the inter-war years these patrician Tories sought to guide the party along a course which, as F. E. Smith had put it when defending the activities of the Unionist Social Reform Committee, stood 'midway between [the] conflicting extremes' of individualism and socialism.

NOTES

1 Cited in W. F. Monypenny and G. F. Buckle, *The Life of Benjamin Disraeli, Earl of Beaconsfield, Vol. II 1860–1881*, new edn. London: John Murray, 1929, p. 709.
2 Robert Cecil,'The Reform Bill', *Quarterly Review*, Vol. 119, 1866, p. 552.
3 'Parliamentary Reform, May 8, 1865', in T. E. Kebbel (ed.), *Selected Speeches of the late Right Honourable the Earl of Beaconsfield . . . in two volumes*, Vol. I, London: Longmans, Green, pp. 537, 543.
4 'Speech on Reform Bill of 1867, Edinburgh, October 29, 1867', in ibid., Vol. II, p. 488.
5 Paul Smith, *Disraelian Conservatism and Social Reform*, London: Routledge & Kegan Paul, 1967, p. 223.
6 The point is made with characteristic lucidity by W. H. Greenleaf,

The British Political Tradition: Vol. 2, The Ideological Heritage, London: Methuen, 1983, pp. 215–16.

7 Arthur B. Forwood, 'Democratic Toryism', *Contemporary Review*, Vol. 43, 1883, pp. 294–304.

8 George N. Curzon, 'Conservatism and Young Conservatives', *National Review*, Vol. 47, 1887, p. 587.

9 Randolph S. Churchill, 'Elijah's mantle; April 19th, 1883', *Fortnightly Review*, new series, Vol. XXXIII, 1883, pp. 613–21.

10 See R. E. Quinault, 'Lord Randolph Churchill and Tory Democracy, 1880–1885', *Historical Journal*, Vol. 22, 1979, pp. 141–65.

11 John Morley, *The Life of William Ewart Gladstone, Vol. III (1880–1898)*, London: Macmillan, 1903, p. 173.

12 Martin Pugh, *The Tories and the People 1880–1935*, Oxford: Blackwell, 1985, p. 13.

13 Cited in R. F. Foster, *Lord Randolph Churchill: a Political Life*, Oxford: Clarendon Press, 1981, p. 134.

14 T. P. O'Connor, *Lord Beaconsfield: a Biography*, London and Glasgow: Collins, n.d., p. 3.

15 'Policy of Lord Salisbury's First Ministry. Dartford, October 2, 1886', in Louis J. Jennings (ed.), *Speeches of the Right Honourable Lord Randolph Churchill, M.P. 1880–1888*, Vol. II, London: Longmans, Green, 1889, pp. 68–86.

16 Curzon, 'Conservatism and Young Conservatives', op. cit., p. 582.

17 See Peter Marsh, *The Discipline of Popular Government: Lord Salisbury's Domestic Statecraft, 1881–1902*, Sussex: Harvester, 1978.

18 Joseph Chamberlain, 'The Labour question', *Nineteenth Century*, Vol. XXXII, 1892, pp. 678, 709.

19 Richard Jay, *Joseph Chamberlain: a Political Study*, Oxford: Clarendon Press, 1981, p. 344.

20 See Robert Eccleshall, *British Liberalism: Liberal Thought from the 1640s to the 1980s*, London: Longman, pp. 35–45, 174–213.

21 See Alan Sykes, *Tariff Reform in British Politics 1903–1913*, Oxford: Clarendon Press, 1979; Peter Cain, 'Political economy in Edwardian England: the tariff-reform controversy', in Alan O'Day (ed.), *The Edwardian Age: Conflict and Stability 1900–1914*, London: Macmillan, 1979, pp. 35–59; D. J. Dutton, 'The Unionist Party and social policy 1906–1914', *Historical Journal*, Vol. 24, 1981, pp. 871–84; E. H. H. Green, 'Radical Conservatism: the electoral genesis of tariff reform', *Historical Journal*, Vol. 28, 1985, pp. 667–92.

22 J. L. Garvin, 'Free trade as socialist policy', *National Review*, Vol. 295, 1907, pp. 48, 51.

23 G. R. Searle, *The Quest for National Efficiency: a Study in British Politics and Political Thought, 1899–1914*, Oxford: Blackwell, 1971; Robert J. Scally, *The Origins of the Lloyd George Coalition*, Princeton: Princeton University Press, 1975.

24 'A constructive policy', in Lord Milner, *The Nation and the Empire:*

Being a Collection of Speeches and Addresses, London: Constable, 1913, p. 214.

25 Neal Blewett, 'Free Fooders, Balfourites, Whole Hoggers: Factionalism within the Unionist Party, 1906–10', *Historical Journal*, Vol. II, 1968, p. 123.

26 Geoffrey Butler, *The Tory Tradition: Bolingbroke-Burke-Disraeli–Salisbury*, London: John Murray, 1914, pp. viii–ix.

27 W. A. S. Hewins, *The Apologia of An Imperialist: Forty Years of Empire Policy*, Vol. I, London: Constable, 1929, p. 314.

28 Jane Ridley, 'The Unionist Social Reform Committee, 1911–1914: Wets before the deluge', *Historical Journal*, Vol. 30, 1987, pp. 391–413.

29 J. W. Hills, W. J. Ashley and Maurice Woods, *Industrial Unrest: a Practical Solution: the Report of the Unionist Social Reform Committee*, London: John Murray, 1914, p. vii.

30 See John Campbell, *F. E. Smith: First Earl of Birkenhead*, London: Jonathan Cape, 1983, ch. 13.

31 Jamie Camplin, *The Rise of the Plutocrats: Wealth and Power in Edwardian England*, London: Constable, 1978; G. R. Searle, *Corruption in British Politics, 1895–1930*, Oxford: Oxford University Press, 1987.

32 Gregory D. Phillips, *The Diehards: Aristocratic Society and Politics in Edwardian England*, Cambridge, Mass: Harvard University Press, 1979; idem, 'Lord Willoughby de Broke: Radicalism and Conservatism', in J. A. Thompson and Arthur Mejia (eds), *Edwardian Conservatism: Five Studies in Adaptation*, London: Croom Helm, 1988, pp. 77–104; idem, 'Lord Willoughby de Broke and the politics of Radical Toryism, 1909–1914', *Journal of British Studies*, Vol. 20, 1980, pp. 205–24; J. R. Jones, 'England', in Hans Rogger and Eugen Weber (eds), *The European Right*, London: Weidenfeld & Nicolson, 1965, pp. 29–70; G. R. Searle, 'Critics of Edwardian society: the case of the radical right', in Alan O'Day (ed.), *The Edwardian Age: Conflict and Stability 1900–1914*, London: Macmillan, 1979, pp. 79–96; idem, 'The "Revolt from the Right" in Edwardian England', in Paul Kennedy and Anthony Nicholls (eds), *Nationalist and Racialist Movements in Britain and Germany Before 1914*, London: Macmillan, 1981, pp. 21–39; Alan Sykes, 'The Radical Right and the crisis of Conservatism before the First World War', *Historical Journal*, Vol. 26, 1983, pp. 661–76.

33 J. M. Kennedy, *Tory Democracy*, London: Stephen Swift, 1911, p. 179.

34 Pierse Loftus, *The Conservative Party and the Future: a Programme for Tory Democracy*, London: Stephen Swift, 1912, pp. 10–11, 114.

35 Hansard, *Parliamentary Debates*, 5th series, Vol. XCIII, 1917, cols 2408–10; ibid., Vol. C, 1917, col. 2029.

36 Henry Bentinck, *Tory Democracy*, London: Methuen, 1918, pp. 77–9.

37 See too Henry Bentinck, *Industrial Fatigue and the Relation between Hours of Work and Output, with a Memorandum on Sickness*, London: P. S. King, 1918.
38 Earl of Halifax, *Fulness of Days*, London: Collins, 1957, p. 157.

1. Benjamin Disraeli, first Earl of Beaconsfield

'Conservative and Liberal Principles. Speech at Crystal Palace, June 24, 1872.' In *Selected Speeches of the late Right Honourable the Earl of Beaconsfield . . . in two volumes*, Vol. II, T. E. Kebbel (ed.), London: Longmans, Green, 1882, pp. 523–5, 529–34.

Disraeli succeeded Derby as Prime Minister in February 1868, but in November the government was roundly defeated at a general election, fought principally on the issue of a Liberal proposal to disestablish the Church of Ireland. In opposition Disraeli wrote another political romance, *Lothair*, published in three volumes in 1870. Four years later he headed the first majority Conservative administration since the downfall of Peel. Among the measures of the 1874–80 government were further factory reforms, consolidation of public health regulations, two Trade Union Acts, protection for agriculture tenants, and the empowering of local authorities to clear slums. Disraeli was prompted by illness and exhaustion to move to the Lords in 1876 where, still as Prime Minister, he became increasingly immersed in imperial and foreign affairs. In opposition again he finished the last of his novels, *Endymion*, published in November 1880. Six months later he died of bronchitis.

Gentlemen, some years ago – now, indeed, not an inconsiderable period, but within the memory of many who are present – the Tory party experienced a great overthrow. I am here to admit that in my opinion it was deserved. A long course of power and prosperity had induced it to sink into a state of apathy and indifference, and it had deviated from the great principles of that political association which had so long regulated the affairs and been identified with the glory of England. Instead of the principles professed by Mr Pitt and Lord Grenville, and which those great men inherited from Tory statesmen who had preceded them not less illustrious, the Tory system had degenerated into a policy which found an adequate basis on the principles of exclusiveness and restriction. Gentlemen, the Tory party, unless it is a national party, is nothing. It is not a confederacy of nobles, it is not a democratic multitude; it is a party formed from all the numerous classes in the realm – classes alike and equal before the law, but whose different conditions and different aims give vigour and variety to our national life.

Gentlemen, a body of public men distinguished by their capacity took advantage of these circumstances. They seized the helm of affairs in a manner the honour of which I do not for a moment question, but they introduced a new system into our political life. Influenced in a great degree by the philosophy and the politics of the Continent, they endeavoured to substitute cosmopolitan for national principles; and they baptized the new scheme of politics with the plausible name of 'Liberalism'. Far be it from me for a moment to intimate that a country like England should not profit by the political experience of Continental nations of not inferior civilisation; far be it from me for a moment to maintain that the party which then obtained power and which has since generally possessed it did not make many suggestions for our public life that were of great value, and bring forward many measures which, though changes, were nevertheless improvements. But the tone and tendency of Liberalism cannot be long concealed. It is to attack the institutions of the country under the name of Reform, and to make war on the manners and customs of the people of this country under the pretext of Progress. During the forty years that have elapsed since the commencement of this new system – although the superficial have seen upon its surface only the contentions of political parties – the real state of affairs has been this: the attempt of one party to establish in this country cosmopolitan ideas, and the efforts of another – unconscious efforts, sometimes, but always continued – to recur to and resume those national principles to which they attribute the greatness and glory of the country.

I have always been of opinion that the Tory party has three great objects. The first is to maintain the institutions of the country – not from any sentiment of political superstition, but because we believe that they embody the principles upon which a community like England can alone safely rest. The principles of liberty, of order, of law, and of religion ought not to be entrusted to individual opinion or to the caprice and passion of multitudes, but should be embodied in a form of permanence and power. We associate with the Monarchy the ideas which it represents – the majesty of law, the administration of justice, the fountain of mercy and of honour. We know that in the

Estates of the Realm and the privileges they enjoy, is the best security for public liberty and good government. We believe that a national profession of faith can only be maintained by an Established Church, and that no society is safe unless there is a public recognition of the Providential government of the world, and of the future responsibility of man. Well, it is a curious circumstance that during all these same forty years of triumphant Liberalism, every one of these institutions has been attacked and assailed – I say, continuously attacked and assailed . . .

Gentlemen, there is another and second great object of the Tory party. If the first is to maintain the institutions of the country, the second is, in my opinion, to uphold the Empire of England. If you look to the history of this country since the advent of Liberalism – forty years ago – you will find that there has been no effort so continuous, so subtle, supported by so much energy, and carried on with so much ability and acumen, as the attempts of Liberalism to effect the disintegration of the Empire of England . . .

Gentlemen, another great object of the Tory party, and one not inferior to the maintenance of the Empire, or the upholding of our institutions, is the elevation of the condition of the people. Let us see in this great struggle between Toryism and Liberalism that has prevailed in this country during the last forty years what are the salient features. It must be obvious to all who consider the conditions of the multitude with a desire to improve and elevate it, that no important step can be gained unless you can effect some reduction of their hours of labour and humanise their toil. The great problem is to be able to achieve such results without violating those principles of economic truth upon which the prosperity of all States depends. You recollect well that many years ago the Tory party believed that these two results might be obtained – that you might elevate the condition of the people by the reduction of their toil and the mitigation of their labour, and at the same time inflict no injury on the wealth of the nation. You know how that effort was encountered – how these views and principles were met by the triumphant statesmen of Liberalism. They told you that the inevitable consequence of your policy was to diminish capital, that this, again, would lead to the lowering of wages, to a great diminution of the employment of the people, and ultimately to the impoverishment of the kingdom.

These were not merely the opinions of Ministers of State, but those of the most blatant and loud-mouthed leaders of the Liberal party. And what has been the result? Those measures were carried, but carried, as I can bear witness, with great difficulty and after much labour and a long struggle. Yet they were carried; and what do we now find? That capital was never accumulated so quickly, that wages were never higher, that the employment of the people was never greater, and the country never wealthier. I ventured to say a short time ago, speaking in one of the great cities of this country, that the health of the people was the most important question for a statesman. It is, gentlemen, a large subject. It has many branches. It involves the state of the dwellings of the people, the moral consequences of which are not less considerable than the physical. It involves their enjoyment of some of the chief elements of nature – air, light, and water. It involves the regulation of their industry, the inspection of their toil. It involves the purity of their provisions, and it touches upon all the means by which you may wean them from habits of excess and of brutality. Now, what is the feeling upon these subjects of the Liberal party – that Liberal party who opposed the Tory party when, even in their weakness, they advocated a diminution of the toil of the people, and introduced and supported those Factory Laws, the principles of which they extended, in the brief period when they possessed power, to every other trade in the country? What is the opinion of the great Liberal party – the party that seeks to substitute cosmopolitan for national principles in the government of this country – on this subject? Why, the views which I expressed in the great capital of the county of Lancaster have been held up to derision by the Liberal Press. A leading member – a very rising member, at least, among the new Liberal members – denounced that the other day as the 'policy of sewage'.

Well, it may be the 'policy of sewage' to a Liberal member of Parliament. But to one of the labouring multitude of England, who has found fever always to be one of the inmates of his household – who has, year after year, seen stricken down the children of his loins, on whose sympathy and material support he has looked with hope and confidence, it is not a 'policy of sewage', but a question of life and death . . .

I have touched, gentlemen, on the three great objects of the Tory party. I told you I would try to ascertain what was the position of the Tory party with reference to the country now. I have told you also with frankness what I believe the position of the Liberal party to be. Notwithstanding their proud position, I believe they are viewed by the country with mistrust and repugnance. But on all the three great objects which are sought by Toryism – the maintenance of our institutions, the preservation of our Empire, and the improvement of the condition of the people – I find a rising opinion in the country sympathising with our tenets, and prepared, I believe, if the opportunity offers, to uphold them until they prevail.

2. Joseph Chamberlain (1836–1914)

'Tariff Reform and Unemployment. Limehouse, December 15, 1904.' In *Mr. Chamberlain's Speeches*, Vol. II, Charles W. Boyd (ed.), London: Constable, 1914, pp. 257–60, 262, 265–6, 269–70, 272–4, 277.

Chamberlain, a somewhat austere workaholic, had a depressive tendency which was aggravated by the death of two wives in childbirth. The eldest child of a Unitarian family which owned a shoemaking business in Camberwell, London, he went at the age of 14 to University College School, which was instituted on the principles of Jeremy Bentham, whose utilitarian philosophy inspired his followers to promote the greatest happiness of the greatest number through more efficient government. Joining the family firm in 1852, Chamberlain left after two years to become a partner with his uncle, a Birmingham screw manufacturer. In Birmingham, where his business acumen was soon apparent, he moved in prosperous middle-class circles and participated in debating and amateur dramatics. He became a member of the local Liberal association in 1865, and four years later was elected to the city council. In 1873, now mayor of the city, he established a reputation as the architect of 'Municipal Socialism' by implementing a programme of urban renewal which entailed the public ownership of facilities such as gas and water.

By this time Chamberlain was immersed in wider political affairs. He had been one of the founders, in 1869, of the National Education League, the objective of which was the creation of a national system of free primary education. Annoyed by the Liberal government's failure to implement this scheme and other measures, in 1873 he issued the first of his radical programmes: besides free education, it included Anglican disestablishment, land reform and rights for workers. He stood unsuccessfully at Sheffield in the general election of 1874, and two years later was elected unopposed for Birmingham. Chamberlain initially hoped for 'a new Radical party' to strengthen the ties between middle-class nonconformity and the working class, but spent his early years in Parliament trying to shift the Liberal Party to the left. Made President of the Board of Trade by Gladstone in 1880, he became frustrated by the government's caution. On its resignation in 1885 he contributed the preface to *The Radical Programme*, a co-authored manifesto which sounded 'the death-knell of the *laissez-faire* system' and advocated acceleration 'in the direction of which the legislation of the last quarter of a century has been tending – the intervention, in other words, of the State on behalf of the weak against the strong, in the interests of labour against capital, of want and suffering against luxury and ease'. Later in the year he fought the general election with an 'unauthorized' campaign for free education, land reform and fairer taxation. Appointed President of the Local Government Board in the new Liberal administration of 1886, he soon resigned on the issue of Irish Home Rule and in June was among Liberals and Whigs who voted with the Conservative opposition to defeat the government.

Chamberlain's intention after the Home Rule debâcle was eventually to replace Gladstone as Liberal leader and repair the party. Meanwhile he and his followers threw in their lot with dissident Whigs to form the Liberal Unionist parliamentary party, led by the Marquess of Hartington. In 1887 he and Randolph Churchill toyed with the idea of forming a new centre party from a coalition of people with Tory Democratic sympathies, but in the winter of that year Salisbury sent him on a diplomatic mission to North America. On his return Chamberlain launched the Birmingham Liberal Unionist Association which established a grass-roots electoral alliance between Liberal defectors and Conservatives. He also began to forge closer links with the Salisbury government, which was prepared to enact some progressive legislation for the sake of Liberal Unionist support. Gladstone, moreover, declined to retire and by 1891, the year in which he became Liberal Unionist leader in the Commons, Chamberlain had renounced hope of a Liberal reunion. In 1894, now calling himself a Unionist, he had some success in persuading the Conservative Party to adopt a programme of social reform.

At the Colonial Office, where he was installed by Salisbury in 1895, Chamberlain's determination to pursue a robust imperial policy contributed to the outbreak in 1899 of the South African

Boer War. His reputation was enhanced by the 'khaki' general election of 1900, which Conservatives won on a tide of anti-Boer jingoism. But he was soon disillusioned by the government's timidity on social reform and imperial integration. His crusade against free-trade orthodoxy, begun after a visit to South Africa, was assisted by the propaganda machinery of the Tariff Reform League, a well-funded pressure group of politicians, intellectuals and businessmen. Chamberlain intended his 'unauthorized programme' of tariff reform to deliver a short, sharp shock to his party, thereby transforming the government into an agency of dynamic change. Instead, the party was torn apart by the protracted wrangles over fiscal policy. Balfour conceded the principle of imperial commercial unity soon after the disastrous election defeat of January 1906, and Chamberlain now sought to persuade the party to outflank Liberals on social questions. In July, however, he was incapacitated by a stroke and for the next eight years played only a marginal political role.

> I put before my countrymen two questions. I ask them in the first place whether they think that a policy which is sixty years old, which was based on promises that have never been fulfilled, which was conceived in circumstances altogether different from those in which we move, can be suitable to our modern conditions? I ask them, in the second place, what are to be our future relations with our colonies? what is to be the future of the great Empire of which we are all a part? . . . What has happened in that interval of sixty years? One by one every civilised nation, every civilised state, including the great democratic nation which dominates on the other side of the Atlantic, including every colony under the British flag – one by one they have rejected this extreme doctrine of Free Trade or of Free Imports. One by one they have found it wanting; and we alone remain still adhering to this old superstition . . . I say that, treating the matter by that test, we, who during the last sixty years have stuck consistently to the doctrine of Free Imports, have opened our ports to all the world, while all the world has shut its ports to us – I say that, although we have shared in the general prosperity, the comparative advance has been much more largely with our competitors.
>
> Well, there is another point of view. The doctrine of Mr Cobden was a consistent doctrine. His view was that there should be no interference by the state in our domestic concerns. He believed that individuals should be left to themselves to

make the best of their abilities and circumstances, and that there should be no attempt to equalise the conditions of life and happiness. To him, accordingly, protection of labour was quite as bad as protection of trade. To him a trade union was worse than a landlord. To him all factory legislation was as bad as the institution of tariffs. That is a consistent doctrine. I am not arguing now whether it was right or wrong, but it was upon the basis of that doctrine that we had imposed upon us our present fiscal system by a Parliament which, in those days, was not in the slightest degree representative of the majority of the country, and above all of the working classes.

Now, it cannot be denied that all parties have given up these harsh theories. We now no longer think that we ought to leave human beings like ourselves, born into the world for no fault of their own, to struggle against the overpowering pressure of circumstances. We do not believe in the theory of every one for himself and the devil take the hindmost. Accordingly, we have for years been engaged in considering – I think I may say without conceit no one more seriously than myself – these questions of social reform. Now, note something. During the last thirty or fifty years there has been a great deal of what is called social legislation. By whom has it been promoted? By the Conservative party, and latterly by the Unionist party. You owe all your factory legislation to Lord Shaftesbury as its originator. You owe to the Unionist party free education, and that provision for allotments and small holdings which has, at all events, secured for the labourers in the country something like 100,000 holdings they had not before. You owe to us compensation for workmen in the case of accidents during the course of their business. Now why is that? I do not pretend that the Liberal or Radical party, either now or formerly, are or have been less anxious to do good – less philanthropic, or less considerate for the poor than we are; but they have been prevented from taking this course by the theories by which they have been governed. All this legislation is inconsistent with what they call Free Trade. You must no more interfere to raise the standard of living, to raise the wages of working men, than you must interfere to raise the price of goods or the profits of manufacturers.

I will go further. I will say that what we have done cannot be maintained unless at the same time you go further. Let me give you an illustration. I was myself concerned largely in the Act which gave compensation for accidents . . . By that Act what is it we do? We put upon the employer everywhere an additional obligation. We add thereby to his cost of production. We put him at a disadvantage with his foreign competitor, who has no such legislation. Now, if we do not make a balance somehow or another, one of two things will happen. Either the working classes of this country will have to accept lower wages in proportion to the extra cost which has been put upon the manufacturer, or else they will lose their employment. Trade will go to those foreign countries which are not troubled by any of these humanitarian considerations. This attempt of ours to protect the weak, to raise the general standard of living, to regulate the conditions of trade in the interest of the working men – it is very good; but – take this to heart – remember that it is inconsistent with Free Trade . . .

You are suffering from the unrestricted imports of cheaper goods. You are suffering also from the unrestricted immigration of the people who make these goods . . .

[U]nder our policy of the open door, we have, as it were, built a bridge between the countries in which people suffer and our own country, which is already too full and which cannot, without great injury, suffer the admission of so large a population. I have said that I do not wish to press upon these people hardly. Far be it from me to blame them, considering the circumstances in which they have lived. But it is the fact that when these aliens come here, they are answerable for a larger amount of crime and disease and hopeless poverty than is proportionate to their numbers. They come here – I do not blame them, I am speaking of the results – they come here and change the whole character of a district. The speech, the nationality, of whole streets has been altered; and British workmen have been driven by the fierce competition of famished men from trades which they previously followed. I ask you, is it good for the people themselves that they should be tempted to come here? Is it good for men to be herded together like beasts in a pen, to starve upon a few pence a day, doled out to them by employers who seem to be deficient in the bowels of compassion? I say it is bad for you, that it is bad for them; and so far as I am concerned I have always been, and I am now, in favour of giving to the Executive Government the strongest power of control over this alien immigration.

But the party of Free Imports is against any reform. How could they be otherwise? If they were openly to admit that the policy which I recommend ought to be adopted, they would be giving up their whole theory. Where would Mr Cobden be? Where would the doctrine of free imports be? Where would the doctrine of cheap goods be? They are perfectly consistent. If sweated goods are to be allowed in this country without restriction, why not the people who make them? Where is the difference? There is no difference either in the principle or in the results. It all comes to the same thing – less labour for the British working man . . .

I say that of all the social questions in which any man can interest himself there is none greater, none more promising of valuable result, than the question of how to increase the employment of the working classes. At all events, be that as it may, I tell you I would never have – to use a well-known expression – taken off my coat in this movement unless I believed, as I do believe, that this great result of more remunerative employment for those who have to gain the subsistence of themselves and their families by the work of their hands will be achieved.

But, I am told, 'you will increase the cost of living'. Well, suppose I did; which is the better for a working man – to have a loaf a farthing dearer and plenty of money in his pocket, or to have a loaf for twopence or threepence and no money to buy it . . . In my view the cost of living is not the most important thing for the working man to consider. What he has to consider as most important to him is the price which he gets for his labour.

But, gentlemen, do not be deceived; it so happens that all I want for the purposes of this crusade does not involve a farthing's increased cost of living to any working man. All that it requires is a scientific, a reasonable transposition of taxation. A Government has to take out of the pockets even of the poorest of working men a certain amount of money. I am not going to increase that amount, but it is possible that I may take it out of one pocket rather than out of the other. He has to bear the burden in any case; I may put it on his right shoulder instead of on his left. That is the whole of the change which I propose in the taxation of this country . . .

I told you there were two issues. I am coming to the second. What are to be our future relations with the British colonies across the sea? I do not conceal from you that it is on this side of the question that I feel most deeply, because I believe it is most urgent. You can postpone fiscal reform, and perhaps you will still be able to carry it out when it becomes apparent to you that it is necessary. But at this moment you have an opportunity in your relations with your colonies which may not come again; and if you do not grasp it now, believe me, you will be held responsible when the sceptre of our dominion has passed from our hands; you will be held responsible by your descendants in that you were too feeble, too selfish, to maintain your grasp of the great inheritance which your ancestors have left to you. Now this question of the colonies is also a new question in the sense that it cannot be treated on the principle which prevailed in Cobden's day. Sixty years ago the colonies were in their infancy. They were distant, so distant that they were almost out of mind; and with statesmen of that day there prevailed a tone of indifference, if not worse, and the majority of them appeared to be more anxious to get rid of the colonies amicably than to establish any kind of unity. The idea that all these great populations of our blood should ever combine in one great Empire with one mind in order to protect common interests, and defend them against a common foe – such an idea would have been laughed at as absolutely impracticable. Now, am I wrong in saying that the great majority of the people of this land have no dearer wish than to bring all men of British race into one great and organised union? In these later years it has been brought home to us, I hope, that great as we are, rich as we are told we are, we are not great enough, not rich enough, to bear on our own shoulders alone the whole burden of this mighty fabric of Empire which we and our predecessors have created. Yet we know that if anything happened to destroy it, all the glory which attaches to our history, the continuance of the great traditions on which we live and breathe, our influence in the councils of the world – all would disappear with the Empire to which we belong.

Now, that Empire is supported at the present time by ties of sentiment alone. Is it not conceivable that, if a crisis came under the existing circumstances of the world, with new empires that have sprung into existence, new powers that have to be considered – is it not conceivable that the tie of sentiment alone would not be sufficient in that time of crisis to meet the new contingencies which would arise? . . .

I say we want a constructive policy. During my long stay at the Colonial Office I had more opportunities than most men to meet and consult with the most distinguished of our colonial statesmen; and, needless to say, this matter of closer union was the one which most interested us, which most absorbed our thoughts. I found very soon that these men agreed that all progress must be gradual, and that the line of least resistance would be a commercial union on the basis of preference between ourselves and our kinsmen . . .

[W]e can make a treaty with our own kinsfolk, with our own best customers, . . . by which every man within the Empire shall have better treatment from his fellow subjects than they gave to the foreigners, by which the manufacturer of the United Kingdom shall be placed at least on equal terms with his foreign competitor, and by which the British workman shall be secured from what is now his urgent and most pressing danger – from being ousted from his legitimate employment by the unfair competition of underpaid labour.

3. Frederick Edwin Smith, first Earl of Birkenhead (1872–1930)

'State Toryism and Social Reform.' In *Unionist Policy and Other Essays*, London: Williams & Norgate, 1913, pp. 20, 25–6, 29–31, 44–6

Clever, witty, charming, arrogant, sexist and extravagant, Smith was as ambitious as Disraeli had been to reach the top of the 'greasy pole'. His father, a Tory Democrat, was elected mayor of Birkenhead in 1888 but died a month later. After failing the entrance examination to Harrow, 'F.E.' was educated at Birkenhead School and University College, Liverpool, before winning a scholarship to Wadham College, Oxford, where he was elected President of the Union. Graduating with a first in jurisprudence, he became a Fellow of Merton College in 1896 and during his time there wrote a textbook on international law.

In 1899 Smith became a Liverpool barrister and, having contested the Walton constituency of the city on a tariff-reform platform, entered Parliament in the general election of 1906. He was a dazzling orator and his maiden speech is reputedly the best ever made in the Commons. In the turbulent period following the rejection by the Lords of the 'People's Budget', he was a 'die-hard' opponent of the Parliament Bill and, as a member of Bonar Law's cabinet from January 1912, a reckless supporter of Ulster resistance to Home Rule. Smith nevertheless campaigned for a more progressive Unionist social policy, in part because he was concerned about national efficiency but also because he feared that the party would lose working-class support in its retreat from tariff reform. Also, as a contemporary observed, he 'aspired to be the Llòyd George of the Tories'. Hence his chairmanship of the Unionist Social Reform Committee.

As Attorney-General, after a short spell as Solicitor-General, in the wartime coalition government, Smith prosecuted Sir Roger Casement who was later hanged for his activities on behalf of Irish nationalism. In 1918 he was appointed Lord Chancellor, and two years later argued unsuccessfully for a merger of coalition Liberals and Conservatives into a single party to meet the challenge of Labour – though his manifesto for the proposed party displayed little of the earlier enthusiasm for state intervention. Birkenhead also modified his hard-line attitude on Home Rule to play a prominent role in negotiating the treaty which led to the creation of an Irish Free State. As a coalitionist at odds with Unionists eager to resume the normal pattern of politics, he had no position in the new Conservative government of 1922: indeed, he reverted to the language of Tory Democracy in order to condemn the administration's impoverished social programme. He eventually returned to the Conservative fold and in 1924 became Secretary of State for India, resigning four years later because of financial debts. Birkenhead finally discarded the sheep's clothing of Tory Democracy during the General Strike of 1926, when he urged a tough stand against organized labour.

> The *laissez-faire* Conservative or Whig wishes the State to touch nothing: the Socialist, and in a lesser degree the Radical-Socialist, wishes the State to touch everything and to touch it in the wrong way. The modern Conservative, like the old Tory, wants the State to touch some things but to touch them in the right way . . .
>
> The Socialist has rushed to one extreme and the Individualist to the other. The first has built his State on an imaginary man, who, like the bee or the ant, possesses nothing but the faculty of organisation; the other on an equally vain imagination – a being possessed of nothing but the instinct for self-advancement and self-preservation. The vice of Individualism is that it would hamstring man's power for co-ordinate advance and joint sacrifice; the vice of Socialism is that it would cut the other motor-muscle of character, the desire for the struggle, and for the reward the struggle brings. It is impossible to tamper with the principle of private property, and with the principle of the family and hereditary succession which depends on it . . .
>
> Tory principle must be based . . . first, on the unity of the State, which Individualism denies, and second, on the

conception of the continuity and stability of the State, which Socialism would destroy. In the third place, Toryism must regard the people of these islands not as if they were 'built like the angels with hammer and chisel and pen' to suit a preconceived doctrine, but as they actually are – men animated by those mingled motives of enterprise and self-interest, patriotism and self-sacrifice, daring and prudence, which have inspired citizens and constructed commonwealths from the dawn of history . . .

Disraeli indeed shone in intellect; Lord Randolph in democratic oratory; Mr Chamberlain in hard common sense joined to parliamentary powers hardly inferior to Disraeli's and democratic power as great as Randolph Churchill's. But they all believed in the nation, and in the people as the nation – nor could they conceive of Toryism as a form of class interest, but only as an embodiment of that national unity which binds class to class, or kingdom to kingdom; which makes unity out of difference, and an Imperial whole out of bodies separated by the width of the world. One may follow, however humbly, in their footsteps, and say that a policy of union or of empire which leaves Social Reform and class unity out of account is built upon sand, and not upon the solid rock of political reality.

I have said that the essence of Tory Social Reform is the study of the real aptitudes of the people. It is, precisely, here that Individualism and Socialism fail alike. Humanity is composed neither of men struggling to arrive at all costs nor of men ready to sacrifice anything and everything to a common end. Nor, to put the matter in a more concrete form, does the race consist entirely of individuals ready to gamble their chances on the wheel of fortune, and to risk all in order to better their conditions and position. On the contrary, most individuals tread in the accustomed paths, and demand of life that it shall give them security and prosperity in the state in which it has pleased God to call them . . .

Security of tenure in all classes of life where such tenure is not a national evil: that is the doctrine of Toryism. Opportunity for talent to develop its own potentialities and the resources of the nation where such a development is to the advantage of the State: that is the doctrine of Toryism. Security to those who need it, opportunity to those who desire it, on what better foundation can the state of the future be built? '*Sanitas sanitatum – omnia sanitas*', said Disraeli, in his hackneyed epigram – and we can best carry out the spirit of his words by looking at the needs of the people as they really are, and not as they are conceived to be by the ideologues of either extreme school of thought. We have to deal with men, not with ideas; with the urgent necessities of the democracy of to-day, not with the theories of the past or bubble hopes of the future. In all things we stand midway between conflicting extremes. We are not for the classes or the masses, for their interests are one. We are not for Individualism or Socialism, for neither is founded on fact. We stand for the State and for the unity which, whether in the form of kingdom or empire or class solidarity, the State alone can bring. Above all stands the State, and in that phrase lies the essence of Toryism. Our ancestors left it to us, and not the least potent method of preserving it is to link the conception of State Toryism with the practice of Social Reform.

4. Lord Henry Cavendish-Bentinck (1863–1931)

Tory Democracy, London: Methuen, 1918, pp. 1–3, 45–6. 137–9

A landowner in Westmoreland, where he was Lord-Lieutenant, Bentinck listed his recreations as fox-hunting, fishing and shooting. Educated at Eton and Christ Church, Oxford, he was a colonel in the Yeomanry and served in South Africa in 1900 and the Dardanelles in 1915. He was Member of Parliament for North-west Norfolk between 1886 and 1892, and for South Nottingham from 1895 until losing his seat in the Liberal landslide of 1906. In 1907, the year in which he was elected to the London County Council, Bentinck was at the centre of a minor political storm when the Confederacy, a secret society of extreme tariff reformers, tried to cajole him as Unionist candidate for South Nottingham into declaring in favour of protectionism. His half-brother, the sixth Duke of Portland, complained to the Unionist leaders, who repudiated the activities of the organization.

Bentinck was elected for South Nottingham again in January 1910, retaining the seat until his defeat in 1929. Previously he had rarely spoken in the Commons. From 1910, however, he frequently intervened in debates to advocate Tory Democratic policies; he urged, for example, further factory legislation to curb the exploitation of women and children, comprehensive national insurance, the statutory provision of a minimum wage, and female suffrage. He also became increasingly involved in humanitarian organizations such as the Penal Reform League, the State Children's Association (which campaigned for enlightened treatment of juvenile delinquents) and a 'public utility society' which used state subsidies to build low-cost homes for the working class. In 1917 he was among former members of the Unionist Social Reform Committee who established a 'luncheon club' to plan for improvements in public health.

Besides opposing the coalition government for making deals with the plutocracy, Bentinck condemned its oppression of Irish nationalists, harsh labour policy and indifference to the League of Nations. In 1922, citing J. M. Keynes on the deficiences of uncontrolled investment, he recommended public planning for full employment. Early in that year he supported Lord Robert Cecil's unsuccessful conspiracy to replace the coalition with an administration led by Viscount Grey. As a champion of the rights of workers, especially miners, Bentinck was hardly less critical of the attitude of the new Conservative ministry towards labour. 'As a Conservative of long standing', he told the House in 1924, 'I hold that the only way to prevent strikes and industrial unrest and to safeguard the institutions of this country is to identify those institutions with the happiness and welfare of the people . . . If we are to fight Communism, we must see that wages and conditions of labour in our industries are such as will commend those industries to the people of the country'. On several occasions he called upon the government to convene a conference of capital and labour, with the purpose of devising an industrial charter to secure wages, improve working conditions and extend profit-sharing schemes. But the sole contribution of the Baldwin government to industrial harmony, he concluded in the aftermath of the General Strike, 'is to treat trade union leaders as naughty children and attempt to pour a dose of nauseous medicine down their throats'.

> [T]hese are times of special danger to all our political parties. A force has arisen which is indifferent to them all, except as instruments for its own purpose – a force which has used the war and the passions aroused by it to fortify its position, and now scoffs at all our idealisms. What is the permanent peace of the world to Plutocracy, or Plutocracy to the permanent peace of the world? Its only thought is to turn the British Empire into a bagman's Paradise, and to make the world safe for itself.
>
> While everything generous, self-sacrificing and noble is shedding its blood on the fields of France and Flanders, Plutocracy is on the war-path at home. Its batteries are unmasked and the attack opened. Plugson of Undershot, having conquered shells and cellulose, will capture our political life. A Ministry of

Information, strengthened and enlarged by Imperial financiers and lumber-men, will provide the right brand of synthetic truth or manufactured falsehood. The 'pious Editor' will spread whatever trash will keep the people in blindness. The Labour Party will be split and divided by subtle machinations. The Golden Calf will be set up; those who worship will be rewarded with the crumbs that fall from the rich man's table, while those who refuse will be denounced as Pacifists and Bolsheviks. The Tory Party will be thoroughly commercialized and vulgarized, and a liberal distribution of office and honours will promote contentment in its ranks.

Such is the grand design, the plan of campaign. The longer the War lasts, the stricter will be the monopoly and the larger the spoils, the more will Plutocracy be ennobled, decorated, knighted and enriched. That way lies disruption and damnation. Disruption for the nation; our wonderful war-time unity will dissolve itself into a confused welter of warring factions. Damnation for the Tory Party; for it will inevitably lose its national character and sink into a tariff-mongering faction.

Under the leadership of Disraeli, the influence of Randolph Churchill, and the guidance of Salisbury, the Tory Party realized its true destiny; it rose above the mere interests of a class, and became a great national party; standing for great principles, it identified itself with the welfare and happiness of the people. It was in consequence trusted by the people . . .

It was not till the death of Lord Salisbury that its popularity began to wane. Under his successor its policy suffered a change. It gradually lost its national character, and fell under the influence of sectional interests . . . The Tory Party lost the confidence of the people on the day when it laid itself open to the suspicion that it was engaged in a capitalist conspiracy, and it will not regain it until it clears itself of that suspicion. And that is the beginning and end of the matter.

It would be kinder, perhaps, to draw a veil over the party's career from 1906 to the out-break of the War, but this much must be said, that it alternated from stupidity to factiousness, and from factiousness to stupidity. Whether Mr. Lloyd George's budget was rejected from pure panic, or in the interests of Tariff Reform, is now of no importance, and whether it was wise to hand the Party over bound hand and foot to the goodwill and pleasure of Sir Edward Carson, need not now be argued; but this much is clear, that there was nothing either Tory or Democratic in a policy which for party purposes strained the Constitution, and for the sake of a faction disputed the sovereignty of the Imperial Parliament, and threatened the very existence of Democracy itself.

There seem to be occasions in the history of the Conservative Party when, as Disraeli remarked, its leaders preserve the institutions of the country as they do their pheasants, merely in order to destroy them . . .

This realm of England is an Empire, said one of Henry VIII's Parliaments. It is more; it is a Commonwealth, a Commonwealth that embraces all – all classes, all sections, all interests – in a common life. The glory of our national history is a glory shed by the light of the vision of the Commonwealth. It is true that the light has often been dimmed. It was dimmed when a landed class, in the course of the sixteenth century, pursued low aims of private gain. It was dimmed again when a capitalistic class, during and after the industrial revolution, followed a policy of individual enrichment, and when the working class in a just resentment began to adopt a policy of retaliation and class warfare. But the vision has never faded . . . It has been seen and it has been followed by the Tory Party at all times when the Tory Party has been true to itself . . .

The readjustment and reconstruction of the national economy in the true spirit of the Commonwealth is the supreme task of the future. The Tory Party can only claim the noble responsibility of shouldering that task if it is true to its own best traditions and to the spirit of the Commonwealth. It will not be true to either if it allows itself to be captured by great moneyed interests, which, though they may be sheltered under the name of National Security, are at bottom sectional and even selfish. The State, and the parties within the State, will in the future be more closely connected with national industry than ever before. It is of all things most vital that the connexion should be pure and clean; that neither the State itself nor any of its parties should be yoked to the horses of Croesus; that wealth should be made to serve the Commonwealth, and industry to produce not wealth for a few, but welfare, abundant welfare, for all.

5 *Survival of the fittest 1880–1953*

> Those who claim to wear the mantle of the older economists have fallen on evil times. They are compelled by their principles to regard almost every act of legislation for the past thirty years as fatally mistaken. Mr. Herbert Spencer mournfully tells us that we are steadily tending downwards from freedom to bondage, but he is preaching in the wilderness, and must be painfully aware of his inability to stay the fatal declension.[1]

Some Tory Democrats did not share Chamberlain's conviction that 'the individualists', as he designated proponents of a minimal state, had been trounced. They were alarmed that by the turn of the century opposition to collectivism came largely from a vociferous section of the Conservative Party. Pierse Loftus feared that the party would be diverted from a programme of social reform by the presence in its ranks of men – many of them refugees from the Liberal Party, as was Chamberlain – who, 'saturated with the *laissez-faire* principles of the Manchester school', advanced 'as a main argument against improvement of the conditions of the people the old phrase, "The survival of the fittest"'. He asked, 'Do the people who use this phrase as a defence of slum dwellings and all the other abominable conditions of our industrial civilization, do they ever think?'[2] Loftus had in mind admirers of Spencer, inventor of the catch-phrase to which he referred, who believed that society progresses through a harsh struggle for survival, in which the weak and idle suffer the consequences of their incompetence. Public amelioration of poverty impedes social evolution, on this account, by cushioning inefficient individuals at the expense of the energetic and skilful. Those who gave an evolutionary twist to the science of political economy preached a message not dissimilar from that of Peelites earlier in the nineteenth century. Fearing, however, that both Liberal and Conservative Parties were treading a slippery slope to socialism in their anxiety to secure the working-class vote, the new individualists defended free-market capitalism with unprecedented urgency.[3] Soon after the turn of the century admiration for Spencer diminished among libertarian Conservatives, and the case against socialism was usually detached from evolutionary theory. Yet as late as the 1950s one of the foremost publicists against collectivism was an arden Spencerite.

Spencer had advocated minimal government as early as the 1840s when, like the radicals of the Anti-Corn Law League, his principal target was the landed Anglican Establishment. In subsequent writings be sought to make unbridled economic competition scientifically credible by demonstrating that society evolves in so far as worthy individuals prosper more than those of an inferior type. The robust society therefore is a meritocracy in which the feeble fall into poverty, while the talented are permitted to scale the heights of affluence. Artificial preservation of the undeserving weak reverses the evolutionary process, according to Spencer, by precipitating society's descent into an economic slum inhabited by moral degenerates.

After the appearance in 1859 of Charles Darwin's *The Origin of Species*, Spencer added a gloss of natural selection to his evolutionary individualism, which he now blazoned as 'the survival of the fittest'. What collectivists pejoratively called Social Darwinism – the doctrine that society progresses through struggle – was popularized by the widely-read *The Man versus the State*, published in 1884; in this Spencer regretted the tendency of the modern state to 'further survival of the unfittest' by a misguided philanthropic attempt to improve the lot of the masses. He was particularly distressed by the readiness of Liberals to meddle with natural selection. Instead of releasing individuals from the clutches of an overmighty state, recent Liberal administrations had betrayed their heritage by behaving in the manner of Tory paternalists. The Conservative Party, by contrast, contained a growing number opposed to the rising tide of collectivism:

> Proof is furnished by the fact that the 'Liberty and Property Defence League', largely consisting of Conservatives, has taken for its motto 'Individualism *versus* Socialism'. So that if the present drift of things continues, it may by and by really happen that the Tories will be defenders of liberties which the Liberals, in pursuit of what they think popular welfare, trample under foot.[4]

The Liberty and Property Defence League was one of several right-wing organizations which emerged at this time. Among their patrons were a few wayward ideologues who, exploring the logic of Spencer's evolutionary individualism, anticipated the eventual withering of the state in a system of private enterprise regulated by voluntary co-operation. But most of their supporters, far from countenancing anarchy, were Tory stalwarts afraid that ordered hierarchy would be submerged in a democratic deluge – rather as those who joined Reeves's Association for the Preservation of Liberty and Property against Republicans and Levellers feared that wealth and rank would be swept away in the wake of the French Revolution. These Conservatives, like Peelites, favoured a strong framework of law and order which facilitated market forces.

The league itself was established in 1882 with the intention of throwing a barrier across 'the high road that leads straight to State-Socialism', along which Britain was said to have been travelling since the Reform Act of 1867.[5] Supported by a fair number of Conservative MPs, it acted as a pressure group against 'over-legislation' by lobbying Parliament, scrutinizing each Bill, co-ordinating sympathetic commercial and industrial interests, and issuing endless propaganda.[6] Principal spokesman of the league was the Earl of Wemyss, formerly Lord Elcho, who had been a Peelite in the 1840s, and who still believed that political economy was 'simply the law of gravitation applied to social matters'.[7] The nation had lost sight of economic truths, Wemyss believed, because political parties were busily accommodating to democracy in a frantic bid for mass support. He claimed that 'the dread spectre of Socialism dwells in the tents' of the Liberal and Conservative Parties, and was appalled by Chamberlain's 'vote-catching' programme of 'Social legislative lollipops'.[8] Instead of combating the menace of socialism, Tory Democrats had joined forces with the enemy.

The gap between the libertarian and the collectivist wings of conservatism widened with Chamberlain's tariff-reform campaign. Protectionism was the thin end of a collectivist wedge in the eyes of free-trade Conservatives, who became semi-detached from the party after their disastrous performance in the general election of 1906 and the subsequent adoption of tariff reform as Unionist policy. They were also dismayed by the radical programme of the new Liberal administration, and their dilemma was expressed by Lord Balfour of Burleigh. He was one of the cabinet ministers who had resigned in 1903 because of A. J. Balfour's willingness to compromise with the Chamberlain faction: 'To put it briefly we are between the Devil and the Deep Sea. Shall we go to the Devil of Protection with our friends, or the Deep Sea of Socialism with our political adversaries?'[9] Balfour was among several Unionist free-traders prominent in the British Constitution Association, founded in 1905 to resist 'political Socialism'.[10] Its title, disparaged by a fellow libertarian as 'amazingly inappropriate',[11] was chosen to highlight the current threat to constitutional liberties that had been wrenched from the state over the centuries. Even the slightest extension of government beyond the protection of life and property enraged members of the association, whose aim was to revive an ethos of rugged individualism as a means of securing the foundations of market capitalism. Whereas tariff reformers advocated 'paternal bureaucracy' as a panacea for the evils of poverty, wrote one of its presidents, Unionist free-traders favoured 'the training of personal character under the discipline of liberty and self-help'.[12] Among the policies condemned by the association were public provision of cheap housing for the working class, free meals for poor children, old-age pensions, and regulation of the hours and conditions of employment: a 'thin as water-gruel' programme of 'much economy and no reform', scoffed a tariff reformer, that was 'a sheer godsend to every Socialist on the stump'.[13]

Herbert Spencer was the main philosophical source for the association, which arranged lectures to expound his message that collectivism interfered with the laws of social evolution. Lord Balfour's presidential address in 1908, which was wrapped in Spencerian logic, contained the usual blend of moral and economic arguments on behalf of a self-help society. Economic success or failure was a fair measure of individual merit, which meant that poverty arose from personal incompetence and not from any structural defects within a system of economic competition; legislation in the interests of the weak, far from correcting the flaws of human nature, reinforced the inclination of some towards indolence and inefficiency; so overloaded with loungers and scroungers would the interventionist state eventually become that it would absorb practically the entire resources of the community in support of its least worthy members; society would then undergo a process of moral decay and economic decline. Government's proper function was to give play to those considerations of self-interest which prompted the poor to escape from starvation and spurred the rich to even greater enterprise. Remove those incentives, concluded Balfour, and the mainspring of social evolution would snap.[1]

Not every libertarian Conservative of the period was an unreconstructed Spencerite. The problem Social Darwinism presented for free-marketeers was that it could be used to broadcast diverse political messages,[14] and even commentators who subscribed to the doctrine of the survival of the fittest did not necessarily oppose welfare policies. In his influential *Social Evolution*, published in 1894, Benjamin Kidd contended that progress would accelerate if the state extended opportunities to the 'unfit' to participate in the struggle for survival. This recasting of Social Darwinism in a collectivist mould prompted W. H. Mallock, the most original and prolific Tory publicist between 1880 and 1920, to detach the argument for a minimal state from Spencer's evolutionary theory.[15]

Mallock, who was active in the Liberty and Property Defence League and other right-wing organizations, began his literary career with several fictional and philosophical books which repudiated agnosticism and liberal Protestantism from the standpoint of High Church orthodoxy. These early works reveal some sympathy with the ideals of *noblesse oblige*. In *The New Republic*, a satirical novel published in 1877, Mallock contrasted the benevolent paternalism of the old squirearchy with the rapacity and myopia of 'cotton-spinning plutocrats' who, along with the 'vast and useless body' of the middle classes generally, 'will soon have made vice as vulgar as they long ago made virtue'.[16] Around 1880, however, he became preoccupied with the spread of collectivist ideas through the working and middle classes. Socialism he regarded as a genuine though misguided concern for the condition of the people, but denounced the 'suburban' radicalism of Chamberlain as a selfish venture to displace the privileges of land by those of an upstart bourgeoisie.[17] Common to both, he said, was a propensity to distort facts and disseminate false principles in order to endow collectivism with pseudo-scientific respectability. Conservatives, by contrast, lacked either the statistical information or theoretical sophistication to expose the follies of their opponents. Mallock therefore set about supplying a 'missing science' of human character intended to 'paralyse the power . . . of the democratic spirit' by demonstrating that social evolution depends upon a desire for inequality.[18] This 'scientific Conservatism' was subsequently elaborated in numerous books and articles, where Mallock provided politicians with precise arguments by which to make the truths of political economy comprehensible to the masses.

Whereas Mallock had previously doubted the social utility of plutocrats, his science of progress attributed economic and cultural developments to entrepreneurial ambition. Society had advanced from barbarism to civilization because of the persistent influence of an exceptional minority, whose inventive genius and organizational ability had steadily increased living standards for everyone. These wealth-creators were induced to exercise their energy for the common benefit by the expectation of appropriate rewards. Egalitarian policies, by removing the incentives which prompted the gifted few to exert themselves, would soon result in economic stagnation and cultural mediocrity.

Mallock's vindication of inequality, though robust and extensive, was not essentially different from the conventional insistence of free-market Conservatives that the poor depended for subsistence upon the profits of the rich. In a sense his capitalist élite can be viewed as a Burkean natural aristocracy, renovated to accommodate the rapid expansion of industry. Like Burke, he drew upon the assumptions of political economy to portray society as a chain of discipline, where the body of the people participate 'in benefits which, in the way alike of material comfort, opportunity, culture and social freedom, would be possible for no one unless the many submitted themselves to the influence or authority of the super-capable few'.[19] Unlike earlier Conservatives, however, Mallock used his scientific defence of capitalism to turn socialism upside-down. This he did by challenging the Marxist notion that manual labour is the sole source of wealth, claiming instead that the growth of productive forces is due entirely to the intellectual direction of the few. The explosion of wealth in nineteenth-century society derived not from the productive capacity of employees, which had remained constant, but from the talent of inventors and the acumen of entrepreneurs who grasped the market potential of technical innovation. They alone were responsible for the creation of 'surplus value' which, far from consolidating class exploitation, had raised the masses beyond a condition of near starvation:

> The fundamental facts of the case are, indeed, of a character the precise reverse of that which the theories of the Socialists impute to them. In proportion as the wages of labour rise above a given minimum, the many are the pensioners of the few, the few are not the plunderers of the many, and those who maintain the opposite are mere intellectual gamins standing on their heads in a gutter.[20]

Once deprived of entrepreneurial command the army of the proletariat would soon slip back into penury.

Mallock's science of human character appears in every respect to have confirmed the conclusions of Spencer's evolutionary individualism. But disturbed by Benjamin Kidd's transformation of Social Darwinism into a justification of state intervention to improve the efficiency of the masses, Mallock argued that Spencer's theory was amenable to conflicting interpretations because of a fundamental defect. The problem was that it systematically ignored the 'cardinal social fact' of inequality.[21] Spencer depicted exceptional individuals as agents rather than the cause of social progress, and thereby failed to acknowledge their creative part in the historical process. Yet while Darwinian struggle might explain the gradual adaptation of the human species over a long period, it could not account for the rapid advance of modern industrial society – which was due entirely to the activities of an entrepreneurial élite. Spencer, in relegating great men to the margins of his sociology, had committed the same error as Marx, who also attributed social development to the improved capacity of average individuals. In *Aristocracy and Evolution*, therefore, Mallock discredited the 'monumental claptrap' of Kidd by accusing both Marx and Spencer of obscuring the historical significance of leadership beneath the laws of social progress.[2]

Mallock, of course, had misunderstood Spencer's logic by viewing it from the distorted perspective of Kidd. Spencer reproached him, in private correspondence as well as publicly, for exaggerating the differences between them.[22] Yet Mallock's critique of Spencer's sociology, however misdirected, did highlight the political ambivalence of the doctrine of the survival of the fittest. Social Darwinism could be used by individualists to oppose welfare legislation which favoured the 'unfit' at the expense of the 'fit'; alternatively it could be invoked by collectivists who wished to improve the fitness of the masses as a means of increasing the efficiency of the nation as a whole. Darwinian collectivism grew in popularity during the early years of the twentieth century when imperialists, concerned about 'national efficiency', argued that the country could not flourish in an international struggle for survival without attending to the health and skills of its labour force.[23] A diminishing number of libertarian Conservatives, in consequence, regarded natural selection as a secure anchorage for their advocacy of unconstrained private enterprise.

Instead of becoming entangled in the web of evolutionary theory, many Conservatives preferred to reiterate the lesson of political economy that labour benefits from the unhindered accumulation of capital. The argument was clear enough and did not need to be encumbered by the intricacies of Social Darwinism: self-interest provides the stimulus for wealth-production; rising living standards depend upon the incentives which persuade entrepreneurs to use their talents for the common advantage; any thwarting of private ambition by confiscatory taxation and egalitarian policies would undermine enterprise and eventually reduce wages; the state should therefore be confined to preserving property rights and protecting the nation against foreign invasion. This was the message conveyed among others by John St Loe Strachey, editor of the *Spectator* and a member of the British Constitution Association, in his 'Letters to a working man': 'Socialism would injure instead of benefiting the poor. You will never be able to give every man on a hot day a bigger drink of water if you begin by stopping up the pipe that feeds the cistern.'[24] Challenging, as Mallock had done, the Marxist claim that labour is the sole source of value, Strachey argued that the least extension of the state beyond its narrow sphere – whether in the provision of free school meals or of old-age pensions – was evidence of the socialist threat to individual initiative. Tariff reform, too, 'would by impoverishing the capitalists injure the manual worker'.[25] Strachey's defence of an enterprise culture was characteristic of the way in which many Unionist free-traders before the First World War responded to what they perceived as the collectivist menace.

During the inter-war period the extravagant prophesies of socialist catastrophe made by libertarians since the 1880s became less credible, largely because the pillars of capitalism withstood the 'impact of labour'. Conservatives were in power between 1923 and 1940, apart from two interludes of weak minority Labour governments, in 1924 and 1929–31; the party, led by the avuncular Stanley Baldwin until 1937, adopted a 'safety first' policy which did not dramatically extend the social and economic functions of the state. Nevertheless there were still many on the right of the party eager to popularize the truths of political economy by arguing, as did Strachey, that the poor would become poorer unless the rich were amply rewarded for their entrepreneurial achievements. If potential wealth-creators were deprived of the 'wages of adventure', as Herbert Williams called profits in *Why I am not a Socialist*, they would refrain from taking the risks necessary to produce abundance for all. The language of these free-marketeers often resembled that of Social Darwinists, even though they usually avoided the labyrinth of evolutionary theory. Williams's case against equality, for example, was that 'you cannot drag everyone down to the pay level of the least efficient' without arresting economic progress.[26]

Sometimes more explicit use was made of the doctrine of the survival of the fittest in order to censure the Conservative Party for adjusting to collectivism. Dorothy Crisp, writing in 1931, was as alarmist as any individualist at the turn of the century in predicting inexorable social decline unless Conservatives rediscovered the principles of political economy. Labour's electoral success in 1929 was due in part, she believed, to the complacency of conservatism, which 'has in practice been corrupted during the last twenty-five years into a meaningless half-Socialism'. One sign of corruption was the readiness to follow fashion by attributing poverty and deprivation to insufficient public expenditure on social welfare. Yet the condition of the people would never be improved by schemes which disregarded natural selection. New corporation housing estates, for instance, soon degenerated into 'a garbage heap' because many of their inhabitants were feckless and half-witted:

> [T]hose who sink to slum life are without doubt . . . the weakest and least desirable of the population . . . To-day the unfit are preserved at the expense of the fit, the deserving pay for the maintenance of the undeserving, and physically, mentally and morally there is a levelling down of the whole race.[27]

Only by returning to a *laissez-faire* policy which taught the necessity of individual self-reliance could the Conservative Party prevent further national deterioration.

One fervent disciple of Spencer was described by J. M. Keynes in 1927 as leader of 'the very extreme Conservatives [who] would like to undo all the hardly won little which we have in the way of conscious and deliberate control of economic forces for the public good, and replace it by a return to chaos'.[28] Prior to 1920 Sir Ernest Benn, whose father was a Liberal MP, had written three books urging government to improve relations between capital and labour by involving trade unions in the management of industry. But a visit to the United States of America in 1921 converted him to minimal statism, and a few years later he wrote *The Confessions of a Capitalist* which, drawing on his experience as 'a middle-class person who has had a middle-class success',[29] was the first of many broadsides against collectivism. He was now prominent in a coterie of *laissez-faire* crusaders who in 1926 launched the Individualist Bookshop to advertise and sell books enshrining the truths of political economy; included in Benn's list of sound literature were Spencer's *The Man versus the State*, Mallock's *The Limits of Pure Democracy*, and Strachey's *Economics of the Hour*.[30] By now, too, he was disenchanted with the Liberal Party, believing that it had been hijacked by intellectuals such as Keynes. These people wished to eliminate the inefficiency and injustice of 'cut-throat individualism' through, for example, state direction of investment, expenditure on slum clearance and other public works, industrial profit-sharing schemes, and the statutory provision of a minimum wage for each industry. Their proposals for taming capitalism – contained in *Britain's Industrial Future: Being the Report of the Liberal Industrial Inquiry*, otherwise known as the Yellow Book, published, curiously enough but in true entrepreneurial spirit, by Benn's own company – convinced him that modern liberalism was 'the illegitimate offspring of Socialism'.[31] In 1929 he announced his intention of supporting the Conservative Party. For the next twenty-odd years his reputation as an unrepentant individualist was not dissimilar from that which his nephew, Tony Benn, later enjoyed as a campaigner for undiluted socialism.

As a schoolboy Benn had caused some alarm in his family by acquiring a set of Spencer's works.[32] The pages were then uncut, and judging by Benn's ignorance of the details of Spencer's evolutionary theory, most of them probably remained in their pristine condition. Benn's frequent references to Spencer were almost invariably to *The Man versus the State*, especially the chapter 'The coming slavery', which prophesied the destruction of personal initiative unless the country awoke to the dangers of creeping collectivism, and he cited his mentor to reinforce, not a thorough sociology of his own, but a plain political message. On his account of social progress, which was not unlike that of members of the British Constitution Association, the struggle to emancipate individuals from the clutches of the state had proceeded steadily from the time of royal absolutism until the 'triumphs of the Victorian era',[33] when the achievements of a talented few were matched by the self-reliance and patriotism of common folk. But the nineteenth-century golden age quickly vanished beneath the 'dead-hand' of officialdom, and the nation had since declined to a point not far short of the despotism predicted by Spencer. Evidence of the disastrous effects of state paternalism was everywhere: civil service 'red tape' which strangled so much private enterprise; the 'bureaucratic incompetence' of government monopolies such as the Post Office and telephone system; disruption of the laws of supply and demand through, for example, control of prices and wages, production targets, subsidies to industry, managed currencies, and tariffs on imports and exports; extravagant expenditure on wasteful public schemes; and the servile dependency of a people who expected to be suckled from cradle to grave by a 'wet nurse' state.

Benn's solution was to roll back the state in order to retrieve that system of natural liberty which, from his romantic perspective, had existed in the nineteenth century. Either the nation could continue travelling towards serfdom or, recovering its sense of direction, choose the route known to lead to economic efficiency and moral vigour:

> The wide and easy road leads to the State as a super-business concern, a sort of inflated Marks and Spencer, with an all-powerful civil service to settle the price level, the amount and sort of production, the quantity and direction of imports and exports, the values of currencies and the fate of debts. A brave new world in which brains are required only by a very limited official class.
>
> The older, safer road, is built for the use of independent individuals, and innumerable byways run towards it with refreshment in the manner of the fibrous growths on a healthy root. It is planned by nature to encourage the maximum variety of genius, to give the widest possible scope to each little fibre and to make all conscious of individual personal responsibility to the general growth, to ensure that each shall strive to be strong enough to bear a full share of the common task.[34]

In attempting to persuade his readers to take the latter road Benn repudiated the Marxist theory of value, arguing, like other libertarians, that entrepreneurial profit is the source of prosperity for everyone.

In his early days as a campaigner for the return to *laissez-faire*, Benn believed that the collectivist tide was about to ebb.[35] His confidence diminished somewhat as the years passed, and he was outraged by the massive state regulation of industry during wartime. Fearing that the economy would remain in its political strait-jacket after the cessation of hostilities, he was instrumental in founding the Society of Individualists to protest 'against the neglect of the laws of the science of Political Economy as laid down by the orthodox masters, a neglect or even denial which has arrested natural progress, brought us into an artificial, regulated, troublesome world, quite apart from Hitler and his iniquities, which must sink ever lower in comfort and continue to provide an unending source of wars'.[36] He was no happier, of course, with the record of the postwar Labour administration, and in 1953 published his last book, 'an *ex-parte* statement in the case of The Man *v.* the State',[37] as he put it; it began by celebrating Spencer for his prophetic insight and concluded with excerpts from the master's chapter 'The coming slavery'. Rising rates of divorce and illegitimacy, pervasive moral laxity, lack of respect for law and order, shoddy workmanship and a lowering of commercial standards: all were attributed in *The State the Enemy* to the enormous extension of government which had culminated in the creation of the Welfare State. The nation had departed so far from the Victorian values of self-help and sound economy that citizens were positively encouraged to be 'unfit'.[3]

This kind of minimal statism was now regarded as eccentric even by most Conservatives, who preferred a more-or-less Keynesian middle road between the free market and socialism. Eventually, however, the collectivist tide did turn and libertarianism became the official creed of the Conservative Party. And although the new individualists discarded Social Darwinism, their arguments for an enterprise culture were not essentially different from those of Spencerites such as Benn.

NOTES

1 Joseph Chamberlain, 'The Labour question', *Nineteenth Century*, Vol. XXXII, 1892, p. 679.

2 Pierse Loftus, *The Conservative Party and the Future: a Programme for Tory Democracy*, London: Stephen Swift, 1912, pp. 110–12.

3 See John W. Mason, 'Political economy and the response to socialism in Britain, 1870–1914', *Historical Journal*, Vol. 23, 1980, pp, 565–87. Mason underestimates the influence of the doctrine of 'the survival of the fittest' on individualists, though the article is an admirable survey of the varieties of anti-socialism in the period.

4 Herbert Spencer, *The Man versus the State*, London: Williams & Norgate, 1885, pp. 17, 69.

5 *Socialism at St. Stephen's in 1883. Work done during the Session by the Parliamentary Committee of the Liberty and Property Defence League*, Westminster: Liberty and Property Defence League, 1884, p. 10.

6 See Edward Bristow, 'The Liberty and Property Defence League and individualism', *Historical Journal*, Vol. 18, 1975, pp. 761–89; N. Soldon, 'Laissez-Faire as dogma: the Liberty and Property Defence League, 1882–1914', in Kenneth D. Brown (ed.), *Essays in Anti-Labour History: Responses to the Rise of Labour in Britain*, London: Macmillan, 1974, pp. 208–33.

7 W. H. Mallock, *Socialism and Social Discord*, London: Liberty and Property Defence League, 1896, p. 19. Wemyss was proposing a vote of thanks to Mallock for his address to the league.

8 Earl of Wemyss, *The Socialist Spectre*, London: Liberty and Property Defence League, 1895, pp. 5, 9.

9 Cited in Richard A. Rempel, *Unionists Divided: Arthur Balfour, Joseph Chamberlain and the Unionist Free Traders*, Newton Abbott: David & Charles, 1972, p. 172.

10 The association has been largely ignored by historians, though see W. H. Greenleaf, *The British Political Tradition: Vol. 2, The Ideological Heritage*, London: Metheun, 1983, pp. 281–5.

11 Sir Roland Wilson, *The Province of the State*, London: P. S. King, 1911, p. 292.
12 Lord Hugh Cecil, 'The Unionist Party and its fiscal sore', *Nineteenth Century*, Vol. 65, 1909, p. 597.
13 J. L. Garvin, 'Free trade as socialist policy', *National Review*, Vol. 295, 1907, p. 51.
14 On the varieties of Social Darwinism, see Greta Jones, *Social Darwinism and English Thought: the Interaction Between Biological and Social Theory*, Sussex: Harvester, 1980.
15 See D. J. Ford, 'W. H. Mallock and socialism in England, 1880–1918', in Brown (ed.), *Essays in Anti-Labour History*, op. cit., pp. 317–42; Albert V. Tucker, 'W. H. Mallock and late Victorian conservatism', *University of Toronto Quarterly*, Vol. XXXI, 1962, pp. 223–41.
16 W. H. Mallock, *The New Republic: or Culture, Faith, and Philosophy in an English Country House*, London: Chatto & Windus, 1900, pp. 35–7, 246–7.
17 W. H. Mallock, 'The radicalism of the market-place', *National Review*, Vol. I, 1883, p. 529.
18 W. H. Mallock, 'A missing science', *Contemporary Review*, Vol. XL, 1881, pp. 934–58.
19 W. H. Mallock, *The Limits of Pure Democracy*, London: Chapman & Hall, 1918, p. 392.
20 W. H. Mallock, *Memoirs of Life and Literature*, London: Chapman & Hall, 1920, p. 195.
21 W. H. Mallock, 'Mr. Herbert Spencer in self-defence', *Nineteenth Century*, Vol. XLIV, 1898, p. 315.
22 Mallock, *Memoirs of Life and Literature*, op. cit., pp. 197–8; Herbert Spencer, 'What is social evolution?', *Nineteenth Century*, Vol. XLIV, 1898, pp. 348–58.
23 See Bernard Semmel, *Imperialism and Social Reform: English Social-Imperial Thought 1895–1914*, London: George Allen & Unwin, 1960, ch. II.
24 J. St Loe Strachey, *Problems and Perils of Socialism: Letters to a Working Man*, London: Macmillan, 1908, p. 20.
25 John St Loe Strachey, *The Adventure of Living: a Subjective Autobiography*, London: Hodder & Stoughton, 1922, p. 450.
26 Herbert G. Williams, *Why I am not a Socialist*, London: The Anti-Socialist & Anti-Communist Union, 1930, pp. 63, 75.
27 Dorothy Crisp, *The Rebirth of Conservatism*, London: Methuen, 1931, pp. 8, 81, 83. She later became chairwoman of the Housewives League, launched in 1947 to resist, not only the welfare policies of the Labour government, but creeping socialism within the Conservative Party. Miss Crisp, according to contemporary accounts, intended 'to form her own political party and become Britain's first woman Prime Minister'. Cited in Beatrix Campbell, *Iron Ladies: Why do Women Vote Tory?*, London: Virago, 1987, p. 80.
28 J. M. Keynes, 'Liberalism and industry', in Robert Eccleshall, *British*

Liberalism: Liberal Thought from the 1640s to the 1980s, London: Longman, 1986, pp. 217–20.

29 Ernest Benn, *Happier Days: Recollections and Reflections*, London: Ernest Benn, 1949, pp. 8–9.

30 Deryck Abel, *Ernest Benn: Counsel for Liberty*, London: Ernest Benn, 1960, pp. 43–5.

31 Ernest J. P. Benn, *The Return to Laisser-Faire: the Case for Individualism*, London: Ernest Benn, 1928, p. 16.

32 John Benn, 'Foreword' to Abel, *Ernest Benn*, op.cit., p. 8.

33 Benn, *The Return to Laisser-Faire*, op. cit., p. 76.

34 Ernest J. P. Benn, *Debt (Private and Public, Good and Bad)*, London: Ernest Benn, 1938, p. 147.

35 Benn, *The Return to Laisser-Faire*, op. cit., pp. 10–11.

36 Ernest J. P. Benn, *Benn's Protest: being an argument for the Restoration of our Liberties*, London: Right Book Club, 1945, p. 9.

37 Ernest J. P. Benn, *The State the Enemy*, London: Ernest Benn, 1953, p. 9.

1. Alexander Hugh Bruce, sixth Baron Balfour of Burleigh (1849–1921)

'Presidential Address to the British Constitution Association at the Whitehall Rooms, February 12, 1908.' In *Political Socialism: a Remonstrance. A Collection of Papers by Members of the British Constitution Association, with Presidential Addresses by Lord Balfour of Burleigh and Lord Hugh Cecil*, Mark H. Judge (ed.), Westminster: P. S. King, 1908, pp. 1–3, 5, 7, 14–15, 30–2.

Born at Kennet, Clackmannanshire, Bruce was educated at Loretto School in Edinburgh, then at Eton and Oriel College, Oxford, where he graduated with a second in law and history. Balfour succeeded to the barony in 1869 – the title having been revived after a long lapse – and seven years later became a representative peer for Scotland, remaining in the Lords in that capacity until his death. An active member of the Church of Scotland, he played a leading role in resisting its disestablishment and later in working for the union of the Scottish Presbyterian Churches. His *An Historical Account of the Rise and Development of Presbyterianism in Scotland* was published in 1911.

Balfour chaired numerous commissions during his parliamentary career. He was Parliamentary Secretary to the Board of Trade from 1889 to 1892, and Secretary of State for Scotland from 1895 until resigning in September 1903 over the issue of tariff reform. In 1905, the year he became a vice-president of the Unionist Free Trade Club, Balfour wrote:

> If Mr Chamberlain was really loyal he would lie low too, but it is clear that he means to push everyone out if he can who does not agree with him, and I for one am not going to take it lying down. I value the Conservative party as much as anyone, but I object to seeing it tied to a policy which I think absolutely disastrous to every interest in the Empire. I would far sooner see it smashed into fragments than see it committed to taxation of staff articles of food for the sake of preference.

Balfour was pushed out the following year, in so far as the Chamberlainites expelled him from the Constitutional Club for supporting the free-trade candidate in Chelsea against the sitting tariff reformer. During the next few years the British Constitution Association, which survived until 1918, was the focus of several abortive attempts to form a new centre party of Unionist free-traders and of Liberals unsympathetic to Lloyd George's radicalism.

> The watch-words of our Association are personal liberty and personal responsibility. Its object is to increase liberty and to inculcate responsibility, and as we believe that self-help is the mainstay of national character, we desire to maintain the freedom of the individual, which freedom ought to be limited only in so far as is necessary for the enjoyment of equal freedom by others.
>
> We resist the usurpation of power by government, or the subjection, either of the individual or of the minority, to coercion on the part of the majority of the community. We believe that the only safe path of progress lies in the continued advance of that freedom, and in the ever-increasing emancipation of the individual from interference by the community in the management of his personal affairs . . .
>
> The justification of our Association is that at the present time there appears to be a danger that both parties, though one in a greater degree than the other, are losing sight of what has been our chief glory in the past, namely, that without abating our national strength and unity, we have been able to secure that ever-broadening liberty for the individual which we so earnestly desire to preserve . . .
>
> We think that the spread of ideas of a socialist type threatens to destroy the moral fibre of our people, and that if these ideas are allowed to grow and develop the result must be the destruction of the ideals alike of self-help and of personal liberty . . .

We describe as 'Political Socialism' all legislation in the interest of one special class, namely, those that are least efficient. Our desire is to advocate the maximum of individual liberty; it is, therefore, totally removed from anarchy, which is that state of affairs in which the freedom of the individual as to his life and his property would be at the mercy of those who desire to interfere with them . . .

We advocate the maximum of individual liberty in order to render as easy as possible the normal course of social evolution. We do not deny the evils which exist in the present state of society; but we do affirm not only that Socialism is not the remedy for them, but that if ever carried out in practice it would make the position of the average individual many times worse than it is at present.

Socialists seem to forget that society is composed of individuals, and that so long as the characters of individuals are imperfect it will be impossible to have a state of society which is devoid of evils. It is easy enough to see now where difficulties exist, but it is utterly unscientific to think that an ideal state can be devised so long as the characters of those who will have to form it remain imperfect as is now the case. We advocate individual freedom because of its encouragement to the efficient, and because it alone can prevent them from being unduly burdened for the benefit of those less capable. It may be a hard doctrine, but we do say that for the State to follow any other principle must lead to disaster . . .

Socialists say that poverty is the main evil they wish to eradicate, but the thing is impossible. There exist among the people many who are excellent in character, in thrift, and in every virtue, but there are some who are bad, who are idle, it may be immoral, and who, at any rate, will not work. Now these must be and ought to be poor. If poverty is to be prevented by the government – an impossibility, of course, but take it for the moment as a hypothesis – if no one was allowed to become extremely poor, it is quite clear that many people will do no work at all. A large number of persons, including all the worthless of the nation, would not work at all if they were to be relieved from the fear of hunger, and if they did not work, the community as a whole would become so poor that it would be impossible to continue the system of subsidising the poorest and those whose claims are at present acknowledged. There would be nothing to give them. It follows therefore that if poverty were, as suggested, to be abolished, the incentive to work is abolished. The amount of work done would be greatly diminished, and the whole nation would be rapidly reduced to penury . . .

The State is to the Socialist a mother on whose lap the idle and the lazy are to fall, pour out their tears, and be pauperised by gifts until their cries are stilled . . .

How do you hope to get good work out of men for the sake of a mysterious abstraction called the State, who will not work for themselves? Will men work for the collective benefit who will not work for their own? The question carries its own answer. Does it not stand to reason that if men who strive are to get no more personal advantage than those who do not, it would not only appear but would be, absurd to strive at all?

Personal advantage is really the sole motive power to the immense majority, and so it will remain. To give alike to the efficient and the non-efficient, to the idle and to the industrious, is nothing but the perennial endowment of sloth.

If a man is not to enjoy what he earns, if he is to stand by and see another man who has not earned enjoy equally with himself, why should he not cease to earn also? If it is just that the non-efficient is to be made equal with the efficient, it also is just that he should do as little.

Socialism appeals to those elements in human character that make for inefficiency and for decay. The legitimate aspiration of every man worthy of the name is to improve his circumstances: he does this by putting forth his best efforts. It does not matter whether his form of energy lies in his brains or in his capacity for manual skill. But the fact that he is encouraged to put forth his best efforts is the root of progress for himself and of wealth for the community.

If you disallow him the legitimate fruits of his toil you cut off is ambition, his enterprise, and his zeal. While, if this is the result to the individual, the result to the community is that the quality of labour is lessened and probably destroyed. Once carry the demands that are made to their logical conclusion, and there will remain no stimulus to industry, no incentive to progress, and no reserve of power.

2. William Hurrell Mallock (1849–1923)

Aristocracy and Evolution: a Study of the Rights, the Origin, and the Social Functions of the Wealthier Classes, London: Adam & Charles Black, 1898, pp. v, 130–2, 144, 149–50, 160–1, 372, 379–80

Mallock, a flamboyant bachelor, was a free-lance writer who, when not resident in London, divided his time between continental Europe and British country houses. Eldest son of the rector of Cheriton Bishop in Devon, he was educated privately and at Balliol College, Oxford, winning the Newdigate prize for poetry and graduating in 1874 with a second in classics. Benjamin Jowett, Balliol's famous Master, regarded the undergraduate Mallock as a dilettante. He, in turn, was affronted by the Master's liberal Anglicanism, and in *The New Republic*, begun at Oxford, he satirized a fictional Jowett, and other guests at a weekend house-party, for abandoning religious orthodoxy. The book's publication in 1877 established Mallock's literary reputation; Disraeli, for instance, writing to Lady Dorothy Nevill, predicted that its author would 'take an eminent position in our future literature'. Henry James, by contrast, found the new celebrity 'a most disagreeable and unsympathetic youth, with natural bad manners increased by the odious London affectation of none. He strikes me as "awfully clever"; but I opine that he will produce no other spontaneous or fruitful thing.' Mallock pursued the theme of *The New Republic* in two further novels: *The New Paul and Virginia, or Positivism on an Island* (1878) and *A Romance of the Nineteenth Century* (1881), as well as in two philosophical books which subjected religious belief to scientific analysis, *Is Life Worth Living?* (1879) and *Atheism and the Value of Life* (1884). Among other novels was *The Old Order Changes*, published in 1886, which Mallock later disowned for its undue sympathy with the ideals of benevolent paternalism.

By now he had determined to expose the fallacies of radicalism, and in 1882 he published *Social Equality, or a Study in a Missing Science*. The following year he resigned as Conservative candidate for St Andrews, having decided the important task was 'that of providing facts and principles for politicians, rather than playing directly the part of a politician myself'. Among the many books in which he subsequently elaborated his scientific vindication of capitalilsm were *Labour and the Popular Welfare* (1893) and *Classes and Masses, or Wealth, Wages and Welfare in the United Kingdom* (1896), both of which were used by the Conservative Central Office as textbooks for speakers. Mallock was a publicist for the Liberty and Property Defence League, and later helped to found a School of Anti-Socialist Economics. He was also involved in the Anti-Socialist Union which in 1908 issued a popular edition of his *A Critical Examination of Socialism*, a collection of lectures given on a tour of the United States.

The thesis of *Aristocracy and Evolution*, wrote Mallock in his *Memoirs of Life and Literature*,

> was similar to that of *Social Equality*, and of *Labour and the Popular Welfare* – namely, that in proportion as societies progress in civilisation and wealth, all appreciable progress, and the sustentation of most of the results achieved by it, depend more and more on the directive ability of the few; and this thesis was affiliated to the main conclusions of evolutionary science generally . . . Looking back on *Aristocracy and Evolution*, I now think that . . . I should modify, not its argument, but the manner in which this argument was presented. Much of its substance I have incorporated in what I have written since; but, as it stood when I finished it, I felt it so far satisfactory that it expressed all I had then to say as to the subjects of which it treated, and my house of political thought was for the time empty, swept and garnished.

The word *aristocracy* as used in the title of this volume has no exclusive, and indeed no special reference to a class distinguished by hereditary political privileges, by titles, or by heraldic pedigree. It here means the exceptionally gifted and efficient minority, no matter what the position in which its members may have been born, or what the sphere of social progress in which their exceptional efficiency shows itself. I have chosen the word *aristocracy* in preference to the word *oligarchy* because it means not only the rule of the few but of the best or the most efficient of the few . . .

[T]he *great man*, as here understood, does not in any way correspond with the *fittest man* in the Darwinian struggle for existence. The fittest man in the Darwinian sense merely promotes progress by the physiological process of reproducing his slight superiorities in his children, and thus raising in the slow course of ages the general level of capacity throughout subsequent generations of his race. The great man, on the contrary, promotes progress, not because he raises the capacity of the generations that come after him, but because he rises individually above the general level of his own. This, however, is only one of the differences by which the great man is distinguished from the fittest. There are two others, of which the first that we must consider is as follows.

The fittest man, or the survivor in the Darwinian struggle for existence, is, so far as his own contemporaries are concerned, greater than his inferiors only in respect of what he accomplishes for himself, or for those immediately dependent on him. He is the man who lives and thrives whilst others die or languish, because whilst they can secure for themselves but little of what is requisite for life and health, he, by his superior gifts, is able to secure much. '*Families*', says Mr Spencer, '*whom the increasing difficulty of obtaining a living does not stimulate to improvement in production are on the high road to extinction, and must ultimately be supplanted by those whom the difficulty does so stimulate.*' That is to say, Mr Spencer, and all our modern sociologists with him, conceive of the fittest as a man, or a man and his family, who fight for their food in isolation, like a lion and lioness with their cubs, and who affect their contemporaries only by being better fed than they, or as a race-horse affects its competitors only by being first at the winning post.

But the great man, as an agent of progress, shows his greatness in a way precisely opposite to that in which the fittest man shows his fitness. This it is that our contemporary sociologists all fail to perceive, and endless error is the consequence. The great man, unlike the strongest lion, promotes progress by increasing the food-supply not of himself, but of others; or if he increase his own, as he no doubt generally does, he does so only by showing others how to increase theirs. He is like a lion who should be better fed than the rest of the lions in his region, not because he took a carcase from them for which they all were fighting, but because he showed them how to find others which they never would have found unaided, and took for himself in payment a small portion of each. The great man, in fact, as an agent of social progress, is great not in virtue of any completed results which he produces directly, by the action of his own hands or brains, or which he exhibits in his own person, but in virtue of the completed results which, by some simultaneous influence which he exercises over the brains or hands of others, he enables others to exhibit in themselves, or produce or do in the form of products or social services . . .

We are now coming to a third point, which is, for practical purposes, even more important than the preceding . . .

[T]he struggle which produces economic progress – and progress of every kind is produced in the same way – is not a general struggle which pervades the community as a whole; neither is it a struggle between the majority and an exceptionally able minority, in which both classes are struggling for what only one can win, and in which the gain of the one involves the loss of the other; but it is a struggle which is confined to the members of the minority alone, and in which the majority play no part as antagonists whatsoever. It is not a struggle amongst the community generally to live, but a struggle amongst a small section of the community to lead, to direct, to employ, the majority in the best way; and this struggle is an agent of progress because it tends to result, not in the survival of the fittest man, but in the domination of the greatest man . . .

Karl Marx conceives of the capitalists as a body of men who, so far as production is concerned, are absolutely inert and passive. Owing to a variety of causes, he says, during the past four hundred years all the means of production have come under their control, and access can be had to them only, as it were, through gates, of which these tyrants hold the key. Outside are the manual labourers, who are the sole producers of wealth, but who, without the means of production, naturally can produce nothing – not even enough to live on; and the sole economic function which the capitalist fulfils is to let the labourers in every day through the gates, on the condition that every evening the unhappy men render up to him the whole produce of their labours, except that insignificant fraction of it which is just necessary to fit them for the labours of the day following. Now it is no doubt theoretically possible that a society might exist, composed of a mass of undifferentiated and undirected manual labourers on the one hand, and on the other of a few passive monopolists who extracted from them most of what they produced, as the price of allowing them the opportunity of producing anything; but it is perfectly certain that a society of this kind would exhibit none of the increasing productive power which, as even Marx and his school admit, is one of the most distinctive features of industry under the capitalistic wage-system. Under that system productive power has increased, not because capital has enabled a few men to remain idle, but because it has enabled a few men to apply, with the most constant and intense effort their intellectual faculties to industry in its minutest details. It has increased not because the monopoly of capital has enabled the few to say to the many, 'We will allow you to work at nothing, unless you give us most of what you produce', but because it has enabled them to say to the many, 'We will allow you to work at nothing, unless you will consent to work in the ways that we indicate to you . . .'

> [T]he inequalities which socialists regard as accidental are the natural result of the inequalities of human nature, and constitute also the sole social conditions under which men's unequal faculties can co-operate towards a common end . . .
>
> The human race progresses because and when the strongest human powers and the highest human faculties lead it; such powers and faculties are embodied in and monopolised by a minority of exceptional men; these men enable the majority to progress, only on condition that the majority submit themselves to their control; and if all the ruling classes of to-day could be disposed of in a single massacre, and nobody left but those who at present call themselves the workers, these workers would be as helpless as a flock of shepherdless sheep, until out of themselves a new minority had been evolved, to whose order the majority would have to submit themselves, precisely as they submit themselves to the orders of the ruling classes now, and whose rule, like the rule of all new masters, would be harder, and more arbitrary, and less humane than the rule of the old.

3. Sir Ernest John Pickstone Benn, second baronet (1875–1954)

The State the Enemy, London: Ernest Benn, 1953, pp. 13, 17–18, 23–9, 59

Sir John Benn, Ernest's father, was chairman of the London County Council, leader of the Progressive Party, and until 1910 a Liberal MP. His younger son, William Wedgwood, was also a Liberal Member of Parliament but eventually changed party allegiance, becoming a Labour minister and entering the Lords in 1942 as Viscount Stansgate. The two bothers were educated in Paris and at the Central Foundation School in Finsbury, London, and in 1891 Ernest joined the family firm which had been established eleven years earlier to publish *The Cabinet Maker*. Having quickly taken control of the business he gradually acquired other trade journals, and in 1923 launched the separate book-publishing company of Ernest Benn Ltd. In 1927 he founded the Boys' Hostels Association to provide residential clubs for homeless boys in London. He became President of the National Advertising Benevolent Society, the Readers' Pensions Committee, and the Advertising Association, and for fifteen years was chairman of the United Kingdom Provident Institution for Life Assurance.

Benn's experience as a temporary civil servant at the Ministries of Munitions and Reconstruction during the First World War – the period when his first three books, *Trade as a Science* (1916), *The Trade of Tomorrow* (1917) and *Trade Parliaments and their Work* (1918) were published – persuaded him that Britain's economic performance could be improved through a system of statutory trade councils supervised by a minister of commerce. He was also involved in implementing the recommendations of the Whitley Report to improve relations between capital and labour, but became impatient with Whitehall bureaucracy and by the early 1920s believed that government should refrain from meddling with industry. The opening of the Individualist Bookshop, a focus of regular lectures and meetings, marked the beginning of his career as a campaigner for unfettered economic competition. During the months preceding the general election of 1931 Benn led the Friends of Economy, which arranged demonstrations and distributed leaflets protesting against excessive public expenditure, and two years later he launched and edited a short-lived libertarian weekly newspaper, *The Independent*.

Although Benn was invited to become the Conservative candidate for East Surrey in 1935 (the plan came to nothing because the motion for his candidature was technically invalid) he preferred to conduct his crusade for individualism without the restrictions of party discipline. His most sustained offensive against big government began in 1941 with a series of articles and pamphlets complaining about wartime bureaucracy. The following year he helped to draft a 'Manifesto on British Liberty', advocating reduction of the state to a minimum to prevent 'the country's lapsing into one or other of the forms of totalitarian government', and in January 1943 was elected president of the Society of Individualists at an inaugural meeting attended by industrialists like Lord Leverhulme. Within two years the society amalgamated with the National League for Freedom, an anti-state organization supported by many Conservative back-benchers.

Writing in *The Economist* under the headline 'All out of step but Johnny', a reviewer of *The State the Enemy* claimed that 'Sir Ernest embodies the *reductio ad absurdum* of nineteenth-century capitalism'. No one, the reviewer continued,

> can approach the radiance of his simple faith that the boundaries of the state's competence were laid down once and for all by Herbert Spencer; that the hidden hand is the only trustworthy and indeed tolerable regulator of economic affairs; that

a moral and intellectual blackout automatically descends on any individual taking service under public authority; and that all the troubles besetting Great Britain today can be ascribed not to two devastating wars, not to the machinations of that same hidden hand which determines, in despite of governments, the terms of trade, but solely and exclusively to the welfare state.

To the Individualist the State is the enemy. Herbert Spencer put the whole matter into five words in the title of his book *The Man Versus the State*. Talk of the people, the country, or the nation stirs the emotions, but the word State has a hard steely ruthless suggestion, and the notion of a State with a soul or a heart does not occur because it cannot exist.

We are so much involved in detail, which for the most part is no proper concern of the State, that we are reduced to almost total inability to see the wood for the trees. The individual citizen is lost in a jungle of benefits, doles, subsidies and pensions from which he can do no other than grab what he can; and of rules, restraints and charges from which he strives to escape. He is no longer governed by the natural laws of political economy but is reduced to scheming to secure from the common pool more than he puts into it . . .

Every strengthening of the State machine means a weakening of the individual, but every improvement in the individual means a strengthening of the nation. We were at our strongest when we put the onus on the man and are now weak because the initiative has passed to the dead hand of the State . . .

The social conscience, or more correctly the social heart, has come to regard the survival of the fittest as a barbarian conception, and applied itself with great vigour to the removal of the natural hardship implied in the Darwinian theory. The revolution in thought, or more correctly sentiment, has gone the full circle until there are large and growing categories in which it is a positive material advantage to be unfit.

'Each according to his worth' was the basis of Victorian economics, resulting in a general endeavour to be worth while. The substitution of the idea of 'each according to his needs', encourages the cultivation of needs without the corresponding obligation to make provision for them . . .

The State is not content with the pretence of provision for the needy, but having no soul of its own has arrogated to itself the power and will to reform the moral character of the delinquent and even of the criminal. This final arrogance has already exposed its own emptiness. The figures are conclusive and disastrous; they show that the function of the State is to punish, and that reformation and reform are matters for the voluntary principle only to be found in human movements, missions, love of one's fellow man – spiritual things which cannot thrive when mechanised by the State.

Most of us used to think of crime as something with which we were not personally concerned, and were content to leave its suppression in the competent hands of the police. In 1910, before the People's Budget, one in every 3,000 of us was convicted of an indictable offence and the other 2,999 were justified in taking no more than an academic interest in the matter; but today one in every ninety is entered in the criminal calendar for having committed a breach of the law, and our traditional respect for law and order has suffered a serious and obvious deterioration . . .

In 1910, before '*Laisser Faire*', 'The Law of the Jungle', 'The Devil take the hindmost', and all the other supposed evils of Individualism were removed by the politicians, the population numbered 36,000,000, but the convictions for crime of all kinds diminished to the lowest figure on record and only 12,000, or one in every 3,000, suffered the indignity of fine or punishment . . .

The working of the Welfare State is perhaps seen in its most striking form when through the machinery of the Children's Court the black sheep of the family can enjoy, in some public institution, living conditions far better than those available to his law-abiding brothers and sisters. It is almost true to say that there is no need for personal character or individual conscience in the Welfare State, but on the contrary in many respects honesty is a positive handicap.

This unpleasant state of affairs is in the very nature of things. A big central pool, containing half the national income, is surrounded by 50,000,000 people striving to establish claims upon it and at the same time searching for excuses to relieve them of the need to contribute to it. To describe us as a nation of dole-drawers and tax dodgers is merely to face the horrid facts. From the moment of its birth the infant is a source of more pressure for orange juice and allowances, although the parent may be declining to work overtime because it will increase the tax upon his income. The wealthiest cannot escape the receipt of a dole – by way of subsidy on his food, and is in duty bound to arrange his affairs in such a way as to attract no taxation that can legally be avoided. Looked at in this way the Welfare State is in a hopeless position; it may be compared to a bank with no willing depositors and every customer anxious for an overdraft. Nothing lower than a nation of angels could make a success of a society with such a constitution; perhaps the best that can be said of us is that we have become a nation of escapists, and escapism does not make for morality or strength of character.

The argument is supported by the distressing story of divorce and illegitimacy, disclosing a very rapid and remarkable change in general attitude of mind . . .

It is difficult, perhaps impossible, to establish by argument any direct connection between the serious change of mind towards moral laxity and the silver-spooning of a Welfare State, but few will fail to feel that the two things have a definite relationship one to the other.

The State is a mechanical apparatus not to be confused with a nation or society; it is of necessity a calculating machine, a thing of forms and figures. It can be used by a nation but cannot supply the pride, patriotism and urge to help oneself and others by personal endeavour; on the contrary, it must act as a deterrent to these old-fashioned characteristics . . .

The encouragement of the unfit in human material has its corollary in the loss of fitness in things in general. A sheet or a blanket or a carpet is no longer expected to have the wear, or give the satisfaction, previously required. Butter is merely butter and such interest as was found in personal preference among the several varieties has simply vanished from the list of finishing touches once regarded as evidence of advancing civilisation . . .

Does the Man keep the State or can the State keep the Man? All Victorian parties accepted the first solution and rejected the second absolutely; all twentieth century parties have denied or doubted the first, and all, in varying degrees, have accepted the second. At the start it was thought that the State could keep the Man out of the surplus of the landlords and the wealth-possessing classes, but as that surplus has been gradually collected and exhausted it is now widely believed that the good work can be continued out of the resources of the State itself. The old conception of the State as a proud liability on the self-supporting individual has given way to the absurd supposition that by planning and control the State is able to relieve the citizen of his responsibilities.

6 *A middle way 1924–64*

Harold Macmillan, writing in the 1960s, recorded how, in the aftermath of the General Strike, he and other dissident Conservatives attempted to formulate an alternative programme to socialism that discarded 'the old Liberal *laissez-faire* concepts' which had been absorbed into his own party:

> Some coherent system, lying in between unadulterated private enterprise and collectivism. It was a policy which I afterwards called 'The Middle Way'; an industrial structure with the broad strategic control in the hands of the State and the tactical operation in the hands of private management, with public and private ownership operating side by side . . . After a lapse of forty years, it appears that what then seemed so visionary has now become commonplace and generally accepted. The tide has indeed flowed on; and although we are still struggling with the problems of what is now termed 'the mixed economy', all parties in the State have, in effect, accepted this concept as a necessary practical basis for a nation such as ours.[1]

Initially, *avant-garde* Conservatives such as Macmillan failed to convert their party to the ideal of a managed economy that would remedy the imperfections of unrestrained competition without stifling individual initiative in socialist bureaucracy. By the 1950s, however, most Conservatives were proclaiming the efficacy of an enlarged state which promoted prosperity and secured the welfare of the people. Not unnaturally they often portrayed their middle way as a continuation of the route taken by Disraeli and other Tory Democrats.

Tariff reformers were among those Conservatives in the 1920s who insisted that their party's doctrine was distinct from individualism and socialism.[2] As in the years preceding the First World War, however, Tory reformers tended to distinguish their arguments for a more interventionist state from the case for protectionism; this was partly because the latter remained a divisive issue, but also because they were not convinced that every economic problem would be resolved by the erection of tariff barriers. These progressive Conservatives were, in the main, young MPs who returned from the trenches imbued with a sense of social responsibility towards the men they had commanded, and who were persuaded by the wartime direction of industry that government could do much more to master economic forces. Exasperated by their party's postwar inertia, they often urged a Disraelian revival to inspire more constructive policies.[3] In Parliament they formed a small group, nicknamed the YMCA, led by Noel Skelton; in 1923 he wrote several articles for *The Spectator* in which he advocated industrial profit sharing and 'co-partnery' so as to defuse class hostilities by enabling the worker to acquire property and to participate in managerial decisions.[4] Skelton's influence was acknowledged in *Industry and the State*, written by Macmillan and three other members of the group in response to the Baldwin government's indifference to industrial relations after the collapse of the General Strike of 1926. The book, described by Macmillan as 'an unpretentious effort',[5] contained proposals not dissimilar to those of the more elaborate Liberal Yellow Book, published in the following year, which so outraged individualists such as Sir Ernest Benn. Included in its 'unauthorised programme' were schemes to improve the status and welfare of employees (the statutory provision of collective bargaining, and the extension of trade boards to fix the hours and conditions of work) and also to enhance economic performance through, for example, the compulsory merger of certain enterprises. Macmillan and his co-authors were clear that they were charting an unfamiliar political terrain lying somewhere 'between Marxian Socialism and complete "laissez-faire"'.[6]

Macmillan, who located himself in the paternalist tradition of Disraeli, Young England and Shaftesbury, now embarked upon a more solitary exploration of the landscape of the middle way.[7] He was initially preoccupied with the conditions of employment and on one occasion joined with Lord Henry Bentinck in urging government to implement an eight-hour working day. Then, as unemployment rose sharply because of economic recession, he set about devising an overall strategy to correct the disorders of the capitalist market. His proposals for economic planning, outlined in various articles and pamphlets in the early 1930s, were developed in a book, *Reconstruction*, which advocated the creation of National Councils for each industry to co-ordinate production and regulate prices. These bodies were to be supervised by a Central Economic Council with responsibility for stimulating demand through control of the flow of investment. Macmillan depicted his design for 'orderly capitalism' as a 'synthesis' of individualism and collectivism that would prevent the nation being engulfed by one of the fascist or communist dictatorships sweeping through much of the world.[8] Three years later, in *The General Theory of Employment, Interest, and Money*, the most influential economic treatise since Adam Smith's *The Wealth of Nations*, J. M. Keynes was to make the same political case for managed capitalism.

Macmillan next became involved in various inter-party ventures intended to build a broad alliance in favour of planning. In 1934 he was instrumental in establishing the Industrial Reorganisation League, consisting of businessmen, economists and MPs, which for two years publicized the need for economic reconstruction, and which also drafted an Enabling Bill to make statutory provision for voluntary schemes of industrial rationalization. The following year he was among fifteen MPs who published a little book, *Planning for Employment*, indicating the institutional mechanisms required to formulate and implement 'a national economic policy'. By now he was a member of the economic affairs committee of the Next Five Years Group, which side-stepped 'the old arguments between individualism and Socialism' to devise a programme for securing the country against the threat of totalitarianism.[9] The outcome was a book, signed by over a hundred public figures, proposing the creation of a Government Planning Committee and of an Economic General Staff to initiate and co-ordinate, for example, town and country planning, industrial reorganization, public investment in housing, transport and electrification, and a more adequate system of social services; the latter was 'to attack most vigorously the grosser inequalities which still divide our democracy into what a Conservative Prime Minister was the first to call "The Two Nations"'.[10] Macmillan fought the general election of 1935 on what he described as the 'little Left of Centre' manifesto of *The Next Five Years*.[11] Later he took virtual control of *New Outlook*, a monthly periodical launched by the Next Five Years Group in June 1936, and used its pages to popularize his views about planning.

For a brief period Macmillan flirted with the idea of a new centre party to rally progressive opinion. But he was now engaged in bringing together themes pursued since the beginning of the decade into a comprehensive argument for planned capitalism. The programme of *The Middle Way*, like that of the less sophisticated *Reconstruction*, was intended to strengthen democracy by removing the causes of economic dislocation and social discontent. Macmillan's recommendations fell into three broad categories: the reorganization of production through amalgamation of older enterprises, together with public ownership of certain essential industries such as coal; government direction of investment by means of a nationalized Bank of England and Keynesian fiscal policies; and the extension of social welfare to establish an irreducible minimum standard of life. The objective was a mixed economy in which there would be both central co-ordination and ample scope for private enterprise: a 'half-way house', as Macmillan put it, between the free market and state socialism.[1]

Between the wars Conservative governments introduced piecemeal economic and social reforms without embracing Macmillan's concept of managed capitalism. But during the Second World War the Churchill coalition quickly streamlined the economy by adopting many of the proposals previously advocated by the Conservative left: Keynesian fiscal techniques; town and country planning; industrial reorganization; mechanisms for involving the state, employers and trade unions in decisions about production; and a move towards industrial self-government through joint consultative committees for management and the labour force. The extension of government was due initially to the necessities of war, but by 1943 all parties were in varying degrees swept along by a mood of popular radicalism – a feeling that direction of the economy had been largely successful, coupled with a belief that further social reconstruction was required to elevate the condition of the people.[12]

Conservatives responded to this mood in Disraelian manner by claiming that they would promote the common welfare without uprooting established institutions, and could therefore be trusted to steer a steady course towards a brighter tomorrow. They meant, in effect, that an enlarged state was acceptable if it entailed neither the crushing of private enterprise nor too much redistribution of wealth. 'Perhaps one man in every ten will have the capacity for leadership, or the enterprise to back his own ability with his savings', wrote David Stelling with a wartime readership in mind. 'The other nine will be the workers in the hive. Democracy needs its officers and N.C.O.s no less in civil life than in the military field, and as a good Tory Democrat, I set my face firmly against the idea of equality which is sometimes mistaken for sound democratic doctrine.' Many Conservatives – with the exception, of course, of individualists such as Sir Ernest Benn – did not object to helping secure what Stelling termed 'the orderly development of political and economic conditions', so long as their party did not succumb to fashionable egalitarian notions.[13]

Yet some MPs who claimed a Disraelian pedigree – many of them recently demobilized – felt that their parliamentary colleagues were lagging behind the public mood, and so formed themselves into an 'advance guard' to revitalize the Conservative Party and extend the progressive legislation of the wartime coalition.[14] They first clashed with the recalcitrant section of the party in January 1943 on the provisions of a Bill to establish a minimum wage and improved conditions in the catering industry. The following month 41 Conservative MPs signed an amendment urging the formation of a Ministry of Social Security to implement the proposals of the Beveridge Report for a comprehensive system of social insurance whereby, in return for flat-rate contributions, everyone would be entitled to receive benefits during sickness, unemployment and old age.[15] The Tory Reform Committee was now formally inaugurated and met weekly to agree a common approach to the business of the Commons. In addition, specialist sub-committees were formed to draft policy on a range of issues. Among the many publications of the Reform Committee during the next couple of years were bulletins and pamphlets on workmen's compensation, land utilization, coal, aviation, agriculture, housing, war pensions, and education, as well as two booklets – *Forward – by the Right!* (1943) and *Tools for the Next Job* (1945) – containing a programme of postwar reconstruction.[16]

The committee continued the exploration of the middle way, though its publications usually cited Keynes rather than the dissident Conservatives of the pre-war years. Government was to plan for full employment and the elimination of class conflict through control of investment, extension of public ownership, industrial co-partnership, a statutory minimum wage in industries such as coal, and improvements in education, housing and social welfare. In endorsing managed capitalism, members of the committee consigned the laws of political economy to the dustbin of history, declaring that 'to follow Adam Smith in the age of Keynes is like adhering to the Ptolemaic astronomy after Copernicus'.[17] Ideological disputes between free-marketeers and socialists were declared obsolete, the problem now being to find the precise mix of state intervention and private enterprise that would stimulate economic growth without curbing individual ambition. Like Tory Democrats earlier in the century the reformers believed that social progress was threatened by those financiers and industrialists who had strayed from the Liberal Party 'into the fold of Conservatism', as the first chairman of the committee put it, bringing with them the kind of 'obnoxious policies' favoured by 'Sir Ernest Benn and the "Individualist Press"'.[18] Besides castigating individualists for opposing economic planning, progressive Conservatives repudiated the concept of a self-help society in which 'the whip-lash of economic necessity is the only incentive to effort, and the chimera of Want the only spur to enterprise'.[19] Idleness and inefficiency were the consequence rather than the cause of poverty, in their view, which meant that the condition of the people could be elevated by a programme of social reform but never through a process of natural selection.

The Tory reformers located themselves in the paternalist tradition stretching back through 'F. E. Smith's Conservative Social Reform Committee' to Chamberlain, Randolph Churchill, Young England, Shaftesbury and Sadler.[20] Government planning and adequate social welfare were portrayed as strategies to secure the ideal of One Nation, and, as might be anticipated, Disraeli was continually lauded as the architect of authentic Toryism. In 1943 Quintin Hogg, soon to succeed Viscount Hinchingbrooke as chairman of the committee, called for a Disraelian revival to heal class divisions and quell popular unrest. His speeches and articles for that year, collected into a single volume, constitute the most cogent expression of the ideas of the wartime reformers.[2]

The Tory Reform Committee, which survived until 1946, failed to equip conservatism for what Hogg called 'revolutionary times'. Its activities were opposed by right-wing MPs, who in November 1943 formed a clandestine counter-group, the Progress Trust,[21] and also by Conservatives in the wartime coalition who were dismayed by the irresponsibility of the reformers. In March 1944 members of the committee helped to defeat the government when, joining with Labour back-benchers on the second reading of the Education Bill, they supported an amendment providing equal pay for men and women teachers. Irritated by what R. A. Butler, the minister responsible for the Bill, described as the 'jubilant and overweening attitude' of the rebels,[22] the government ensured that the amendment was rejected the next day by making it a vote of confidence. The party as a whole was less eager than the committee to keep pace with the mood of popular radicalism, even though a Post-War Problems Committee chaired by Butler had been in existence since 1941, and the general election manifesto of 1945 contained a programme of social reconstruction. Yet during the election campaign many Conservatives, taking their cue from Churchill, denounced planned capitalism as a leap towards totalitarian socialism.

The party was jolted from its complacency by the Labour landslide of 1945, and various 'think-tanks' were quickly created or revived to reformulate policy. So effective were these research bodies that within a short time most Conservatives were happily striding along the middle way. Butler, who was immersed in this process of doctrinal readjustment, played a central role in transforming the radicalism of the Conservative left into party orthodoxy. After the election defeat Hogg wrote to him urging the need for a new Tamworth Manifesto. Butler, agreeing that Conservatives must demonstrate their readiness to accommodate to a 'social revolution', was untroubled by the charge of individualists like Sir Herbert Williams that he was a 'pink' socialist:

> I had derived from Bolingbroke an assurance that the majesty of the State might be used in the interests of the many, from Burke a belief in seeking patterns of improvement by balancing diverse interests, and from Disraeli an insistence that the two nations must become one. If my brand of Conservatism was unorthodox, I was committing heresy in remarkably good company. In fact, Conservative principles adapted to the needs of the post-war world meant that we should aim for a 'humanized capitalism'.[23]

The party got its Tamworth Manifesto endorsing 'humanized capitalism' in the form of an *Industrial Charter*, which emerged from an Industrial Policy Committee established in 1946 with Butler as chairman. Macmillan was a member of the committee and a leading influence in its deliberations. Indeed, the *Charter* reads like an abridged version of *The Middle Way*, with an emphasis on 'central direction' of the economy to secure full employment and comprehensive social security, allied with industrial co-partnership and other proposals for improving the pay and status of the labour force. The overwhelming support which the document received at the annual conference of 1947 signified that the party had at last come to terms with the Keynesian age.

The *Industrial Charter* was an effective piece of internal party propaganda because of the skill with which Keynesianism was recast in a Conservative mould: the language advocating an enlarged state was deliberately bland, yet there were sparkling passages defending individual initiative and entrepreneurial rewards; the regimentation and bureaucracy of a socialized economy were denounced, while the case was being made for nationalization of the Bank of England, coal and the railways; and the authors of the report, particularly Butler, stressed that Conservatives had favoured the efficient and benevolent use of state power since the time of the first factory legislation. In these ways the *Charter*'s policies were portrayed as a pragmatic alternative to socialism by which Conservatives could continue to safeguard the national interest. Numerous Tory publicists took up the theme. Occupying a non-dogmatic 'central position between the extremes of Manchester and Moscow',[24] they announced, the party now withstood the excesses of collectivism as vigorously as it had once resisted rapacious individualism. Everything depended upon preserving a balance between strategic co-ordination of the economy and the tactical operations of private enterprise:

> The crux of the matter is that Keynes recognised that economic forces need to be 'curbed and guided'. The Socialists, busy fighting yesterday's battles against *laissez-faire*, interpreted this as an argument for full state control. The Tories, on the other hand, understand that what is required is a synthesis between the two extremes so that to the *direction* provided by the State can be added the immense *motive* power of individual enterprise.[25]

Macmillan had said it all, of course, a decade earlier.

Similar policy statements followed the *Industrial Charter*, and with the manifesto for the general election of 1950 – *This is the Road*, which Butler was instrumental in drafting – the party became formally committed to maintaining full employment in a Welfare State. In 1951 Conservatives were returned to power, and for the next thirteen years presided over a period of economic expansion and consumer affluence. They did so by administering the system of 'humanized capitalism' largely installed by their Labour predecessors.[26] Butler succeeded the Labour Chancellor, Hugh Gaitskell, at the Treasury, and commentators invented the word 'Butskellism' to indicate that both men 'spoke the language of Keynesianism'. Yet they spoke it, as Butler noted, with different accents.[27] Conservatives continued to depict themselves as the guardians of individual freedom against the threat of collectivist uniformity. Whereas socialist egalitarianism led to cultural mediocrity and economic decline, it was their intention to preserve diversity and increase prosperity. While ensuring that everyone enjoyed a minimum standard of income, housing and education, they would not thwart ambition by confining individuals within a strait-jacket of universal provision. Only a society which gave talented people opportunity to rise above the average could produce enough wealth to sustain its weaker members. This was Butler's message to the National Summer School in 1954. In adopting 'A

Disraelian approach to modern politics', according to Butler, the Conservative Party was healing class divisions, 'not by levelling the few, but by elevating the many'.[3]

Seven years later he announced that the chasm which Disraeli perceived between the two nations had been bridged by the creation of an affluent and meritocratic society where the politics of class envy were irrelevant.[28] Quintin Hogg, who by now had succeeded his father as Viscount Hailsham, made the same point, arguing that economic prosperity and greater social justice 'have rendered obsolete the whole intellectual framework within which Socialist discussion used to be conducted'.[20] The prospect for the future depended upon the extent to which politicians turned their attention from the distribution of wealth, the obsession of socialists, to its production:

> We are not interested in levelling down, only in lifting up. In our belief the fundamental problem in Britain today comes not from any remaining inequalities of existing wealth, but from the risk that too little new wealth will be created in which all can share. It is, therefore, to the strengthening of incentive and reward, that statesmanship needs to turn its hand.[30]

Conservative trusteeship of managed capitalism had secured what Hailsham called 'the balanced society',[31] though others preferred alternative descriptions: 'one nation', 'the opportunity state', 'the responsible society', 'a property-owning democracy' and so forth. Macmillan, now Conservative Prime Minister, settled for the phrase he had coined twenty years earlier, though he too urged those who followed the middle way to be vigilant against assault from the left. A Labour government, however well-intentioned, would not succeed in transforming Britain 'into an egalitarian society without, as we have seen in Eastern Europe, a gigantic exercise in despotism'.[32] The Young Turks of earlier decades had become exponents of party orthodoxy.

Middle-way ideology survived the Conservative Party's defeat in the general election of 1964. In the late 1960s, however, the politics of managed capitalism came under attack from a growing number of Conservatives for whom Keynesianism was an interruption of the proper business of safeguarding the economy against state control. Eventually economic individualism became the party's official creed, and on their return to power in 1979 Conservatives embarked upon a triumphal mission to turn the collectivist tide.

NOTES

1 Harold Macmillan, *Winds of Change 1914–1939*, London: Macmillan, 1966, pp. 223–4.
2 E.g. L. S. Amery, *National and Imperial Economics*, Westminster: National Unionist Association, 1923.
3 E.g. L. H. Lang, 'The young Conservative', *National Review*, Vol. LXXXIII, 1924, pp. 73–4.
4 Noel Skelton, *Constructive Conservatism*, Edinburgh and London: William Blackwood, 1924.
5 Macmillan, *Winds of Change*, op. cit., p. 173.
6 Robert Boothby, Harold Macmillan, John De V. Loder and Oliver Stanley, *Industry and the State: a Conservative View*, London: Macmillan, 1927, p. 20.
7 An account of his political journey is given in Alan Booth and Melvyn Pack, *Employment, Capital and Economic Policy: Great Britain 1918–1939*, Oxford: Blackwell, 1985, ch. 3.
8 Harold Macmillan, *Reconstruction: a Plea for a National Policy*, London: Macmillan, 1933, pp. 22, 128.
9 Macmillan, *Winds of Change*, op. cit., p. 376.
10 Harold Macmillan, *The Next Five Years: an Essay in Political Agreement*, London: Macmillan, p. 178.
11 Macmillan, *Winds of Change*, op. cit., pp. 375, 426.
12 See Keith Middlemas, *Politics in Industrial Society: the experience of the British system since 1911*, London: André Deutsch, 1979, ch. 10.
13 David Stelling, *Why I am a Conservative*, London: Conservative Headquarters, 1943, pp. 8, 26. For a wartime account of conservatism based upon Disraeli's Crystal Palace speech of 1872, see Richard V. Jenner, *Will Conservatism Survive*?, London: Staples Press, 1944.
14 Olive Moore, 'Can the Tory reform?', *Persuasion*, Summer 1944, p. 20.
15 See Hugh Molson, 'The Beveridge Plan', *Nineteenth Century and After*, Vol. CXXXIII, 1943, pp. 22–30.
16 On the committee, see Hartmut Kopsch, *The Approach of the Conservative Party to Social Policy during World War II*, PhD thesis, London University, 1974, pp. 43–63. There is a succinct account of the committee's ethos and objectives in Thelma Cazalet-Keir's autobiography, *From the Wings*, London: Bodley Head 1967, pp. 142–3.

> 'When the so-called Beveridge Plan on the future of social insurance was produced in 1943, a number of Conservative backbenchers formed a Tory Reform Committee, of which I was a member, to encourage the Government to act on Sir William Beveridge's recommendations. A ginger group of this kind was not superfluous. It has been forgotten that the Beveridge Report

had not been received with undiluted enthusiasm by the Conservatives. When I invited Sir William to address a meeting of London Conservative women a fierce die-hard, Sir Herbert Williams, protested violently.

This attitude was contrary to that of the Tory Reform Committee which was quite determined not to return to the economic and social policies prevailing between the wars. There were about forty of us, and we gave our brand of Conservatism the blessed label 'progressive'. It was really not a misnomer. We worked hard on all the main measures produced by the Government; and we believed that a political party must model itself on biology, that is to say, if it is to remain alive and kicking it must adapt itself to the changes in a changing world. Dogmatic parties would die as surely as the dinosaur.'

17 Hugh Molson, 'The Tory Reform Committee', *New English Review*, Vol. XI, 1945, p. 250.

18 Viscount Hinchingbrooke, *Full Speed Ahead! Essays in Tory Reform*, London: Simpkin Marsall, 1944, pp. 20–1. See too Molson, 'The Tory Reform Committee', op. cit., p. 248; idem, 'Election issues', *Contemporary Review*, Vol. 168, 1945, pp. 4–6.

19 Hinchingbrooke, *Full Speed Ahead!*, op. cit., p. 31.

20 Molson, 'The Tory Reform Committee', op. cit., p. 245; Olive Moore, 'Can the Tory reform?' op. cit., p. 25; Viscount Hinchingbrooke, 'The course of Conservative politics', *Quarterly Review*, Vol. 284, 1946, p. 116.

21 Kopsch, *The Approach of the Conservative Party to Social Policy*, op. cit., pp. 70–2.

22 Lord Butler, *The Art of the Possible*, Harmondsworth: Penguin, 1973, p. 121.

23 ibid., pp. 135–7.

24 John Boyd-Carpenter, *The Conservative Case*, London: Wingate, 1950, p. 11.

25 Bernard Braine, *Tory Democracy*, London: Falcon Press, 1948, p. 115.

26 Postwar conservatism is dealt with by Andrew Gamble, *The Conservative Nation*, London: Routledge & Kegan Paul, 1974; and Nigel Harris, *Competition and the Corporate State: British Conservatives, the State and Industry 1945–1964*, London: Metheun, 1972.

27 Butler, *The Art of the Possible*, op. cit., pp. 162–3.

28 R. A. Butler, 'Trustees of posterity', in *Accents on Youth*, London: Conservative Political Centre, 1961, pp. 7–15.

29 Viscount Hailsham, 'Introduction' to *Prospect for Capitalism: Strength and Stress*, London: Conservative Political Centre, 1958, p. 8.

30 Viscount Hailsham, *Toryism and Tomorrow*, London: Conservative Political Centre, 1957, p. 17.

31 Viscount Hailsham, *National Excellence*, London: Conservative Political Centre, 1963.

32 Harold Macmillan, *The middle way: 20 years after*, London: Conservative Political Centre, 1958, p. 9.

1. Harold Macmillan, first Earl of Stockton (1894–1986)

The Middle Way: A Study of the Problem of Economic and Social Progress in a Free and Democratic Society, London: Macmillan, 1938, pp. 5–6, 102–3, 116, 185–6, 192

Daniel Macmillan, founder of the family publishing company, was a Christian Socialist: his grandson, Harold, when censuring the Conservative Party in the 1930s for clinging to *laissez-faire* principles, claimed that Toryism had always been a form of paternal socialism. Harold was educated at Eton and at Balliol College, Oxford, where he read as much as possible about his hero, Disraeli, and where the influence of a tutor confirmed his High Anglican convictions. His sense of *noblesse oblige* was reinforced by wartime experience – he became a captain in the Grenadier Guards after obtaining a first in moderations – and also by his marriage in 1920 to Lady Dorothy Cavendish, daughter of the Duke of Devonshire, whom he had met in the previous year on becoming ADC to the duke, the newly appointed Governor-General of Canada.

In 1924 Macmillan, now working for the family firm, became Member of Parliament for Stockton-on-Tees, having unsuccessfully contested the seat the previous year. Distressed by the effects of economic depression upon his constituency, he was increasingly frustrated with the Baldwin government's failure to reduce unemployment, and by 1929, the year he lost the seat, had established a reputation as a maverick. On regaining Stockton in 1931 he began the quest for a coherent policy that led to *The Middle Way*. By the time of its publication he was preoccupied with foreign affairs, being outraged by the willingness of Neville Chamberlain (who had succeeded Baldwin as Conservative Prime Minister in 1937) to appease Hitler: in 1938 Macmillan campaigned for an anti-appeasement independent, A. D. Lindsay, Master of his old College, against the Conservative candidate, Quintin Hogg, at an Oxford by-election; he also wrote a pamphlet, *The Price of Peace*, calling for rearmament and an alliance of Britain, France and Russia against the German menace.

At the outbreak of war Macmillan made speeches urging a co-ordinated economic policy, and from 1940, as Parliamentary Secretary at the Ministry of Supply in the National government, implemented some of his ideas about planning through the creation of Area Boards, representing government, industry and the trade unions, which were responsible to an Industrial Capacity Committee chaired by himself. In 1942 he became Under-Secretary of State for the Colonies, and a few months later was made Resident Minister in North Africa, where he achieved a reputation for diplomacy. At the end of the war he was appointed Secretary of State for Air in Churchill's brief caretaker administration. He lost Stockton in the Labour landslide of 1945, having fought the election on the platform of *The Middle Way*. But at a by-election shortly afterwards he won Bromley, North Kent, and retained the seat until his departure from the Commons in 1964.

Macmillan joined the shadow cabinet and in 1946 became a member of R. A. Butler's Industrial Policy Committee, whose report, the *Industrial Charter*, installed as official policy many of his long-cherished ideas about planning. One newspaper described the *Charter* as 'the second edition' of the *The Middle Way*, and Macmillan claimed that it belonged to 'the tradition of Disraeli'. From 1951 he was successively Minister of Housing – becoming a minor folk-hero because of his house-building programme – Minister of Defence, Foreign Secretary, and Chancellor of the Exchequer. On Anthony Eden's resignation in 1957 after the Suez crisis, he became Prime Minister, being unexpectedly preferred to Butler.

As premier, Macmillan secured a consumer boom through expansionist policies, telling the people that they had 'never had it so good', and enjoying the nickname 'Supermac'. Always an actor and dandy, like his hero, Disraeli, he now cultivated the image of a languid grandee. In the words of Anthony Sampson, one of his biographers, he 'presented a modernised "Tory democracy", with the same kind of panache as Disraeli or Lord Randolph Churchill, and the same confidence that the British people would prefer, in the end, the rule of patricians to plebs'. In 1959 he led the party to election victory on a manifesto, 'The next five years', bearing the same name as the group to which he had belonged in the 1930s. Macmillan, who resigned as Prime Minister in 1963 after a prostate operation, lived long enough to see the Conservative Party abandon the middle way. He remained a public figure, partly through his Chancellorship of Oxford University, to which he had been elected in 1960, and at the age of ninety accepted an earldom. In the Lords he made several elegant speeches critical of the Thatcher government, on one occasion likening its policy of denationalization to selling the family silver.

This book is offered as a contribution towards the clearer formulation of the new ideas of society that have been slowly emerging since the political crisis of 1931. I hope it will be given sympathetic consideration by men and women of all parties who recognise that some new theory of social evolution must be conceived if we are to retain our heritage of political, intellectual, and cultural freedom while, at the same time, opening up the way to higher standards of social welfare and economic security . . .

I want to argue, therefore, for the deliberate preservation of private enterprise in a field lying outside the range of minimum human needs. I support it for the purely economic reasons that it ensures initiative, the adoption of new methods, the exploration of the market possibilities of new products, and speculative experimentation with new scientific discoveries. But, more than that, I mean to submit that freedom of individual initiative and enterprise in these fields is essential to the preservation of liberty, to the freedom of each person to live his life in his own way, and to provide for that diversity which is characteristic of the human mind.

But I do not propose to employ this defence of private enterprise in the fields for which it is best suited in order to condone or excuse the poverty and insecurity in the basic necessities of life, which we have today as a legacy of unrestrained competition and uneconomic waste and redundancy. I shall advocate all the more passionately on grounds of morality, of social responsibility, as well as of economic wisdom, a wide extension of social enterprise and control in the sphere of minimum human needs. The satisfaction of those needs is a duty which society owes to its citizens. In carrying out that responsibility it should adopt the most economical methods of large-scale co-operative enterprise. The volume of the supply of these necessities, the prices at which they are sold, and the power of the consumer to buy them should not be left to the determination of the push and pull of competitive effort. We have to evolve a new system by which the supply of those articles which we have classified as being of common need and more or less standardised in character, would be absorbed into an amplified conception of the social services . . .

The argument in favour of planning is not . . . some new and unheard-of principle. It is merely an extension of that principle of interference and regulation which has been common to the political thought of England since the first Factory Act was passed. But, if we are to become masters of our fate instead of slaves of circumstance, the principle must now be extended, and applied to a much wider field, because this has become essential in the changed conditions of today . . .

For as far ahead as we can see, it is both possible and desirable to find a solution of our economic difficulties in a mixed system which combines State ownership, regulation or control of certain aspects of economic activity with the drive and initiative of private enterprise in those realms of origination and expansion for which it is, by general admission, so admirably suited.

I realise, of course, that it is contended both by Socialist Planners and by Anti-Planners that this mixed system – this half-way house between a Free Capitalism and complete State Socialist planning – is an impossibility. They unite in claiming that we must be whole-hoggers or nothing; that we must, as it were, either leap forward into the twenty-first century or retreat into the nineteenth. I profoundly disagree with that view. Britain has been moving along the road towards economic planning for many years now in accordance with the traditional English principles of compromise and adjustment. Unless we can continue this peaceful evolution from a free capitalism to a planned capitalism, or, it may be, a new synthesis of Capitalist and and Socialist theory, there will be little hope of preserving the civil, democratic, and cultural freedom which, limited as it may be at the moment by economic inefficiency, is a valuable heritage. It is only by the adoption of this middle course that we can avoid resorting to measures of political discipline and dictatorship. Such methods, whether exercised by the 'right' or by the 'left', are the very opposite of that liberation and freedom which mankind should be striving to achieve . . .

An adequate policy must therefore provide for –

(a) A form of industrial organisation which curbs unwise speculative over-expansion of any industry and assists by an intelligent system of market anticipation in guiding capital investment into the correct channels and in the correct proportions, to maintain a balance in the quantities of separate goods which, if stability is to be preserved, must exchange for one another.

(b) A method of ensuring that financial policy is conducted in such a way as to keep the factors of production at the highest possible degree of permanent employment.

(c) A method of insuring the consumer against a loss of purchasing power arising from unforeseen fluctuations, and which, by maintaining his standard of life at an irreducible minimum by means of social provisions, would check in its early stages any tendency towards depression that might still arise.

2. Quintin Mcgarel Hogg, Baron Hailsham of Saint Marylebone (1907 –)

One Year's Work, London: Hutchinson, 1944, pp. 43–4, 49, 80–1, 91–3, 95

'Scholastically brilliant, emotionally turbulent' – this description of Hogg when chairman of the Tory Reform Committee has been echoed many times since. His father, the first Viscount Hailsham, was twice Lord Chancellor, and Hogg himself was to have three spells on the woolsack. Educated at Eton and Christ Church, Oxford, he graduated with a first in 1930, and the following year was elected a Fellow of All Souls. In 1932 he was called to the bar at Lincoln's Inn, and in 1938 was the successful 'Peace with Honour' candidate at an Oxford by-election which became a mini-referendum on Neville Chamberlain's Munich agreement with Hitler. Among those who campaigned for Hogg's opponent, the anti-appeasement A. D. Lindsay, were two future Conservative Prime Ministers, Harold Macmillan and Edward Heath. Hogg retained his Oxford seat until 1950.

Returning from active service in December 1942 he was soon prominent on the Conservative left. He argued during the parliamentary debate on the Beveridge Report, for example, that 'as long as there remain people who cannot have enough to eat, the possession of private property is a humiliation and not an opportunity'. He succeeded Viscount Hinchingbrooke as chairman of the Tory Reform Committee in 1944, and for a brief period the following year was Parliamentary Secretary of Air. Among his publications at this time were *The Left was never Right* (1945), a robust defence of Conservative foreign policy between the wars, and *The Case for Conservatism* (1947), an elegant exposition of Conservative philosophy which, citing Burke and Disraeli, portrayed the British nation as an organic community unfolding under the guidance of divine providence. 'Conservatives do not believe that political struggle is the most important thing in life', he contended in one memorable passage, 'the simplest among them prefer fox-hunting – the wisest religion.'

Succeeding to the peerage in 1950 Hailsham subsequently held various government posts: First Lord of the Admiralty (1956–7); Minister of Education (1957); Deputy Leader of the Lords (1957–60); Leader of the Lords (1960–3); Minister for Science and Technology (1959–64); and Secretary of State for Education and Science (1964). In 1957 Macmillan appointed him Chairman of the Party to enliven its image, which he did at the annual conference of that year by appearing in a bathing-suit on Brighton beach and by rousing the delegates with what he termed 'campanological eccentricities' – the continuous ringing of a hand-bell. Encouraged by Macmillan, who thought him one of the few 'men of real genius in the Party who were the true inheritors of the Disraeli tradition of Tory Radicalism, which I had preached all my life', Hailsham announced in 1963 that he would renounce his peerage to enter the contest for the premiership. Many Conservatives were offended by his exuberance, however, and Macmillan eventually advised the Queen to appoint Lord Home Prime Minister.

Hogg was Member of Parliament for St Marylebone from 1963 until 1970, when he accepted a life peerage. He was Lord Chancellor from 1970 until 1974, and again from 1979 to 1987 in the first two Thatcher administrations. In various speeches and publications at this time Hailsham suggested that the 'elective dictatorship' of Parliament should be curtailed by means of a written constitution, with provision for judicial review and a Bill of Rights acting as a higher law beyond parliamentary repeal. As elder statesman of the Thatcherite counter-revolution he staunchly defended the government against the charge that it had abandoned genuine Toryism: commenting, for instance, on Lord Stockton's accusation that privatization was analogous to selling the family silver, Hailsham claimed that 'our respected colleague, to whom we all owe so much, was talking nonsense on this occasion'. After retiring as Lord Chancellor, however, he became critical of aspects of government policy, and in 1989 castigated 'meddlesome Maggie' (as he called the Prime Minister) for seeking to extend market principles into the judiciary. The legal profession, according to Hailsham, could not be regulated like a corner shop in Grantham.

> Benjamin Disraeli . . . saw that the new was not really the enemy of the old, yet that if the people were not given social reform by the Parliament, the Parliament would be given social revolution by the people; that if our institutions were to be preserved they were to be preserved only by a rigid insistence

on social justice – by welcoming the new with understanding and real gladness in the name of the old instead of with obscurantist opposition or with timid compromise. Thus he hit upon the role of Conservatism in revolutionary times – to lead and dominate revolution by superior statesmanship, instead of to oppose it, to bypass the progressives by stepping in front of current controversy instead of engaging in it, to seek an objective study of the actual nature of social forms rather than indulge in political bromides. This is the real meaning of *Coningsby*.

Does it offer any hope for today? Surely it does, almost with mathematical parallelism. The New Conservative . . . sees in the modern extra-political forms of public control a Nationalisation which has lost its terrors, and in the larger joint-stock companies with limited liability a private enterprise which has lost its meaning. He is not impressed by the fear of schemes for social security as destructive of enterprise. On the contrary, he sees in them the basis for social stability necessary to the restoration of industry . . .

This twentieth-century society demands a measure of control to prevent chaos. The price of ignoring this need is unemployment, cut-throat competition, unbalanced economy, unjust distribution of wealth, slums, ignorance, bitterness, squalor, and in the end war . . .

It is no mere coincidence that on an average of about twice or more during a century there arises within the Tory Party a movement of young men, decried by their elders as revolutionary, who preach reform in the name of Conservatism.

Such a one was Disraeli: such too was Lord Randolph Churchill. To such a movement in the Tory Party belonged F. E. Smith's Social Reform Committee of 1911. There is reason for thinking that this attitude has become particularly appropriate to the solution of the problems of the present day, and that there is already in existence an organised movement in the Tory Party in the true tradition capable of expressing it . . .

The thesis of the reforming Tories is that current political controversies have become petrified in the use of phrases and theories which are no longer relevant to social forms. We Tories believe that this stage had already been reached before the beginning of hostilities, and that the tragedy of the pre-war years would only be re-enacted if we permitted public opinion to remain divided on the old issues such as

'Socialism' versus 'Private Enterprise', 'Nationalisation' versus 'Free Competition' . . .

It was not to be wondered at that the gospel of self-help produced social insecurity. It was meant to do so. The idea was that man was by nature an idle creature who would not work unless spurred for ever by the apprehension of poverty. This fear could hardly be a real one unless the danger were reasonably close. Therefore a man must fend for himself; there must be poor in order to provide an example to those who would be thrifty. The comparable theory in the realm of health is that boys must be hardened in order to make sturdy, healthy men. Unhappily the facts do not wholly bear out the theory. Those boys make the best men who have always been well and sufficiently clothed, housed, and fed. Those men are the most self-reliant and the most enterprising who under proper discipline have been carefully guarded by their parents in youth and by their position in maturity from the pressing fear of being unable to provide the means of life for themselves and their dependants. Want and disease, vice, shiftlessness, malice and ignorance are the results as well as the causes of poverty. Fear is an evil master and a bad counsellor. Its pupils are concerned chiefly with present emotions and improvised expedients. Confidence and foresight are the products of reasonable security . . .

The history of social progress during the past forty years does not countenance the theory that it is part of the law of God that one class in society, and that collectively among the most useful, should be in perpetual fear of disaster. The members of this class . . . think their needs, and by their needs they mean the things which make life tolerable for sensitive and civilised people, should be a first charge on the proceeds of commerce, agriculture and industry. They have no hostility to private profit as such. But they do not understand why the law should give profits priority over their needs.

These considerations have led to a widespread discontent. If this discontent has found expression in envy, hatred and malice; if it has led to disloyal and unworthy reflections upon our national institutions or achievement, to want of enthusiasm in our Empire, or to cynicism about the ultimate validity of moral or religious values, it is not those who have erred who are to blame. The Duke of Wellington, that great Tory, once observed: 'There are no bad troops. There are only bad officers.' Until the full validity of the criticisms which the rank and file of our peoples make of the social structure is fully recognized, there will be no peace or dignity in this realm, and we shall be condemned during the period of reconstruction to the same fruitless impotence as characterised our political history before the war . . .

To a Conservative the remedy of these grievances is a matter of practical necessity. It binds him to no economic or political theory of the State. He sees it to be a necessary step to the maintenance of our institutions and the preservation of our Empire, and by proclaiming it as part of his view of national policy he commits himself neither to Socialism nor to the theory of class war, nor to the abolition of private property or enterprise.

3. Richard Austen Butler, Baron Butler of Saffron Walden (1902–82)

'A Disraelian approach to modern politics', in *Tradition and Change: Nine Oxford Lectures*, London: Conservative Political Centre, 1954, pp. 10–12

Rab, as he was known, came from a dynasty of Cambridge dons and public servants. Born in India, where his father, Montague, was an official, he was educated at Marlborough and at Pembroke, the Cambridge College which in 1937 was to elect Sir Monty Butler as Master; he became President of the Union, and graduated in 1925 with a first in history. For a year he held a fellowship at Corpus Christi College, where his uncle, Sir Geoffrey Butler (author of *The Tory Tradition* and MP for Cambridge University) was also a Fellow, and at this time married Sydney Courtauld, heiress of the famous textile firm. In 1929 he was elected to Parliament as the Member for Saffron Walden, holding the seat until his retirement from politics. With his appointment in 1938 as Under-Secretary at the Foreign Office, after nearly six years at the India Office and a spell at the Ministry of Labour, he became spokesman for Neville Chamberlain's policy of appeasing Hitler. Three years later he was promoted President of the Board of Education and had responsibility for the Bill of 1944 which laid the foundations of postwar education, and was Minister of Labour in the caretaker administration of 1945.

By now Butler was emerging as 'the shrewd, hardworking brain of modern Toryism', as *The Sunday Times* called him in 1950, through his involvement in policy making. He had been chairman of the party's Post-War Problems Central Committee for much of the period since its formation in 1941, and a member of the Reconstruction Committee from 1943. After the election defeat of 1945 he became head of both the moribund Conservative Research Department and the new Advisory Committee on Policy and Political Education, and was also instrumental in setting up the Conservative Political Centre. In 'Fundamental issues: a statement on the future of the Conservative education movement', a speech published by the Conservative Political Centre in 1946, Butler exhorted Conservatives to

> enter the battle of ideas . . . a battle fought in a changing world for the middle ground of politics, a battle in which old weapons and old methods of warfare are out of date. No longer can the forces on our side sit in entrenched positions or rely on holding old-fashioned fortresses. The warfare is mobile and the prize will go to the most daring tactician.

The endorsement of the *Industrial Charter* signified his success in severing the party from some of its pre-war ideological roots, against the accusation of right-wingers that he was a 'milk-and-water' socialist.

Butler was Chancellor of the Exchequer from 1951 until his appointment four years later as leader of the House of Commons. In 1957 he became Home Secretary after unexpectedly failing to succeed Sir Anthony Eden as Prime Minister, combining the post from 1959 to 1961 with the chairmanship of the Conservative Party. In 1963 Butler, now Deputy Prime Minister, again failed to reach the top of the greasy pole, partly because he was insufficiently ruthless. But it was also because his ascent was blocked by Macmillan, the outgoing premier; he thereafter enjoyed the reputation of being 'the best Prime Minister we never had'. He was Foreign Secretary until the Conservative election defeat of 1964, and the following year accepted both a life peerage and the Mastership of Trinity College, Cambridge, remaining there until 1978.

> The classical role of Conservatism has always been to find the right mean between its dynamic and its stabilising aspects.
>
> When there was an excess of *laissez-faire* we leaned towards the authority of the State; now that we see an excess of bureaucracy we are leaning towards individual enterprise and personal liberty. We should continue to lean, but without losing our balance.

Society is a partnership, and so underlying all our differences there should be a fundamental unity – the very antithesis of the 'class war' – bringing together what Disraeli called the Two Nations into a single social entity. The Tory record and contribution to social unity and welfare are unrivalled; and the present administration has sought faithfully to maintain this honourable tradition, particularly by our housing programme, by increases in insurance benefits, and by legislation to improve working conditions, for example in the mines.

But if Disraeli provided us with inspiration, he was no less prescient in warning us of the pitfalls. He cautioned us, for example, that posterity was not a pack-horse always ready to be loaded with fresh burdens. He cautioned us no less strongly that we should seek to secure greater equality, not by levelling the few, but by elevating the many. I think it very important, in looking to the future of the Welfare State, to concentrate on these points, using the social services as a basis from which human nature and individual enterprise can strive for better things . . .

We are confronted now with the Socialist concept of the social services as a levelling instrument, a means of securing that everyone shall have just the same average uniform standard of life. Wherever we meet it, we can see how self-defeating this concept must be.

In education, a blind faith in the unproven virtues of the comprehensive secondary school, to which all must go, could mean denial of opportunity to the most able children. (By all means carry out the spirit of the Education Act, and have experiments of all sorts, but do not put all your money on one runner.) In health, an obsession with the principle of a free service could mean, and did mean between 1948 and 1951, a denial of adequate treatment to those in greatest need. Then there is housing. A complete concentration on Council building could mean, and did mean throughout the period of Socialist Government, a denial of homes to tens of thousands who could have been housed, and are now being housed, under methods which impose less burdens on their fellow taxpayers and ratepayers. I do not say for a moment that in slum clearance and in many of the working-class homes of this country an element of subsidy is not necessary. I do say that we shall have to find a much more just system of awarding the subsidy and seeing that it is used for those who really need it.

In all these fields it is our policy to give real help to the weak. It is no part of our policy to repress the initiative and independence of the strong. Indeed, unless we allow men and women to rise as far as they may, and so allow our society to be served by what I describe as *the richness of developed differences*, we shall not have the means to earn our national living, let alone to afford a Welfare State.

7 *Turning the collectivist tide 1963–*

So strong was the collectivist tide, Professor Beloff told the Conservative Political Centre Summer School in 1978, that it would not be turned without at least a decade of Conservative government resolutely challenging 'the orthodoxies of a century'.[1] In the following year Conservatives began a long period of rule in which, as Beloff had hoped, they sustained a crusade to restore a purer from of capitalism. A succession of administrations led by Margaret Thatcher abandoned the commitment of their postwar predecessors to the managed economy, and sought instead to revive market forces by cutting direct taxation, rejecting control of prices and incomes, selling state-owned industries, curbing trade-union power, reducing expenditure on social welfare, and undermining the 'municipal socialism' of local government. One remarkable feature of the Thatcher years is the intellectual ascendancy of the New Right within the party. Individualists in the century following the launch of the Liberty and Property Defence League knew that they were swimming against the tide, and even the age of Peel was also the heyday of Tory paternalism. Since 1979, by contrast, the Conservative counter-revolution has moved through the party like a juggernaut, crushing One Nation dissidents and leaving a mere handful of stragglers along the middle way. In this sense, at least, Thatcherism constitutes a unique phase in the history of English conservatism – the jubilant voices of the 'two-nations strategists' matched only, perhaps, by the triumphal reassertion of royal absolutism during the Restoration.[2]

Less remarkable are the ideas of the modern right, for they have long been the stock-in-trade of free-market Conservatives. Those who now favour an enterprise culture share with earlier individualists a fear of creeping socialism, a conviction that the poor benefit from the wealth created by the rich, a belief that welfare coddling erodes self-reliance and places unfair burdens on the more competent members of society, a preference for a state which withdraws from the economy yet stands firm against social indiscipline, and a tendency to extol the nineteenth century as a golden age of moral vigour and economic success. What makes the New Right novel is not its individual ideas, but rather the reassembling of arguments which Keynesians had pronounced obsolete into a radical and electorally potent image of the self-help society.

There had always been some Conservatives who disapproved of the party's postwar conversion to 'humanized' capitalism. Their dissent was endorsed by the arguments of a few intellectuals for a minimal state enforcing rules of conduct. Reviewing Quintin Hogg's *The Case for Conservatism* in 1947, the philosopher Michael Oakeshott censured the Conservative Party for failing to perceive that the only safeguard against arbitrary government is 'a rule of law which has emphasized duties at least as much as rights between private individuals'.[3] More accessible than Oakeshott's writings were those of the Austrian economist, F. A. Hayek, who also declared that centralized economic planning is incompatible with individual freedom. In *The Road to Serfdom*, published in 1944, when he was teaching at the London School of Economics, Hayek contended that Britain was rapidly moving towards totalitarian socialism because most people falsely believed in the possibility of 'some Middle Way between "atomistic" competition and central direction'.[4] His book is the flagship of postwar libertarianism, and from the 1970s was often cited as a prophetic warning of the ratchet effect of collectivism. In the 1950s and 1960s, however, most Conservatives supposed that the route from a free-market economy could end far short of despotism.

The only influential Conservative who seriously challenged the Keynesian consensus before the late 1960s was Enoch Powell. In 1958 he resigned from the government because of its refusal to cut public spending, and within a few years was a persistent critic of the planned economy. Powell, unlike some of the Spencerites, did not become an unqualified minimal stater. He continued to advocate selective provision of social security, for example, claiming that 'a capitalist state can also be a welfare state; indeed, other things being equal, a state which is capitalist can provide more welfare than one that is not'.[5] His significance is that he retrieved, in lucid and elegant prose, the arguments of political economy for a society in which government refrains as far as possible from tampering with the laws of supply and demand. A free-market economy generates prosperity and maximises freedom, he asserted in speeches made in 1963 and 1964, by calling into play individual choice and initiative. In Burkean manner, moreover, Powell incorporated this system of natural liberty into a picture of the organic community evolving through the accumulated experience of centuries.[1] This depiction of an island race of ruggedly independent individuals, nourished by an ancestral wisdom, was intended to arouse hostility to the expansion of state power, and also to rekindle patriotism in a country which had lost its empire. Powell's romantic nationalism later led him to oppose an immigration policy he believed would submerge Englishness in a sea of alien cultures, as well as to condemn Britain's entry into the EEC as an assault upon that symbol of a glorious heritage, the sovereignty of Parliament. He was sacked from the shadow cabinet in 1968 for his alleged racism, and eventually broke with the party over the Common Market. Yet among Thatcherites he is revered as a prophet of the new enlightenment.

Postwar Conservative advocates of managed capitalism repudiated egalitarianism, because it was not their intention to promote social justice at the expense of economic efficiency. The termination in 1964 of thirteen years of Conservative government prompted a thorough policy review which gave added emphasis to the production rather than the distribution of wealth. Economic growth was to be stimulated by lower rates of direct taxation, greater selectivity in the social services, and constraints on trade union power. 'We must create a Britain that is bold', announced Edward Heath, who led the party from 1965, 'in which the spirit of adventure and enterprise can be given full play'.[6] But this promise to emancipate entrepreneurs from the clutches of the state failed to rally those on the right of the party who were eager for a frontal assault on economic planning. In their view, Heathite policies for modernizing Britain were merely a bluish version of the Labour government's programme of technological innovation. After another election defeat, in 1966, a rising number of Conservatives applauded Powell for having 'made his escape from the socialist dream',[7] and urged the adoption of 'libertarian' policies 'to dismantle the vast structure of controls and restrictions by which this nation is now stifled'.[8] The evacuation of the middle ground had begun.

This shift to the right did not stem from a belief that Keynesianism had completely failed in its objectives. A persistent claim in the 1960s was that the interventionist state had been only too successful in spreading affluence through society. The foundations of social order were being undermined as a consequence, for the citizens of an indulgent Welfare State had little respect for those who had traditionally exercised authority. This was said to be a problem which Heathite Conservatives not only failed to address, but seemed intent on aggravating by their preoccupation with economic growth. Hence the call to revive market forces, with their attendant inequalities, was conceived as a dual strategy to rejuvenate the economy and restore social discipline. The strategy was made plain by the political journalist and High Tory, Peregrine Worsthorne. Although keen for the Conservative Party 'to clamber back on capitalist terra firma', he warned that the electorate would not be persuaded to embrace the free market merely through an exposition of the truths of political economy. 'The argument that if the rich are allowed to get richer, the poor will eventually get less poor, although demonstrably true, has never, in this country, proved politically viable.' Instead, Conservatives should exploit a growing fear of social disintegration in order to vindicate the traditional bases of authority. And this required them, wrote Worsthorne in the manner of a latter-day Burke, to use 'the authentic language of Toryism' in celebration of the bourgeoisie, not only as the mainspring of a dynamic economy, but as a bulwark of order and the source of civilized values.[9]

Free-market capitalism was linked to a mission to defend civilization through denunciation of the permissive society. Traditional values were challenged in the 1960s by a more liberal attitude on such issues as abortion and pornography, campaigns for gay rights and women's liberation, and especially by the dress, music, pot-smoking, communal living, demonstrations and university sit-ins of rebellious youth. For the right, permissiveness was a symptom of moral decadence, and counter-cultural unruliness demonstrated that self-discipline had been weakened by a nursemaid state. A lurid picture was painted of a nation polluted by libertines, enfeebled by egalitarians, and – as Powell, too, was claiming – culturally diluted by immigration and politically threatened by the Common Market. The moral flabbiness, hedonistic frivolity and social dislocation of welfare capitalism were contrasted, moreover, with the self-reliance, thrift and discipline of the Victorian enterprise culture. In this way, the offensive against collectivism was incorporated into a plea for the restoration of traditional codes of conduct. The state was to safeguard the British way of life by releasing its hold upon the economy, while taking firmer action against both internal laxity and intrusion from without. And this required the Conservative Party to engage in a patriotic crusade to preserve the organic unity of 'our island race', so that, as of old, entrepreneurial daring might co-exist with the sturdy independence, industry, sobriety and decency of common people. Only by taking such a 'right turn', argued Rhodes Boyson with the fervour of an apostate from the Labour Party, could Conservatives halt 'the slow-quick-quick–slow foxtrot to socialism and spiritual and material impoverishment'.[2]

A focus for this type of thinking in the late 1960s was the Monday Club, founded in 1961 by younger Conservatives who objected to the rapid British de-colonization of Africa and were alarmed by 'the leftward drift of the party' under Macmillan's leadership. After the election defeat of 1964, the club expanded into 'a party within a party', with an executive council, mass membership and branches throughout the country.[10] In numerous pamphlets its publicists advocated a 'self-help' society of low public expenditure,[11] coupled with a strong law-and-order state to combat left-wing subversives, truculent workers, civil libertarians, revolting students and all the other 'enemies within'.[12] Ridiculing the 'mythical "middle ground of politics"', John Biggs-Davison told an audience at The Queen's University of Belfast in 1969 that the club had 'done a special service to Conservatism and to Britain. It has given new hope to many who had begun to despair of both. It has rescued Toryism from tepidness, from trimming and from toadying to an intellectual, cultural and political establishment that is pink and permissive.'[13] Of course, he was making exaggerated claims on behalf of the faction, which was more often regarded as a repository for the 'loons and ultras' of the party. A sea change within conservatism was presaged, nevertheless, by the persistence with which the club's growing membership called for a government that would loosen the state's grip on the economy while attending more resolutely to the nation's security.

There was nothing irregular in this combination of 'the free economy and the strong state'. *Laissez-faire* Conservatives since Burke had wanted government to constrain individuals who failed to respond to the imperatives of market forces. In extolling the moral prowess and economic dynamism of Victorian society, too, the emerging New Right was echoing Sir Ernest Benn and others. But in the 1960s the rhetoric of economic freedom and political order coalesced into an unusually resonant appeal for national revival. In the past the patriotic card had been played by Tory Democrats, who, taking their lead from Disraeli, eulogized a national party determined to preserve the empire and to elevate the condition of the people at home. Now, however, Conservatives were being urged to abandon illusions about imperial grandeur and the efficacy of social reform, and instead to articulate popular anxieties about race, crime, cultural unrest, licentious behaviour, heavy taxation, welfare officialdom, the EEC and so forth. They were to become, in this view, sentinels of a fortress Britain besieged from within and without. And the instrument at the disposal of the new model army of conservatism in its defence of national identity, according to the radical right, was to be a state which, though stripped of many of its economic functions, had been re-equipped to maintain social cohesion. Romantic nationalism had contracted into Little Englandism.

What eventually swung many Conservatives against collectivism was the collapse of the Heath government. Heath came to power in 1970 with the promise of a 'quiet revolution' that would reverse national decline by reducing public expenditure, rolling back the state from industry, curbing trade unions, and restoring law and order. But the government was faced with rising inflation and unemployment, and within a couple of years had abandoned much of its free-market strategy in a dramatic U-turn. State intervention in the economy was increased through subsidies to the unprofitable 'lame ducks' of industry as well as by a comprehensive statutory prices and incomes policy, which was soon challenged by striking miners. Dwindling coal stocks led to the imposition of an emergency three-day working week throughout industry, and in February 1974 a general election was called on the theme of 'Who governs Britain?' The government lost, and Conservatives were defeated more decisively at another election in the following October.

The failure of Heath's interventionism convinced a growing number of Conservatives that it was 'time to move on' to a market-oriented economy,[14] and from the mid-1970s there was a clamour for 'our Big Brother State' to be dismantled.[15] Moreover, resurgent economic libertarianism spread beyond the publications of the Conservative Political Centre. Keynesian orthodoxy was increasingly repudiated by academics and journalists, and especially by various 'think-tanks' which emerged or flourished at this time. Anti-collectivist groups now burgeoned, just as Spencerite bodies such as the Liberty and Property Defence League and the British Constitution Association had sprung up a century earlier to combat socialism. Most of these organizations were not formally connected with the Conservative Party, and many of their members remained aloof from the crusade of Rhodes Boyson and others against permissiveness. Instead of articulating the themes of 'authoritarian populism',[16] they sought to discredit the postwar settlement by expounding the arguments for market capitalism advanced by writers such as Hayek and the American economist, Milton Friedman. Unlike the free-marketeers at the turn of the century, who never seized the intellectual initiative, the libertarian right of the 1970s did help to change the climate of public debate. Suddenly it became fashionable to subscribe to individualism, particularly within the Conservative Party, where the remaining defences of Butskellism fell almost as swiftly as the walls of Jericho.

One of the oldest groups to disseminate free-market ideas in the 1970s is Aims of Industry, saluted by Margaret Thatcher on its fortieth anniversary in 1982 as 'a tireless crusader for our great liberties'. Launched by industrialists amidst wartime regulations, it has persistently campaigned for lower taxation, less public spending, and fewer controls upon industry. The link between free enterprise and individual liberty is emphasized, and in the 1970s the organization was preoccupied by the alleged threat of industrial militancy to the open society. Conservative MPs are among the authors of its numerous pamphlets, the titles of which convey the group's outlook: *The Pleasant Face of Capitalism*, *Galloping Bureaucracy and Taxation: the Radicalism the Case Requires*, *Reducing the Growth of Civil Servants*, *A Practical Guide to Denationalization*, *Redistribution in Reverse: More Equal Shares of Wealth Mean Less Equal Shares of Spending*, *Dealing with the Marxist Threat to Industry*, and the like.

Another long-standing organization is the Institute of Economic Affairs which, in the words of its former editorial director, has 'systematically mustered and presented in modern dress the truths of classical political economy', publishing in the process more than three hundred pamphlets and books.[17] Its authors continually condemn the inefficiency and bureaucracy of extensive government, and like earlier libertarians applaud the entrepreneur as 'the prime mover of progress'.[18] The IEA has challenged what Ralph Harris, General Director since its inception in 1957, calls 'the KCC: the Keynesian-Collectivist Consensus' by formulating a range of policies to reduce the activities of government.[19] It wants market forces to operate in health and education, for example, through individuals being given greater opportunity to opt out of the public provision of these services. The institute was once considered eccentric outside a small group, but its founders subsequently claimed with some plausibility to have won the battle of ideas. Harris, who describes himself as a 'radical reactionary',[20] worked for R. A. Butler after the war, but left the party to establish the institute because of the drift to collectivism. There was a *rapprochement* in the changed intellectual climate of the 1970s, however, and he was ennobled in Margaret Thatcher's first honours list. In a tribute to the IEA in 1983, she remarked that her policies were 'firmly founded' on the ideas which it had explored over the years.

Among the newer 'think-tanks' is the Adam Smith Institute, which was founded in the late 1970s by graduates from St Andrew's University, a seedbed of the New Right. The ASI advocates massive cuts in public spending and taxation, as well as a rolling programme of privatization and de-regulation. In 1982 it set up various working parties, whose members included Conservative MPs, with the task of formulating policies to contract the state to a minimum. The outcome was *The Omega File* of 1985 which the Institute's President, Dr Madsen Pirie, described as 'an almanac of the future of Britain'. In more than six hundred proposals for releasing market forces its authors recommended the abolition of many departments of central government and the virtual disappearance of local authorities, the privatization of coal, prisons and the railways, a BBC financed by advertisements, the closure of job centres, and the replacement of the Welfare State by a system of compulsory private insurance.[21]

There is also the Freedom Association, established in 1975 after the murder, by the IRA, of Ross McWhirter, a leading right-wing campaigner.[22] Rhodes Boyson was among the Conservative MPs co-opted on to its council, and Margaret Thatcher attended the inaugural subscription dinner as guest of honour. At its formation the Association, known initially as the National Association for Freedom, had no doubt that it stood on the side of individualism in a battle against encroaching government. In the words of Norris McWhirter, Deputy Chairman and later Chairman of the Association, and brother of the murdered Ross:

> In the three decades of post-war Britain there has been a consistent policy of corporatism – the macro-economic approach epitomized by high taxation, universal welfare, centralized planning, state control, high public spending, massive bureaucracy, income and price policies, trade unions with legal immunities and ever diminishing individual freedom. The alternative of low taxation, selective welfare, decentralized planning, limited government, essential public expenditure, small bureaucracy, free wage negotiation, market force pricing, non-monopoly trade unions subject to democratic ballot and increasing personal freedom is attainable only if there is the zest, zeal and motive to attain it.[23]

Its founders believed, as did the British Constitution Association seventy years earlier, that individual liberties wrenched from the state over the centuries were now endangered by collectivism. The Association therefore proposed a written constitution and a Bill of

Rights to fetter Parliament and safeguard individuals against the abuses of power. Its own fifteen-point *Charter of Rights and Liberties*, however, was largely an agenda for liberating private enterprise and emasculating trade unions.

The ideas of this organizational network were transmitted to the heart of the Conservative Party by the Centre for Policy Studies, whose success in persuading Conservatives to abandon the middle way is comparable to that of R. A. Butler's research outfits in enticing them along it after the war. The Centre was founded within six months of the downfall of Heath's government by Sir Keith Joseph and Margaret Thatcher in order to 'reshape the climate of public opinion'. It quickly became both a base for the challenge to Heath's leadership and, largely through Joseph's speeches, an intellectual power-house; it generated alternative policies in 'the belief that it is only through the operation, as unfettered as possible, of the free market that the lives of the citizens of our country will be enhanced'. Once Thatcher became party leader, and eventually Prime Minister, the CPS provided a platform for expressions of the new orthodoxy, and through its working parties initiated fresh policies to maintain the momentum of the counter-revolution.

A recurrent claim of the Centre's pamphleteers is that postwar Conservatives were deluded into supposing that a haven existed somewhere between capitalism and socialism. Hijacked by Keynesians and assailed by egalitarians with 'class on the brain',[24] the party had imagined that it could both fine-tune the economy and, by amply providing welfare, promote social justice. Conservative governments had therefore helped to construct 'an overblown, dropsical state, a gorged and sluggish Leviathan' of heavy taxation, high public spending, prices and incomes policies, a bureaucratic stranglehold on industry, and the legislative cushioning of trade unions.[25] The outcome was rising inflation, unemployment and economic stagnation, which is why Conservatives needed to be re-educated in the truths of political economy. For Nigel Lawson, who was to become Chancellor of the Exchequer, this meant rediscovering the road originally taken by the Peelites.[26] Illusions about intervention had to be discarded so that the state could be reduced to its proper function of preserving the framework of a stable economy. Here the centre promulgated the doctrine of monetarism, derived from Milton Friedman, which was fashionable during the first Thatcher government. Keynesian administrations had accelerated inflation, in this view, by printing money to stimulate demand. Instead of indulging in demand management, however, government should preserve the value of the currency by removing inflationary pressures such as excessive public expenditure. A principal source of inflation is said to be the power of trade unions. In the past, according to monetarists, workers priced themselves out of a job through high wage demands and restrictive labour practices such as overmanning, and governments responded by expanding the money supply to reduce unemployment. The centre therefore urged the restoration of the laws of supply and demand in the labour market through the removal of legal immunities such as picketing and the closed shop, as well as by the abolition of councils safeguarding the wages of the low paid,[27] measures which were implemented during the Thatcher years.

These ideas became the subject of public debate through the speeches of Sir Keith Joseph, who had been a loyal and high-spending minister in the Heath administration. But the manner of the government's defeat made him 'a late convert to sanity',[28] and he now tried – with little success – to convince his shadow cabinet colleagues of the error of their ways. Shortly before the second general election of 1974, in consequence, he began to preach the gospel of monetarism in the first of many speeches throughout the next few years which combined intellectual rigour with born-again zeal.

Joseph believed, as did Boyson, that the summit of British endeavour had been reached in the nineteenth century, when common habits of self-reliance, hard work and respect for the law had complemented the entrepreneurial success of a gifted minority. With the expansion of government the nation had slid steadily downhill towards economic lassitude, cultural mediocrity and political coercion. A principal cause was 'the pursuit of crude redistribution' by which 'rewards to effort and thrift and enterprise and sanctions against sloth and fecklessness are diluted'.[29] The pace towards a uniformly socialist state had been quickened by Keynesian policies of excessive taxation and public spending, demand management, regulation of industry, and control of incomes and prices. In *Stranded on the Middle Ground?*, a selection of his speeches and articles in 1975 and 1976 published by the Centre for Policy Studies, Joseph attributed the massive postwar concentration of state power to the ratchet effect of socialism. The middle ground was continually shifting leftwards, because in their search for consensus Conservative governments had adjusted to the agenda set by their Labour predecessors. Hence inflation and the other problems which now vexed the country. His solution, of course, was to retrieve 'the spontaneous dynamism' of a market economy by pushing back the state to its legitimate tasks of preserving a stable currency and maintaining public order.

Interestingly, Joseph dissociated minimal statism from Social Darwinism, claiming that the independence and initiative of individuals in a free-market economy was not a licence for the strong to trample on the weak in an unregulated struggle for survival. A competitive economy framed by the rule of law, on the contrary, would foster civilized behaviour among people conscious of their civic responsibilities, as well as creating the wealth for alleviating poverty.[3] Nevertheless, Joseph's political message – with its praise of the Victorian enterprise culture, condemnation of overmighty government, conflation of collectivism with socialism, and prophecy that egalitarianism would lead to a 'totalitarian slum' – was not essentially different from that of the ardent Spencerite, Sir Ernest Benn.

One reason why the ideas expounded by Joseph aroused interest at this time was that the Labour government appeared to be no more successful than its Conservative predecessor in managing economic crises. The Labour Party was returned to power in 1974 with the promise of more extensive government regulation of the economy, but was soon confronted by rising unemployment and rampant inflation. In 1976, under pressure from the International Monetary Fund, the government engaged in its own version of a U-turn by reducing public expenditure and imposing monetary targets. Its incomes policy was also challenged, like that of the Heath administration, by industrial militancy, and the government lost the general election of 1979 after a wave of unpopular strikes in the public sector. By confirming a widespread suspicion that Keynesian techniques had been exhausted, the record of the Labour administration made even more Conservatives receptive to the arguments of those in their party who wanted a 'revolutionary' departure from the postwar settlement.[30]

Without the unexpected election in 1975 of the forceful Margaret Thatcher as leader, however, the bulk of the party would not have lurched so far to the right. Unlike Sir Keith Joseph, her mentor and co-founder of the Centre for Policy Studies, Mrs Thatcher never confessed to a dramatic conversion to genuine conservatism. Instead she gave the impression that monetarism provided an intellectual framework for values she had imbibed as a child living in a corner shop in a small provincial town. Among these homespun virtues are self-reliance, hard work, thrift, family support, respect for law and order, and patriotism. The nation is often described by Thatcher as a household writ large, and as Prime Minister she views herself as a super-housewife charged with the responsibility of prudently balancing the books, 'with a little left over for a rainy day'. This inclination to eulogize the respectable petty-bourgeois family as the fount of political wisdom reveals her populist instincts. Thatcher has led an offensive against the middle way not by expounding the intricacies of economic philosophy, but by portraying her mission to restore sound finance and repair the social fabric as the pursuit of common sense. Largely through her simple homilies, usually delivered in strident tones, free-market ideology has both captured the soul of the Conservative Party and been transformed into a potent electoral message.

Central to this message is the evil of socialism, which in Thatcher's elastic usage means redistributive taxation, demand management, extensive social welfare, and most of the other policies pursued by postwar Conservative as well as Labour governments. After her first administration she claimed to have 'offered a complete change in direction – from one in which the state became totally dominant in people's lives and penetrated almost every aspect – to a life where the state did do certain things, but without displacing personal responsibility'.[31] Five years later she proclaimed that Britain had 'come out of the long, dark tunnel of socialism. We are the first post-socialist society.'[32] Socialism is denounced through a mixture of economic and moral arguments. One reason for a sluggish economy in the 1970s is said to be punitive taxation, which discouraged potential wealth-creators by stifling individual ambition. Lower taxes, according to Thatcher, restore incentives to those risk-takers without whom there would be insufficient prosperity to sustain a safety net of social services for the poor. A country where entrepreneurial success is justly rewarded 'might in some ways be a chillier, bumpier, less cosy place – but infinitely more invigorating'.[33]

There is also the claim that an overbearing state gnaws at the moral fibre of its citizens by depriving them of choice and responsibility. In part this argument stems from the familiar belief that the unsuccessful are not entirely blameless for their predicament, which means that the poor will not improve themselves unless permitted to bear some of the consequences of their incompetence. Thatcher despises people who 'drool and drivel about caring', she let slip in a television interview, because they naïvely call for the kind of universal welfare provision which reinforces habits of dependence, idleness and improvidence. Individuals who are continually pampered by a 'nanny state', she has said many times, soon become 'moral cripples' eager to delegate their responsibilities to officialdom.

More unusual for a twentieth-century politician is the suggestion – also made by Burke in *Thoughts and Details on Scarcity* – that a bountiful state reduces opportunities for the rich to discharge their Christian obligation of charity. Government should encourage rather than usurp the exercise of virtue by individuals who, she reminded the General Assembly of the Church of Scotland in 1988, have obeyed the scriptural injunction to create wealth. And this requires ample scope for them to engage in voluntary philanthropy. 'When the State steps in, generosity is increasingly restricted from all sides', she announced elsewhere, and 'when the money is taken away and spent by government, the blessing goes out of giving and out of the effort of earning in order to give.'[34] On another occasion she turned the parable of the good Samaritan upside-down, claiming that a less affluent person would not have been able to assist the unfortunate man who fell among thieves. A society can be neither economically vigorous nor morally healthy, then, unless government stands aside to enable the rich to exercise initiative and the poor to acquire self-discipline.

Thatcher, like Joseph and Boyson, contrasts the postwar period with more heroic moments in the nation's past. Britain's ascent, which she believes to have begun in the first Elizabethan age, led to the enterprise, moral rectitude and philanthropy of the nineteenth century. 'We, who are living off the Victorians' moral and physical capital, can hardly afford to denigrate them.'[35] In wishing to roll back the state so as to recover the market economy which served the nation so well in the past, she also wants to restore the discipline of Victorian society. Thatcher is clear that a limited state should be neither weak nor inactive, and a major complaint against excessive government is that it cannot perform the essential tasks of maintaining stable finance and safeguarding security. Hence the economic decline, inflation, insufficient defence expenditure, union militancy, rising crime rates, and general unruliness of a Britain corrupted by socialism. Human beings are 'inherently sinful', she told listeners at a London church in the year before becoming Prime Minister, 'and in order to sustain a civilised and harmonious society we need laws backed by effective sanctions. Looking at this country today, I am bound to say that upholding the law is one area of life where I would wish the State to be stronger than it is.'[36] These themes of a free economy and strong state, as well as her castigation of collectivism and approbation of enterprise, self-reliance and philanthropy, emerge in a couple of speeches, one delivered in 1977 and the other in 1980, which are included in a collection, *In Defence of Freedom*.[4]

Since 1979 successive Thatcher administrations have pursued a broadly consistent strategy of pruning the state to enable it to discipline a market-oriented society. To reduce the range of government responsibilities, demand management of the economy has been abandoned, state-owned industries and public utilities such as British Airways, British Gas, British Steel, British Petroleum, British Telecom, Rolls-Royce, electricity and water have been privatized, much of the public stock of housing has been sold, employment legislation protecting women, teenagers and the low paid has been repealed, personal taxation has been cut, and – though the Welfare State has not been dismantled – the value of social security benefits has been eroded and market principles have been imported into the National Health Service. Measures to strengthen the state, on the other hand, have included laws to weaken trade unions; higher expenditure on defence and internal security; additional powers for the police and judiciary to deal with criminals, demonstrators and strikers; removal of the right of accused persons to remain silent; the introduction of military-style detention centres to deliver a 'short, sharp shock' to young offenders; a broadcasting ban on people representing terrorist organizations and Sinn Fein; investigations and prosecutions to preserve official secrecy; an Official Secrets Act which conflates the public interest with the interests of government; a campaign against 'loungers and scroungers' receiving social security; and the eradication of 'municipal socialism' through the abolition of the Greater London Council and metropolitan counties, as well as by stripping away the power of remaining local authorities to set rates, shape the school curriculum and rejuvenate inner cities. All this amounts to a determined effort to accommodate a free economy within a strong state, even though the pace of radical reform has not been swift enough for every counter-revolutionary enthusiast.

Nor has the fusion of the free economy and strong state in Thatcherite rhetoric and policy satisfied some dissident intellectuals, who claim that undue emphasis on competitive individualism obscures the essential Conservative task of maintaining public order. The Salisbury Group, named after a Prime Minister admired for his mistrust of political panaceas and resolve to defend property rights against the 'masses', emerged in 1976 as a reaction to evangelical monetarism. Two years later the group (many of whom are either Fellows or former students of Peterhouse College, Cambridge) produced a collection called *Conservative Essays*, and in 1982 founded a journal, the *Salisbury Review*. Its editor, the philosopher Roger Scruton, has also written *The Meaning of Conservatism* to remind his co-ideologues 'of the uncomfortable truth that they are always in danger of forgetting, in their impatience to "roll back the frontiers of the state", namely, that the state is necessary, and must be large and strong'.[37] These sceptical Conservatives are not opposed to free-market capitalism. Their complaint is that 'libertarian crackpots' have confused conservatism with a particular economic doctrine which, when not incorporated into an image of society as an ordered hierarchy, enjoins its adherents to champion individual rights against the state instead of seeking to enforce the duties of citizenship.[38] Free-market zealots are liberals masquerading as Conservatives, on this account, who endanger the organic nation by making individual liberty a primary value and overriding political objective. 'But it is not freedom that Conservatives want; what they want is the sort of freedom that will maintain existing inequalities or restore lost ones, so far as political action can do this.'[39] And this requires Conservatives to integrate their advocacy of a market economy, Burkean style, into a positive conception of the state which subordinates rights and liberties to obligation and authority.

Interestingly, the arguments of the Salisbury Group against economic libertarianism are not unlike those used by Tories and conservative Whigs to repudiate contractualism and the radical interpretation of the Glorious Revolution: as publicists who employed the language of natural liberty and equality were once accused of undermining political stability by encouraging notions of popular sovereignty, so Hayekians who castigate postwar collectivism as a totalitarian infringement upon market freedom are censured by the Salisbury Group for arousing suspicion among the citizenry of any form of rule; and as Reeves and Burke blamed the spirit of Jacobinism on the emotive simplicity of natural rights, so the abstract logic of free-marketeers is now condemned for fostering potentially subversive illusions about the availability of an earthly paradise. Authentic conservatism, by contrast, portrays civil society, neither as a structure of equal rights nor as the approximation of some ideological blueprint, but as a fragile chain of command linked by coercion, tradition, and sentiments of allegiance and patriotism.

Laissez-faire principles, according to the Group, are singularly ill-adapted to justify the kind of rolling forward of the state that is needed to deal with social indiscipline and cultural disintegration. In his contribution to *Conservative Essays*, Peregrine Worsthorne pursued themes he had broached a decade earlier by urging firm action against vandalism, football hooliganism, urban terrorism, unruly behaviour in schools, sexual immorality, pornography, and other manifestations of a general collapse of authority.

> What Britain is suffering from is 'riotous disorder' and to argue as Mrs Thatcher does, that 'setting the people free' will cure it is as senseless as trying to smooth raging waters with a stick of dynamite or to quieten hubbub with a brass band. The urgent need is for the State to regain control over 'the people', to re-exert its authority, and it is useless to imagine that this will be helped by some libertarian mish-mash drawn from the writings of Adam Smith, John Stuart Mill, and the warmed-up milk of nineteenth-century liberalism.[40]

Contributors to the *Salisbury Review* have extended the list of measures government should adopt to restore national cohesion and cultural homogeneity by advocating, for example, corporal and capital punishment, the conscription of unemployed youth, and the compulsory repatriation of immigrants.

If the Institute of Economic Affairs (one of the Salisbury Group's favourite targets) and some other right-wing organizations appear to occupy the narrow ground of political economy, mainstream Thatcherites are usually careful to connect their defence of market forces with the wider project of reimposing traditional patterns of conduct; so scrupulous are they, in fact, that the strictures of the Group seem largely misdirected. Indeed, some of those denounced by the Group are themselves critical of Thatcherism on the grounds that the economic policies of the 1980s were pursued within a context of what Samuel Brittan, a long-time advocate of competitive capitalism, calls 'petty authoritarianism and a highly illiberal rhetoric on social and personal issues'.[41] The Conservative counter-revolution has been persistently presented as a bid to rescue the nation not only from economic ruin, but also from cultural decline and social decay.

An enduring feature of this crusade is the tendency to blame the unrest of the 1960s for any recurrent social problems. Sir Keith Joseph, for instance, was inclined to attribute the ills of the 1970s to the virus of permissiveness which had infected society a few years earlier.[42] And even in the 1980s Conservatives fulminated against the 'decadent decade' with hardly less passion than Rhodes Boyson and others had shown at the time. Margaret Thatcher has taken a lead in castigating the permissive age. After ten years of Conservative government, she said in 1989, Britain was again flourishing as an enterprise culture. Yet the process of restoration had to be prolonged: for 'the hooligans, the louts and the yobs on the late-night trains' were animated not by the success of free-market policies, but by the 'prophets of the permissive society' whose motto

> in dealing with the trade union negotiator, with the criminal, with our international adversaries, or even the child in the classroom . . . was always the same 'Never say no'. And now they see the legacy they've left they try to pin the blame on us. What colossal humbug . . . That's why we've toughened the law on the muggers and marauders. That's why we've increased penalties on drink-driving, on drugs, on rape. That's why we've increased the police and strengthened their powers. That's why we've set up the Broadcasting Standards Council . . . For there can be no freedom without order. There can be no order without authority; and authority that is impotent or hesitant in the face of intimidation, crime and violence, cannot endure.[43]

In this way the canons of political economy are incorporated, as the Salisbury Group prescribes, into a puritanical political theology.

A persistent assailant in the late 1980s of the 'poisoned legacy of the Permissive Society' was Norman Tebbit.[44] One outcome of a lengthy period of Conservative administration had been the forging of a new consensus, according to him, because a growing body of opinion now acknowledged that only a market economy could sustain both prosperity and freedom.[45] The Thatcherite 'revolution' had yet to run its course, however, for individual responsibility – already weakened by the collectivist ethos of servile dependence upon the state – had been more permanently undermined by the collapse of traditional values in the 1960s. The waves of permissiveness were still sweeping through society in the form of high crime rates as well as a widespread disregard for standards of decency and order, which was why the economic emancipation of individuals had to be accompanied by a further tightening of moral and social restraints. Tebbit dealt with these themes in *Britain's Future*, a speech given at St Stephen's Constitutional Club in 1985.[5] In suggesting that permissiveness had reinforced the tendency of the mixed economy to foster individual irresponsibility and social indiscipline, he was transmitting the same message as Peregrine Worsthorne twenty years earlier. Now, however, 'post-war funk' was being blamed for the apparent failures, not only of the corporate state, but also of an era of free enterprise.

Thatcherism has not gone unchallenged within the Conservative Party. Among its most articulate critics are former ministers, many of them purged in cabinet reshuffles for not being 'one of us', who are reluctant to stray far from the middle way. Their objection to the New Right is threefold. They are dismayed, first, by the government's confrontational and sectarian style, and claim that the party has been hijacked by self-righteous fundamentalists intolerant of anyone who does not display the same degree of counter-revolutionary enthusiasm. According to Lord Pym, who was sacked as Foreign Secretary in 1983, the party has contracted from a broad church accommodating diverse opinions into 'a narrow and dogmatic faction' of missionary zealots.[46]

This partisan inflexibility, secondly, is attributed to ideological bewitchment. Thatcherites are not authentic Conservatives, in this view, because they have discarded experience and pragmatism for the abstractions and simplistic nostrums of political economy. And in becoming lost in what Sir Ian Gilmour, the most literate of former Tory ministers, calls 'the fog of Manchester Liberalism',[47] they have created an underclass of the unemployed and underprivileged. Hence, thirdly, the commanders of the new model army of conservatism are said to exhibit none of the traditional concern for the condition of the people. Dedicated to the achievement of acquisitive individualism, they have absolved themselves of the patrician responsibility to attend to the needs of those unable to respond to the imperatives of an enterprise culture. Dryness, writes Pym in a reference to the Prime Minister's description of her cabinet opponents as 'wets', produces 'a cactus society, scratching its members to pieces'.[48]

The call for Conservatives to recover their patrician inheritance is expressed in various ways. Jim Prior, who left the government in 1984, urges a 'balanced' approach in which 'Conservatives once again address themselves to the needs of all sections of society'.[49] John Biffen, who in 1987 was dropped as Leader of the Commons after undergoing a metamorphosis from the driest of monetarists to a 'semi-detached' member of the government, believes that 'the radical crusade cannot last for ever. There must be a blend between the zealots and the basic instincts of Conservatives' through increased public spending on, for example, health, education and the environment.[50] Michael Heseltine, who resigned as Secretary of State for Defence in 1986 during the Westland affair, wants a 'caring capitalism' in which 'those who enjoy the privileges of a free society' discharge their paternal obligations by dispersing the benefits of the enterprise culture to everyone. And this requires the wealthy and powerful to adapt the ideals of *noblesse oblige* to modern conditions by, for example, devising a coherent industrial strategy and facilitating a programme of urban renewal.[51] Peter Walker, the only 'wet' to survive successive cabinet changes – and who in 1989, as Secretary of State for Wales, contrived to give the impression that by means of interventionist policies he was running the principality better than the Prime Minister was governing the country – opts for the route recommended by Macmillan. 'The middle way is a recognition that society is held together only by the moral bond of mutual obligations . . . The most fundamental of all mutual obligations is the obligation to guarantee to even the humblest the means to live and enjoy a decent life.'[52] What these Tories share is a dislike of ideological extremism and, in varying degrees, a desire to 'Return to One Nation' where the practical task of fostering class harmony does not become obscured by adherence to economic dogma.[53]

What the Tory dissidents lack is either widespread support within the party or anything approaching the kind of organizational network through which anti-collectivist ideas were transmitted from the 1970s. Thatcherism may be an aberration, as one of its most virulent critics, the former Prime Minister, Edward Heath, contends, because of its lapse from the tradition of Disraeli and Macmillan.[54] After a decade in power, however, few Conservatives were inclined to believe that they had embraced an alien doctrine which should be discarded in order to retrieve the Tory Democratic legacy. Even some paternalists conceded that the counter-revolution was unlikely to be arrested or reversed, with Michael Heseltine, for instance, calling for its 'frontiers' to be pushed forward through, in effect, the humanizing of Thatcherism.[55]

More remarkable than the dissent of One Nation Tories is the ideological gulf separating Thatcherism from many of the professions and public institutions. The Church of England has expressed reservations about the gospel of individualism and is critical of its effects upon the poor and unemployed, and government supporters have retorted by advising meddlesome prelates to confine their homilies to spiritual matters. The universities have been affronted by successive cuts and by efforts to transform them into training centres for the market economy, while the government has not concealed its contempt for ivory-tower intellectuals. In 1989 the legal profession, infuriated by a scheme to expose it to the operations of the market, declared open warfare on the government, which in turn denounced the hallowed traditions and restrictive practices of the judiciary. In the same year the medical profession, amidst government charges of being backward-looking, mounted a campaign against the proposed regulation of health-care provision by market forces. There are few government sympathizers in the civil service or the arts. And even the royal family, a bastion of *noblesse oblige*, is allegedly disturbed by the government's distaste for the Commonwealth as well as by evidence of an increasingly divided nation at home. Hence, by a strange twist of history, the party which has always portrayed itself as the guardian of altar, throne and other institutional embodiments of national cohesion, now arouses more hostility within the Establishment than any previous Liberal or Labour administration.

Thatcherism has been sustained in power partly by a weak and divided opposition, but largely because numerous people have prospered from lower direct taxes and rising incomes as well as from the sale of council houses and an extension of share-ownership. Moreover, to the surprise of many observers who anticipated a period of consolidation, the third Thatcher administration renewed its assault upon collectivism with a further programme of radical measures. This does not necessarily mean that Mrs Thatcher has won the battle of ideas, as she announced in 1987, or that the libertarian tide is irreversible. By no means all the beneficiaries of 'popular capitalism' share the government's unshakeable faith in market forces, and there remains a large body of support for the public provision of health care, welfare and education as well as for positive action by the state to heal the division between the two nations. Nor is it clear that government policies, while reducing inflation and curbing trade unions, have resolved such long-term problems as the weakness of manufacturing industry. Eventually Conservatives are likely to be swept by a sea change towards new forms of state intervention. They are unlikely to revert to the corporatism of the middle way, however, because one effect of a decade of Thatcherism has been to discredit many aspects of postwar Keynesianism, and even the opposition parties now incline to a more market-oriented approach. Perhaps the post-Thatcher Conservative Party will endorse the kind of revitalized but humane capitalism advocated, for example, by Michael Heseltine. If so a modern style of patrician Toryism – one seeking to accommodate the enterprise culture within the framework of a state which facilitates investment, curtails market forces to prevent environmental damage, and also attends to the condition of the people – will be the fashion of the future.

NOTES

1 Max Beloff, *The tide of collectivism – can it be turned?*, London: Conservative Political Centre, 1978, p. 21.
2 Thatcherism is characterized as a two-nations strategy in Bob Jessop, Kevin Bonnett, Simon Bromley and Tom Ling, *Thatcherism*, Oxford: Polity Press, 1988. There is now a vast literature on all aspects of Thatcherism. Among the more comprehensive books are two by political scientists: Dennis Kavanagh, *Thatcherism and British Politics: the End of Consensus?*, Oxford: Oxford University Press, 1987, and the conceptually more interesting Andrew Gamble, *The Free Economy and the Strong State: the Politics of Thatcherism*, Houndmills: Macmillan, 1988; and also two by political journalists: Peter Jenkins, *Mrs Thatcher's Revolution: the Ending of the Socialist Era*, London: Jonathan Cape, 1987, and the thematically sharper Hugo Young, *One of Us: a biography of Margaret Thatcher*, London: Macmillan, 1989.
3 Michael Oakeshott, 'Contemporary British politics', *Cambridge Journal*, Vol. 1, 1947, p. 479.
4 F. A. Hayek, *The Road to Serfdom*, London: Routledge & Kegan Paul, 1962, p. 31.
5 Enoch Powell, 'Is it politically practicable?', in *Rebirth of Britain: a symposium of essays by eighteen writers*, London: Pan, 1964, p. 266.
6 Edward Heath, *The Great Divide*, London: Conservative Political Centre, 1966, p. 11.
7 Lord Coleraine, *For Conservatives Only: a study of Conservative leadership from Churchill to Heath*, London: Tom Stacey, 1970, p. 118.
8 T. E. Utley, 'Intellectuals and conservatism: a symposium', *Swinton College Journal*, Vol. 14, 1968, p. 31.
9 Peregrine Worsthorne, 'The ideological heritage', in Robert Blake *et al.*, *Conservatism Today*, London: Conservative Political Centre, 1966, pp. 17–33.
10 See Patrick Seyd, 'Factionalism within the Conservative Party: the Monday Club', *Government and Opposition*, Vol. 7, 1972, pp. 464–87.
11 Victor Goodhew, *Self-Help*, London: The Monday Club, 1969.
12 Anthony T. Courtney, *The Enemies Within*, London: The Monday Club, n.d.
13 John Biggs-Davison, 'The speech the People's Democracy tried to drown', in Jeremy Harwood, Jonathan Guinness and John Biggs-Davison, *Ireland – Our Cuba?*, London: The Monday Club, n.d.
14 David Howell, *Time to move on: an opening to the future for British politics*, London: Conservative Political Centre, 1976.
15 Eldon Griffiths, *Fighting for the Life of Freedom*, London: Conservative Political Centre, 1977, p. 6.
16 The New Right is characterized as a form of authoritarian populism by Stuart Hall. See the essays collected in his *The Hard Road to Renewal*, London: Verso, 1988.

17 Arthur Seldon, 'Preamble: the essence of the IEA', in *The Emerging Consensus . . . ? Essays on the interplay between ideas, interests and circumstances in the first 25 years of the IEA*, Arthur Seldon (ed.), London: Institute of Economic Affairs, 1981, p. xvii.
18 *The Prime Mover of Progress: the Entrepreneur in Capitalism and Socialism*, Arthur Seldon (ed.), London: Institute of Economic Affairs, 1980.
19 Ralph Harris, *The End of Government . . .?*, London: Institute of Economic Affairs, 1980. Some of the Institute's policy options are considered in Nick Bosanquet, *After the New Right*, London: Heinemann, 1983, pp. 75–83.
20 Lord Harris of High Cross, *The Challenge of a Radical Reactionary*, London: Centre for Policy Studies, 1980.
21 On the institute see Ruth Levitas, 'Competition and compliance: the Utopias of the New Right', in Ruth Levitas (ed.), *The Ideology of the New Right*, Cambridge: Polity Press, 1986, pp. 80–106.
22 See Neill Nugent, 'The National Association for Freedom', in Roger King and Neill Nugent (eds), *Respectable Rebels: Middle Class Campaigns in Britain in the 1970s*, London: Hodder & Stoughton, 1979, pp. 76–100.
23 Norris McWhirter, 'Freedom of choice', in K. W. Watkins (ed.), *In Defence of Freedom*, London: Cassell, 1978, p. 63.
24 P. T. Bauer, *Class on the Brain*, London: Centre for Policy Studies, 1978.
25 Ferdinand Mount, *Property and Poverty: an agenda for the mid-80s*, London: Centre for Policy Studies, 1984, p. 16.
26 Nigel Lawson, *The New Conservatism*, London: Centre for Policy Studies, 1980, p. 2.
27 E.g. Russell Lewis, *Wages Need No Councils*, London: Centre for Policy Studies, 1984.
28 Sir Keith Joseph, 'Proclaim the message: Keynes is dead!', in Patrick Hutber (ed.), *What's Wrong With Britain?*, London: Sphere Books, 1978, p. 102.
29 Sir Keith Joseph, 'The economics of freedom', in *Freedom and Order: Three Cambridge Studies Based on Lectures Presented to the CPC Summer School at Cambridge*, London: Conservative Political Centre, 1975, pp. 7–8.
30 Patrick Hutber, 'The need for a revolutionary conservatism', in Patrick Hutber (ed.), *What's Wrong With Britain?*, London: Sphere Books, 1978, pp. 107–12.
31 Interview in *The Times*, 5 May 1983, p. 5.
32 Margaret Thatcher, *Speech . . . at the 58th Conservative Women's National Conference*, London: Conservative Central Office, 1988, p. 12.
33 Margaret Thatcher, 'Britain's era of enterprise', *Reader's Digest*, December 1983, p. 25.
34 Margaret Thatcher, *Let Our Children Grow Tall: Selected Speeches 1975–1977*, London: Centre for Policy Studies, 1977, p. 110.

35 ibid., p. 111.
36 Margaret Thatcher, *'I Believe': a speech on Christianity and Politics*, London: Conservative Central Office, 1978, p. 10.
37 Roger Scruton, 'The Right Stuff', *New Socialist*, Vol. 33, December 1985, p. 34.
38 'Editorial', *Salisbury Review*, Vol. 4, no. 4, July 1986, p. 53.
39 Maurice Cowling, 'The present position', in Maurice Cowling (ed.), *Conservative Essays*, London: Cassell, 1978, p. 9.
40 Peregrine Worsthorne, 'Too much freedom', in ibid., p. 149.
41 Samuel Brittan, *A Restatement of Economic Liberalism*, Houndmills: Macmillan, 1988, p. 310.
42 E.g. Sir Keith Joseph, 'Britain: a decadent new Utopia', *Guardian*, 21 October 1974.
43 Margaret Thatcher, *Speech . . . to the Central Council at Scarborough on Saturday 18 March 1989*, London: Conservative Central Office, 1989, pp. 10–11.
44 Norman Tebbit, *The Values of Freedom*, London: Conservative Political Centre, 1986, p. 9.
45 Norman Tebbit, *The New Consensus: Inaugural Address to the Radical Society*, London: Chatham House, 1988.
46 Francis Pym, *The Politics of Consent*, London and Sydney: Sphere Books, 1985, p. x.
47 Ian Gilmour, *Britain Can Work*, Oxford: Martin Robertson, 1983, p. 218.
48 Francis Pym, *The Politics of Consent*, London and Sydney: Sphere Books, 1985, p. 146.
49 Jim Prior, *A Balance of Power*, London: Hamish Hamilton, 1986, p. 263.
50 John Biffen, 'Now it's time for a change', *Observer*, 30 April 1989, p. 13.
51 Michael Heseltine, *Where There's a Will*, London: Hutchinson, 1987; idem, interview in *Marxism Today*, March 1988, p. 18.
52 Peter Walker, *Trust the People: Selected Essays and Speeches*, London: Collins, 1987, p. 45.
53 Edward Heath, 'A return to One Nation: the first Harold Macmillan Memorial Lecture', unpublished, 1988.
54 Interview in *Marxism Today*, September 1988, p. 23.
55 Michael Heseltine, 'There can be no halt to the Tory revolution', the *Mail on Sunday*, 9 October 1988, p. 8.

1. John Enoch Powell (1912–)

A Nation Not Afraid: the Thinking of Enoch Powell, John Wood (ed.), London: Hodder & Stoughton, 1965, pp. 25–6, 145–6

Greek scholar, poet, commentator on Christian doctrine, historian of the House of Lords, Tory renegade and populist politician

– Powell is a remarkable figure, and much has been written about the phenomenon of Powellism. Both Enoch's parents were Birmingham school teachers, and their only child was later to write a book about Joseph Chamberlain, the former 'king' of the city who was also, as Michael Foot characterizes Powell, a political 'loner'. From King Edward VI Grammar School, Birmingham, Powell went to Trinity College, Cambridge, where he won glittering prizes for classics. He was elected to a fellowship at the College in 1934, and three years later became Professor of Greek at Sydney University, New South Wales. At the outbreak of war he enlisted as a private, leaving the army in 1946 with the rank of Brigadier.

Powell, who had served in India since 1943, returned to England determined to oppose the dissolution of the British empire. He joined the Conservative Research Department where, in R. A. Butler's words, he was 'the most intellectually formidable' of the backroom boys who helped cut the party adrift from its pre-war economic and social policies. Failing to win a by-election at Normanton in 1947, he entered Parliament in 1950 as the Member for Wolverhampton South West, retaining the seat until 1974. In his early years in Parliament Powell became secretary of the One Nation group, but even then was wary of socialism by stealth, and in *Change is Our Ally*, which he co-edited and largely wrote for the group in 1954, advocated a partial restoration of market forces. By this time he had come to recognize that imperial disintegration was inevitable. He was made Parliamentary Secretary at the Ministry of Housing in 1955, and was Financial Secretary to the Treasury from 1957 until his resignation the following year in protest against the government's refusal to implement deflationary measures. He became Minister of Health two years later, but refused to accept office when Lord Home succeeded Macmillan as Prime Minister in 1963.

Powell's speeches in defence of the free market after his return to the back benches were intended to re-educate the Conservative Party, as well as to condemn Labour policy. 'Often, when I am kneeling down in church,' he once remarked, 'I think to myself how much we should thank God, the Holy Ghost, for the gift of capitalism.' He was appointed opposition spokesman for transport in 1966, and the following year moved to defence. By 1968 he was involved in an anti-immigration campaign, and at Birmingham made a speech containing an anecdote about a Wolverhampton widow allegedly harassed by her black neighbours. 'As I look ahead,' he concluded,

> I seem to see 'the River Tiber foaming with much blood'. That tragic and intractable phenomenon which we watch with horror on the other side of the Atlantic but which there is interwoven with the history and existence of the United States itself, is coming upon us here by our own volition and our own neglect. Indeed, it has but come. In numerical terms, it will be of American proportions long before the end of the century. Only resolute and urgent action will avert it even now. Whether there will be the public will to demand and obtain that action, I do not know. All I know is that to see, and not to speak, would be the great betrayal.

Powell was sacked by Edward Heath for the notorious 'rivers of blood' speech, but his opposition to coloured immigration transformed him into a folk-hero whose popularity exceeded that of his party leader.

Powell did not seek re-election for Wolverhampton in February 1974, and at the two general elections of that year advised the electors to vote Labour. This was partly because he disagreed with Conservative prices and incomes policy, but also because

> [I] saw the Conservative party not merely agree to cede, in the most complete and formal manner, that sovereign omnipotence of Parliament which for Britain is the essence of political independence, in order to become a member of the European Economic Community, but proclaim that to amalgamate the United Kingdom into a new West European State was the very object and justification of this act . . . I explicitly identified membership of the Community as one of those supreme questions over which, like Joseph Chamberlain over Home Rule, politicians not merely quit but destroy the parties they were reared in.

In October 1974 he became Ulster Unionist MP for South Down, and staunchly supported the integration of Northern Ireland with the rest of the United Kingdom. Although celebrated as a forerunner of Thatcherite economic policies, moreover, he remained a bitter critic of the Conservative government. Infuriated by the Anglo-Irish Agreement, he attributed its signing to a conspiracy of the Foreign Office and the USA to unify Ireland. He also castigated Conservative nuclear defence policy, commending Labour's unilateralism to the voters in the general election of 1987. At the election Powell narrowly lost South Down.

'It was Enoch Powell who first sowed the seeds whose harvest Margaret Thatcher reaped last Thursday', Peregrine Worsthorne wrote in the *Sunday Telegraph* after the general election of 1983, 'and to his great voice should credit go for shattering the Butskellite glacis, the dissolution of which led to the avalanche.' Despite the mixed metaphor there is some truth in this judgement.

> [We] are a capitalist party. We believe in capitalism. When we look at the astonishing material achievements of the West, at our own high and rising physical standard of living, we see these things as the result, not of compulsion or government action or the superior wisdom of a few, but of that system of competition and free enterprise, rewarding success and penalising failure, which enables every individual to participate by his private decision in shaping the future of his society. Because we believe this, we honour profit competitively earned; we respect the ownership of property, great or small; we accept the differences of wealth and income without which competition and free enterprise are impossible . . .
>
> But our reasons for upholding the free economy of capitalism are not merely, perhaps not even mainly, material ones. We believe that a society where men are free to take economic decisions for themselves – to decide how they will apply their incomes, their savings, their efforts – is the only kind of society where men will remain free in other respects, free in speech, thought and action. It is no accident that wherever the state has taken economic decision away from the citizen, it has deprived him of his other liberties as well. It is not that there was some peculiarity in the character of the Russians or the other Communist nations which predisposed them to servitude. It is that state Socialism is incompatible with individual liberty of thought, speech and action. You may choose one or the other: you cannot have them both.
>
> We uphold the capitalist free economy, then, as much more than a mechanism for ensuring that the nation gets the best material return from its energies and resources: we uphold it as a way of life, as the counterpart of the free society, which guarantees, as no other can, that men shall be free to make their own choices, right or wrong, wise or foolish, to obey their own consciences, to follow their own initiatives.
>
> We believe that the outcome of a nation thus exercising its own free choice will be wiser and better than any caucus of economists or any committee of sociologists could have contrived for it.

Unlike our opponents, we are not so conceited as to ascribe a superior wisdom to government or the state, just because it is government or the state. On the contrary, we have a healthy scepticism about them, which predisposes us not to ask them or allow them to manage things which people can manage for themselves. We think we see not one or two but many instances 'in our rough island story' where the nation's instinct has found out a wiser and better path than any statesman or administration would have laid down if they had been given the power. We believe this is true of our constitution; we believe it is true of our economic life . . .

For the unbroken life of the English nation over a thousand years and more is a phenomenon unique in history, the product of a specific set of circumstances like those which in biology are supposed to start by chance a new line of evolution. Institutions which elsewhere are recent and artificial creations, appear in England almost as works of nature, spontaneous and unquestioned. The deepest instinct of the Englishman – how the word 'instinct' keeps forcing itself in again and again! – is for continuity; he never acts more freely nor innovates more boldly than when he most is conscious of conserving or even of reacting.

From this continuous life of a united people in its island home spring, as from the soil of England, all that is peculiar in the gifts and the achievements of the English nation, its laws, its literature, its freedom, its self-discipline. All its impact on the outer world, in earlier colonies, in later *pax Britannica*, in government and lawgiving, in commerce and in thought, has flowed from impulses generated here. And this continuous and continuing life of England is symbolised and expressed, as by nothing else, by the English kingship. English it is, for all the leeks and thistles and shamrocks, the Stuarts and the Hanoverians, for all the titles grafted upon it here and elsewhere, 'her other realms and territories', Headships of Commonwealths, and what not. The stock that received all these grafts is English, the sap that rises through it to the extremities rises from roots in English earth, the earth of England's history.

We in our day ought well to guard, as highly to honour, the parent stem of England, and its royal talisman; for we know not what branches yet that wonderful tree will have the power to put forth. The danger is not always violence and force: them we have withstood before and can again. The peril can also be indifference and humbug, which might squander the accumulated wealth of tradition and devalue our sacred symbolism to achieve some cheap compromise or some evanescent purpose.

2. Sir Rhodes Boyson (1925–)

'Right Turn', in Dr Rhodes Boyson (ed.), *Right Turn: a symposium on the need to end the 'progressive' consensus in British thinking and policy*, London: Churchill Press, 1970, pp. 3–4, 6–13.

A colourful character who lists as a recreation 'inciting the millenialistic Left in education and politics', Boyson was regarded even by many Conservatives as a wild man of the right until Thatcherism became party orthodoxy. He was educated at Haslingden Grammar School in Lancashire, Manchester University and the London School of Economics, and was awarded a PhD by London University in 1967. His thesis was on Henry Ashworth, a Lancashire cotton manufacturer who was a brother-in-law of Richard Cobden of the Anti-Corn Law League, and a devotee of the Manchester school's free-market philosophy, which Boyson later espoused. A fervent opponent of factory legislation and trade unions, Ashworth aroused considerable interest among Tory paternalists because of his reputation as a model, though somewhat despotic, employer. Two of the characters in Disraeli's Young England novels are supposedly based on him, and Lord Ashley described the Ashworth mills as 'quite astonishing' with 'much discipline + order'. *The Ashworth Cotton Enterprise: the Rise and Fall of a Factory Firm 1818–1880* was published by Oxford University Press in 1970.

From 1957 until 1961 Boyson was a Labour councillor in Haslingden, where his father had been a trade union secretary and was still a Labour alderman. Leaving the Labour Party in 1964, Boyson joined the Conservatives three years later. Between 1955 and 1974 he was head of secondary modern, grammar and comprehensive schools in Lancashire and London, and his early forays against collectivism concentrated upon postwar trends in education. In the *Black Papers on Education*, jointly edited by him from 1969 to 1977, and in publications such as *The Crisis in Education* (1977) he blamed fashionable egalitarianism for declining standards of literacy, school indiscipline, low-calibre teachers, 'the recruitment of university lecturers whose qualifications and perhaps attitudes would not have gained them interviews for university appointments in the 1930s and 1940s', cultural malaise and a general breakdown of authority.

After unsuccessfully contesting Eccles in 1970 he was elected to Parliament for Brent North in 1974, becoming opposition spokesman for education two years later. He continued to urge the Conservative Party to tilt rightwards, and his book *Centre Forward: a Radical Conservative Programme*, published in 1978, concluded with an imaginary 'seven-day re-creation of Britain programme':

> Day one, taxes would be reduced for all, with a top rate of 50 per cent. Day two, a declaration that government expenditure would be cut by 5 per cent a year in real terms each year of the five-year term of government. Day three, the statutory monopoly of the nationalised industries would be ended and existing nationalised industries would be both offered for sale and opened to internal and international competition. Day four, all exchange controls would be repealed and a pledge made to let the pound continue to find its own level. Day five would see the announcement that the present welfare state would give way to a system of topping up individual spending power by money or specific vouchers to put the consumer in charge of all the welfare services. Day six, increase police pay and numbers and declare war on crime and the moral pollution of our cities. Day seven, rest like the Creator and stroll in our gardens apart from attending the funerals of socialist suicides for whose widows we must care.

From 1979 Boyson was Parliamentary Under-Secretary at the Department of Education, and successively Minister of State for Social Security, Northern Ireland, and Local Government. In 1986 the Prime Minister came under pressure from the 92 Group (a bunch of disgruntled back-benchers who believed that the Conservative counter-revolution had stalled) to appoint Boyson to the cabinet in succession to Sir Keith Joseph, whose departure from Education was anticipated. But Boyson, though bubbling with ideas, was never a particularly competent minister, and in 1987 he was sacked from his Local Government post with the consolation of a knighthood.

> My own move to Conservative party membership arose from the effect of my research into the cotton industry and the Manchester school of liberal economic philosophy. Here was a body of men who believed that a free enterprise economy was not only efficient but brought moral growth to all men. The employer risked his capital on his judgement and must care for his workers as part of his stock in trade, and the workers would be enabled to become prosperous and through

their own industry, thrift and moral courage could establish their own business enterprises and their personal independence to the advantage of themselves, their families and society. Cobden had a moral view of society and believed that free enterprise would not only bring prosperity but social harmony at home and peace abroad within a system of universal free trade . . .

Our modern state, as fashioned largely by intellectuals of the Labour party, now takes more unto itself by taxation and regulations, decides how a man's children shall be educated, what rent he shall pay for his house or flat, how much he shall save for his old age, and what standards of health provision he shall receive. It has become destructive of the self-reliance and responsibility which were the pride of the 19th-century nonconformists. State ownership limits choice of employment in basic industries and heavy taxation severely limits a man's chance to become self-reliant . . .

If taxation is to be cut on moral grounds, the functions of the state must be carefully examined and reduced to those outlined by the classical economists. External defence and internal law and order are the basic necessities without which civilised life is not possible. Compulsory basic (though not necessarily state) education, anti-monopoly legislation linked with secure patent laws, and concern for general prosperity and for those suffering from mental and physical handicaps are the only other concerns of the state, apart from the neglected obligation to safeguard our environment for our successors. Any further responsibilities taken by the state cut into the responsibilities of the individual . . .

The move to a freer economy with less government will mean moral growth as well as much higher prosperity since it will pay a man to take business risks. The theology of Christianity stipulates that a man can choose between good and evil and that such choice is necessary for his moral salvation. This concept also applies to the economic plane: a man will grow to his full stature only when he has the maximum of free choice. The powerful state is the enemy of moral man no less than of the free society.

There are two other factors which must be faced in any new morality of the right: the freedom of individual morality and the pride in one's country and its institutions, its society and its history. On individual morality, economic freedom is simply a help to the good life . . . Just as economic freedom must not lead to monopoly or the restriction of others' freedom to enjoy our common environment, so moral freedom must not disturb the lives of fellow citizens, corrupt the young, nor threaten the stability of society . . .

If all authority is attacked and rendered suspect, the end result is not freedom but anarchy with the prospect of a new slavery when people clamour for order again. A minority of intellectuals and their imitators have attacked our history, our institutions, our way of life, our religion. These men are socially disturbed and like medieval flagellants parade about beating themselves and any others who will join in the sport of cleansing society from its imaginary sins. Their disproportionate success is, however, a sign that no political party is channelling the national conscience. Freedom in our society has become equated with stage nudity, lack of censorship, drugs, and four-letter-words, and the press and television take notice of such mental adolescents to the disgust of the general populace. Some degree of censorship is the written and oral equivalent of the protection of our environment and beautiful countryside from despoilers who selfishly see only their own desires and would ride rough-shod over the rest of the community. The organic unity of our society is also threatened by troublesome, restless and often rootless minorities which are dramatised by the media until it appears that such groups are determined to provoke the use of increased state power in order to justify their own use of force . . .

The Conservative party has combined in unique measure a respect for individual freedom with a concern for the organic unity of British society and the state. It can again by word and action teach the people in authority to exercise their power proudly as part of a continuing British society. Our schools and centres of higher learning can again teach that duties come before rights. They can again be brought to realise that their task is to train men and women to fit into our society, instead of producing crowds of unkempt young people running amok proclaiming that the end of the world is at hand. If our religion again concentrates upon its true task of saving souls, emphasising uncomfortable moral precepts and preparing people truly to serve our society, then we shall have less false religion like 'anti-apartheid demonstrations', 'racial integration', and 'unilateral nuclear disarmament'.

Once we realise again that there is a unique British way of life which must be preserved for the sake of all mankind as well as ourselves, the problem of widespread alien immigration will be seen in its true light. Those who oppose this immigration can then be seen to do so on moral grounds because they wish to preserve a society which has served the world in a way unequalled by any other nation. This claim is not based on arrogance but on humble common-sense and duty. It will then be seen clearly that the argument on immigration is between two different but moral viewpoints: on one side that of the patriot who feels his country can best serve mankind by retaining its unity and helping to make the world a better and more interesting place by preserving variety and diversity; and on the other side the equivalent viewpoint of the educational egalitarians who sadly but on moral grounds wish to reduce all the world to a drab sameness and conformity.

Patriotism within this concept will once again be a word with moral appeal and the Tory party will again link with the feelings of the ordinary person who objects to the common market and widespread immigration, who cheers our world cup team and wishes for a morally satisfying society. The Conservative party firmly established on a free economic society of responsible men, minimum central government . . . and boasting a wise and profound patriotism and determination to save and cherish the British environment and way of life, will have a strong moral appeal which will again make it the national party.

3. Keith Sinjohn Joseph, Baron Joseph of Portsoken (1918–)

Stranded on the Middle Ground? Reflections on Circumstances and Policies, London: Centre for Policy Studies, 1976, pp. 20–3, 55, 60–2, 70–1, 75–9

Sir Samuel Joseph, the first baronet, was a Jew, a wealthy businessman and Lord Mayor of London. His son, who succeeded to the baronetcy in 1944, was educated at Harrow and Magdalen College, Oxford. After serving in the war he was elected a Fellow of All Souls College, Oxford, and became a barrister at the Middle Temple. From 1946 to 1949 he was an alderman for the City of London, and in the 1955 general election unsuccessfully contested Baron's Court. In 1956 Sir Keith was elected to Parliament as the Member for Leeds North-East, retaining the seat until 1987. Between 1957 and 1964 he was Parliamentary Under-Secretary at the Commonwealth Relations Office, Parliamentary Secretary at the Ministry of Housing, and successively Minister of State at the Board of Trade and for Housing and Welsh Affairs.

Joseph was Secretary of State for Social Services throughout the Heath administration, but after its defeat became convinced of the folly of state intervention. 'It was only in April 1974 that I was converted to Conservatism', he commented after founding the Centre for Policy Studies. 'I had thought that I was a Conservative but now I can see that I was not one at all.' His assault on the politics of the middle ground made him a likely successor to Edward Heath as leader of the party. As an introspective intellectual lacking political antennae, however, Joseph presented minimal statism in an insensitive manner. His monetarist arguments against inflation were interpreted as a prescription for unemployment, while in October 1974, in a speech that would have appealed to some Social Darwinists, he appeared to advocate more effective contraception among the lower classes as a means of preserving the 'human stock'. 'First he wants to make the workers unemployed', someone remarked at the time, 'now he wants to castrate them.' Joseph, who was acutely conscious of his flaws as a politician, stood aside to enable Margaret Thatcher to challenge Heath.

Once Thatcher became leader in 1975 Joseph was made responsible for party research and policy development. Continuing his crusade against excessive government, he suggested, like Lord Hailsham and the Freedom Association, that Britain needed a Bill of Rights as part of a new constitutional settlement 'to replace that of 1689 which gave Parliament the unfettered sovereignty which it did not press to excess for another two and a half centuries'. His book *Equality*, jointly written with Jonathan Sumption and published in 1979, used traditional libertarian arguments to demonstrate that egalitarianism is neither compatible with a system of natural liberty nor capable of improving the human condition:

> A society of autonomous individuals is the natural condition of mankind . . . Men are so constituted that it is natural to them to pursue private rather than public ends . . . It is no part of a government's function to disapprove of those ambitions or to seek to change or frustrate them, for it owes its existence to them. Men have a natural right to their ambitions because it was not for the purpose of abolishing competitiveness that they submitted to government; it was for the purpose of regulating competitiveness and preventing it from taking violent, fraudulent or anti-social forms . . . If there is no natural right to equality the only possible justification for the redistribution of wealth is that it is in the interest of everybody . . . The supposed economic advantages

> of narrowing class differences, the political benefits of preventing destitution, the suggestion that a society without differences of wealth will be a more contented one, are all legitimate arguments for equality based on the belief that society as a whole will benefit from it. They are legitimate arguments but they fail on their own terms. For class distinctions will not evaporate when we all own the same amount of money. Equality will not relieve destitution but will spread it equally. Equal societies are not contented ones but wretched societies based on the frustrations of ordinary human instincts.

In 1979 Joseph became Secretary of State for Industry, and two years later moved to Education. A perceptive portrait of him as a government minister has been drawn by Jim Prior, a former cabinet colleague, in his political memoir, *A Balance of Power*. Commenting on Joseph's appointment to Industry, Prior writes,

> he simply was not the right choice as he was constantly regaled with tales of woe from industrialists and pleas to be baled out from the state-owned industries. Being a decent, soft-hearted man, he found this unbearably difficult. Margaret admired him, treasured him, looking upon him like a mother who cannot refrain from indulging a favourite son, even though she knows it will do him no good. In the end it all became impossible and Keith was moved to Education . . . This thoroughly honourable man was not suited to being a departmental Minister . . . He would invariably indulge in a mea culpa exercise, before moving blithely on to adopt some other hare-brained scheme.

At Education Joseph abandoned 'hare-brained schemes' such as student loans and education vouchers, though among his reforms was that of the 16-plus examination system. As an evangelical monetarist, however, he deprived schools of resources and fomented a bitter pay dispute with teachers; and though purporting to be raising standards in the universities, presided over a dark age of severe cuts, the downgrading of subjects whose economic value was not immediately apparent, and the implementation of managerial techniques more appropriate to a chocolate factory. Joseph left Education in 1986 and was made a life peer the following year.

> In retrospect, it is clear that the middle ground was not a secure base, but a slippery slope to socialism and state control, whose present results even socialists now disown. Of course, we did

not see it that way at the time. The middle ground gambit was accepted by us, the vast majority of us, as the apex of political sophistication. By locating and holding the middle ground, we were enjoined to believe, we should be guaranteed power in perpetuity. And if, by any mischance, we should lose office briefly, this would only be because Labour had been even more finely discriminating in locating the middle ground and more self-denyingly skilful in seizing it: hence, we thought, they could be relied on to act moderately . . .

As things worked out, with the socialists of nearly all shades committed to moving towards their promised land at whatever rate seemed practicable, while we Conservatives were basically reconciled to the *status quo* as of that moment, it was inevitable that the party pendulum should be replaced by the ratchet. When the socialists were in power they moved it forward as fast as they considered politic; when we were in office, we either kept things as they were, or let them move on under their own momentum, e.g., the Price Code and Industry Act . . .

The public sector, including central and local government, and more accurately named the state-sector, or wealth-eating sector, was bound to spread like bindweed at the expense of the non-state sector, the wealth-creating sector, strangling and threatening to destroy what it grew upon. It took up a disproportionate share of investment capital, scientists, and technologists, starving the private firms on which we depend for wealth and exports. It employed many more workers than needed, leaving labour-shortages in other parts of the economy and infecting many segments of the private sector with its tendency to overman. It paid above the odds in terms of productivity, at taxpayers' expense, thereby forcing up wages and expectations in the private sector. This impinged partly on prices, partly on profitability. The duty imposed on itself by the state to maintain full employment was partly fulfilled by subsidizing inefficiency and technological obsolescence – whether generated by unions' refusal to come to terms with labour-saving investment, or by any other cause. The infection spread from the state sector to segment after segment throughout the economy.

Declining profits, unwillingness of unions to accept labour-saving technology, patchy management-quality, and the unpredictability and apprehensions generated by capricious and changeable government intervention, all undermined the level of investment. This, in turn, stunted economic growth, the creation of new well-paid employment and the higher incomes and state spending needed to meet the very high expectations which we politicians had created with our usual mixture of good intentions and political calculation.

This sluggishness in growth and employment set up interlocking vicious circles. Governments were naturally concerned so they sought ways of stimulating investment, growth and employment. But we were inhibited from looking into the true causes of this sluggishness: the excessive state expenditure, the nature of nationalization and job-subsidization, decreasing returns to exaggerated expectations. The socialists were inhibited because it was their creation. We were inhibited because we had accepted these policies as the middle ground, so that to criticize them would be regarded as 'immoderate', 'right-wing', 'breaking the consensus', 'trying to turn the clock back', in short unthinkable, taboo.

So, instead of remedying the causes, we tried to suppress symptoms. As you know, it became fashionable to argue that if only we raised effective demand by government expenditure and money creation, growth and fuller employment could be achieved. And, as you know, this fallacy was sanctified in the name of Maynard Keynes, on the basis of his prescriptions for the 1930s. More percipient souls who pointed out that you cannot create wealth by printing money were derided as 'monetarists', and accused of desiring unemployment and stagnation.

The pseudo-Keynesians believed, some still believe in face of logic and experience alike, that they could prevent their inflationary policies creating inflation simply by suppressing symptoms through demand management, and wage and price controls.

Predictably, inflationary demand together with all the distortions created by suppressed inflation and arbitrary demand-management generated 'go-stop', stagflation and our present super-inflationary recession; with still worse to come if we do not change our ways . . .

We entered the age of Keynes believing that inflation was a lesser evil, that a little inflation might even do good. We end with the realization that inflation corrodes and erodes economic activity, making life nasty, brutish and above all short-term, eroding a base we once took for granted. Far from being a lesser evil, it is a certain source of all conceivable economic, social and political evils . . .

In the market system individuals are constantly seeking to improve their productivity because the pressure of competition and the search for profit forces people in their own interest to find more economic ways of doing what public demand requires to be done . . .

The market in its constant adjustment to changing public demand is a world of uncertainty. It is the entrepreneur who identifies a demand and subject to competition and within the law, in the hope of profit, seeks to satisfy it. In order to do so, he or she orchestrates skills, machinery, materials, money.

Without entrepreneurs the system will not work. It is not the workers alone – whether they are manual or management workers – who provide goods and services. It is workers mobilized by the entrepreneur.

But there will not be successful entrepreneurs unless there are both substantial rewards for success and sanctions against failure. People are only going to risk money and endure the tensions and anxieties involved if there is hope of substantial reward. The same is true of managers and investors. We must not grudge, as we do now with our vicious taxation, high net rewards. If we continue to do so, we shall not have entrepreneurs in this country: they will emigrate, or they will opt for a more secure existence in one of the bureaucracies . . .

Profit-making free enterprise is the base on which all our public services rest. Free enterprise provides the exports, visible and invisible, to pay for our imports. Free enterprise provides the earnings and profits from which most of our taxes to support the public sector come.

The more efficient free enterprise, the higher the earnings it can pay and the larger the tax base. So the public sector utterly depends upon the efficiency of free enterprise. It is no good urging more money for the National Health Service or for education or for whatever cause and at the same time ignoring the conditions necessary to enable the free enterprise sector to flourish . . .

In brief, the market system is the greatest generator of national wealth known to mankind: co-ordinating and fulfilling the diverse needs of countless individuals in a way which no human mind or minds could even comprehend, without coercion, without direction, without bureaucratic interference.

But the market order does not only, more effectively than any other system, serve our interests as producers and consumers. It also sustains our freedoms . . .

We who value human dignity cherish the differences that reflect the freedom of men to fashion their own lives in their own way. We value a market economy under the rule of law, and we value equality before the law above equality of income, because this is the only social arrangement that enables men to associate and to do things together and, yet, to run their own lives. We oppose socialism because it means a government that runs men rather than makes rules for men who run themselves.

We are not opposed to all interference by government, as socialists claim. We do not advocate a free-for-all when we defend a market economy. A belief in letting individuals decide for themselves how to earn and spend their money is not in any way whatsoever a belief in economic or any other kind of anarchy. We have had quite enough of the nonsense conjured up by that unfortunate phrase, *laissez faire.*

Nor do we believe in a 'natural struggle for existence'. It was Herbert Spencer, the mentor of the socialist Beatrice Webb, who saw relations among men in society as a *natural struggle for existence* in which the strong beat up or eat up the weak. But this is nothing like free enterprise as we understand it.

When we oppose the kind of interference that socialists advocate, we are not denying the importance of what governments, and governments alone, can do. We are advocating a particular conception of government as a maker of rules for men who want to fashion their lives for themselves, who may want to make gardens, write poetry, play darts, chat with friends, watch the sunset; in short, not to be mere drones who 'serve the national interest' or 'increase production' . . .

The rule of law that governs a market economy does not spew forth directions or orders for how to live or even for how to get rich. It allows men to choose whether they want to try to be rich or to live quietly doing something they like which does not bring or require much money . . .

[E]quality before the law and equality of opportunity are both objectives which we should certainly aim, so far as practicable, increasingly to achieve. They both enhance freedom. It is the pursuit of equality of income which endangers freedom, prosperity, and the prospects for eliminating poverty . . .

An egalitarian policy squeezing differentials, high direct taxation on nearly all income levels, discouraging capital accumulation and transmission, narrowing the gap between the incomes of successful and unsuccessful, will discourage wealth-creators . . .

It is no use imagining that we would be better off with a smaller national income equally shared, and do without the wealth-creators. If we discourage enterprise we shall rapidly descend to a national income far too small to maintain anything like our present standard of living, let alone improve the conditions of those who need more . . .

We shall do better for all, including those now poor or hard-pressed, with a market economy precisely because the inequality of rewards and benefits involved will create greater wealth, which is bound to raise general living standards and can be used to increase social benefits for those who need help . . .

Egalitarianism destroys not only prosperity but freedom and culture. The fewer the individuals with independent resources, the greater the dominance of government. Moreover real freedom – in religion, in politics, in art, in enterprise – depends upon there being many possible sources of financial support. If government becomes the only patron, then freedom – and quality – will die . . .

Making the rich poorer does not make the poor richer, but it does make the state stronger – and it does increase the power of officials and politicians, power more menacing, more permanent and less useful than market power within the rule of law. Inequality of income can only be eliminated at the cost of freedom. The pursuit of income equality will turn this country into a totalitarian slum.

4. Margaret Hilda Thatcher (1925–)

In Defence of Freedom: Speeches on Britain's Relation with the World 1976–1986, introduction by Ronald Butt, London: Aurum Press, 1986, pp. 21–2, 26–7, 63–6

Mrs Thatcher, who in 1988 became the longest-serving Premier since the Liberal H. H. Asquith at the beginning of the century, is a workaholic who combines a lawyer's command of detail with an imperious manner. Although shrewd and often cautious, she is more doctrinaire than any recent Prime Minister and describes herself as a 'conviction politician' at war with socialism. She also revels in her reputation as an 'Iron Lady' – a sobriquet which came from the Soviet Union – who, unlike her predecessors, refuses to U-turn.

Alfred Roberts, a Grantham grocer, was a self-educated Methodist lay-preacher and Sabbatarian who became an independent alderman and mayor of the town. 'My policies', his younger daughter remarked when Prime Minister and by then an Anglican, 'are based not on some economic theory but on things I and millions like me were brought up with: an honest day's work for an honest day's pay; live within your means; put a nest egg by for a rainy day; pay your bills on time; support the police'. Margaret Roberts was educated at the local girls' grammar school and at Somerville College, Oxford, becoming President of the University Conservative Association and graduating with a second in chemistry. She worked as a research chemist from 1947 until 1951, the year in which she married Denis Thatcher, then managing director of a family paint firm. Three years later she bore twins and also qualified as a barrister at Lincoln's Inn.

After unsuccessfully contesting Dartford in 1950 and 1951, Thatcher was elected to Parliament in 1959 as the member for Finchley. She was Joint Parliamentary Secretary at the Ministry of Pensions and National Insurance from 1961 until the government's defeat in 1964, and during the subsequent years of opposition held shadow appointments at the Treasury, Power, Transport, and Education. As the 'statutory woman' in the Heath administration she was known as 'Thatcher the Snatcher' when, as Secretary of State for Education, she abolished free school milk. Her unexpected victory over Edward Heath in 1975 was due to a 'peasants' revolt' of backbenchers against an aloof leader who had lost two general elections the previous year.

The popularity of the first Thatcher government, which was elected in 1979, slumped when monetarist policies led to mass unemployment and the decline of manufacturing industry. Thatcher nevertheless resisted pressure from cabinet colleagues to change course, and her reputation for firmness was enhanced by the recapture of the Falklands Islands in 1982. For her the defeat of the Argentinians signalled the renaissance of Britain as a great nation. In a speech at Cheltenham she urged her compatriots to emulate the discipline and co-ordination of the South Atlantic task-force, and, in a passage which echoed the sentiments of W. H. Mallock, likened the directive responsibility of captains of industry to that of 'commanders in the field'. The Conservative landslide in the general election of 1983 was probably due less to the Falklands factor, however, than to divisions among the opposition parties.

In her second administration Thatcher assembled a cabinet largely purged of any 'wet' who was 'not one of us'. Her reputation for honesty and resolve was damaged in 1986 by the Westland affair, which began as a quarrel about how to rescue a helicopter manufacturer from bankruptcy, but ended with the resignation of two ministers from a government in disarray amidst charges of deceit and incompetence against the Prime Minister. She was nevertheless swept into office for a third term with a boast that the battle of ideas had been won. A more likely explanation for the Conservative win of 1987 than a national desire to assist in the task of finally burying collectivism is that many people had prospered under the Thatcher regime – despite a widening gap between rich and poor.

> I have reason to believe that the tide is beginning to turn against collectivism, Socialism, statism, dirigism, whatever you call it. And this turn is rooted in a revulsion against the sour fruit of Socialist experience . . .
>
> In our philosophy the purpose of the life of the individual is not to be the servant of the state and its objectives, but to make the best of his talents and qualities. The sense of being self-reliant, of playing a role within the family, of owning one's own property, of paying one's way, are all part of the spiritual ballast which maintains responsible citizenship, and provides the solid foundation from which people look around to see what more they might do, for others and for themselves.
>
> That is what we mean by a moral society; not a society where the state is responsible for everything, and no one is responsible for the state . . .
>
> [T]he better moral philosophy of the free society underlies its economic performance. In turn the material success of the free society enables people to show a degree of generosity to the less fortunate unmatched in any other society. It is noteworthy that the Victorian era – the heyday of free enterprise is Britain – was also the era of the rise of selflessness and benefaction . . .
>
> Experience has shown that Socialism corrodes the moral values which form part of a free society. Traditional values are also threatened by increasing state regulation. The more the state seeks to impose its authority, the less respect that authority receives. The more living standards are squeezed by taxation, the greater is the temptation to evade that taxation. The more pay and prices are controlled, the more those controls are avoided.
>
> In short, where the state is too powerful, efficiency suffers and morality is threatened . . .
>
> In our party we do not ask for a feeble state. On the contrary, we need a strong state to preserve both liberty and order, to prevent liberty from crumbling and to keep order from hardening into despotism.

The state has, let us not forget, certain duties which are incontrovertibly its own: for example, to uphold and maintain the law; to defend the nation against attack from without; to safeguard the currency; to guarantee essential services.

We have frequently argued that the state should be more strongly concerned with those matters than it has been . . .

What we need is a strong state determined to maintain in good repair the frame which surrounds society. But the frame should not be so heavy or so elaborate as to dominate the whole picture. Ordinary men and women who are neither poor nor suffering should not look to the state as a universal provider.

We should remind ourselves of President Kennedy's great injunction: 'Ask not what your country can do for you, but what you can do for your country.' We should not expect the state to appear in the guise of an extravagant good fairy at every christening, a loquacious and tedious companion at every stage of life's journey, the unknown mourner at every funeral.

The relationship between state and people is crucial to our economic approach. Our understanding of economics, our economic philosophy is an extension of our general philosophy . . .

[I]f, during recent years, we have in Britain done so much less well than we might have done, it is not because we are bad or incompetent, but because a layer of illusion has smothered our moral sense. Let me list a few of the illusions which have blinded us.

The illusion that government can be a universal provider, and yet society still stay free and prosperous;
the illusion that government can print money, and yet the nation still have sound money;
the illusion that every loss can be covered by a subsidy;
the illusion that we can break the link between reward and effort, and still get the reward;
the illusion that basic economic laws can somehow be suspended because we are British.

For years some people have harboured these illusions which have prevented us from facing the realities of the world in which we live. It is time we abandoned them so that we can tackle our problems.

Government and people both have a part to play. For government, facing our national problems entails, above all, keeping the growth in the amount of money in line with the growth in the amount of goods and services. After years of printing too much money, to which the economy has become addicted, this will take time: but it must be done.

But it is not only the total amount of money that matters. It is how that money is distributed between on the one hand the public sector, which produces little real wealth, and on the other hand industry and commerce, the mainstays of our economy.

At present too much is spent on the public sector. It follows that the government's second most important task is to reduce state spending, so that more resources can be put to investment in industry and commerce. This too takes time but it must be done.

Too much money spent by government has gone to support industries which have made and are continuing to make heavy losses. The future requires that industry adapt to produce goods that will sell in tomorrow's world. Older industries that cannot change must be slimmed down and their skills transferred to new products if they are to serve the nation. This too takes time but it must be done.

Economics means harnessing change instead of being dominated by it. But government cannot do it alone. These policies are a necessary but not a sufficient condition for recovery. The British economy is the British people at work – their efforts and their attitudes. Success will only be achieved in so far as people relate the rewards they receive to the efforts they make, and in so far as managers, freed from restrictions imposed by previous governments, respond to their new-found freedom to manage.

5. Norman Beresford Tebbit (1931–)

Britain's Future: a Conservative vision, London: Conservative Political Centre, 1985, pp. 5–6, 14–16

Aggressive, sardonic, and every inch a Thatcherite contemptuous of the patrician wing of the party, Tebbit seems a strange choice for the 'first Disraeli lecture', as *Britain's Future* was styled. The only discernible similarity between the architect of Tory Democracy and the streetwise Tebbit is a strong populist instinct. Explaining how in the 1970s he sought to attract mass support for right-wing policies, Tebbit wrote in his autobiography, *Upwardly Mobile*:

> I had long believed that the Heath aberration of authoritarian centralist corporatism apart, most of the values, ethos and policies of

> conservatism were strongly supported by working-class voters. These voters – especially the socio-economic groups C1 and C2 – I saw as natural Conservatives who nevertheless saw themselves for tribal reasons as Labour voters. However much we tried to reach them by argument, we always failed because they were unable to identify themselves with the representatives of the Tory Party they saw. I was determined to be a Conservative who spoke their language, not just what is often described as my flat North-London accent – which was after all my mother tongue – but their practical realism, lack of humbug and strong attachment to many traditional standards and values. In my judgement they were ready to listen to blunt words – or even colourful words – but not to complex waffle.

The elder Tebbit was variously employed as a shop manager, house painter and clerk. In 1981, when Secretary of State for Employment, Tebbit told the Conservative Party Conference at Blackpool that during the economic recession of the 1930s his father had cycled around North London looking for a job. 'Get on your bike' immediately became a catch-phrase symbolizing the self-help imperative of Thatcherism.

Tebbit left Edmonton Grammar School in 1947 to become a price-room hand at the *Financial Times*. After national service with the RAF he worked in advertising for a short period, and then spent seventeen years as an airline pilot with BOAC, during which time he was active in the pilots' union, BALPA. He was elected MP for Epping in 1970 and then for Chingford in 1974. A member of Thatcher's campaign team in the leadership contest against Heath, Tebbit eventually acquired a reputation as the most abrasive representative of the new style of conservatism. Michael Foot once described him as 'a semi-housetrained polecat', and he was generally dubbed 'the Chingford skinhead'.

In 1979 Tebbit became Parliamentary Under-Secretary at the Ministry of Trade, and the following year was appointed Minister of State at the Department of Industry. As Employment Secretary between 1981 and 1983, he introduced tough legislation against trade unions. After a spell as Secretary of State for Trade and Industry, he was made chairman of the party in 1985, from which position he mounted an attack upon the BBC for its alleged anti-Conservative bias. By now, however, he was out of favour with the Prime Minister, in part because of his apparent ambition to succeed her, but also because she felt that his vitriolic manner was inappropriate at a time when the government was anxious to mellow its image. Tebbit had been seriously injured by the bombing of the Grand Hotel, Brighton during the annual party conference of 1984. After disagreements with Thatcher about the conduct of the 1987 general election campaign, he resigned as party chairman to spend more time with his wife, who was paralysed by the IRA bomb. In semi-retirement from politics and no longer quite 'one of us', Tebbit continued to urge the completion of the 'next stage' of the 'Thatcher revolution': 'the rebuilding of the social restraints which have been greatly weakened by the doctrines of the permissive society'.

> The Conservative Party shares the British people's attachment to freedom. It is to the free society that we are committed. That is a society in which the unavoidable derogations of individual liberty are minimised and take place under only the rule of law.
>
> Of course, many of our opponents also claim to be friends of freedom. But the freedom they offer is always at best highly qualified. They do not understand or acknowledge that political freedom will not long be maintained if it is divorced from economic freedom. They obstinately close their minds to the lesson that state controls are contagious, threatening to spread from sector to sector whenever given the chance. And, above all, they refuse to face their supporters with the awkward truth that the moral and material benefits of freedom itself cannot be enjoyed free from the risks and difficulties of freedom and the burdens of personal responsibility.
>
> Nor can the choices be fudged painlessly away. The path away from economic freedom is, as Hayek long ago demonstrated, the road to serfdom. The road may be a long one: the pace may be swift or slow: but the destination cannot be changed. State ownership, state monopolies, state regulation and state planning, through the centralisation of economic power, inevitably lead to economic failure. They inevitably increase both the temptation and the scope for abuses of political power until freedom itself is threatened. The planned economies, the controlled societies which socialism requires, pervert what are truly economic decisions for the market into political decisions for the politician or the bureaucrat. The fruits of centralised economic planning are corruption, poverty and servility – and in the socialist society the only medicine which

may be prescribed is heavier doses of the same socialist poison . . .

It would be wrong to blame all our ills upon collectivist policies. The effects of those policies have been dramatically worsened by the onset of the politics of the permissive society. Far from encouraging the greater self-discipline and responsibility, for which no doubt Mr Roy Jenkins hoped when he upheld the view that the permissive society is the civilised society, permissiveness compounded by the economic failure and personal irresponsibility engendered by the socialist state leads inevitably to the violent society . . .

Society today is more violent and criminal and corrupt than it was. Only the experts would challenge that: and the experts are, as usual, wrong. Why?

In the past, lack of police where they were most required – on the streets – was certainly one reason. But not today. For we have increased police manpower by almost 13,000, putting more officers back on the beat: we are providing the pay, equipment, technology and moral support to perform their difficult, dangerous task. We shall continue to do so.

Nor has criminal behaviour increased because of poverty or unemployment: the 1930s was a time of very high unemployment but not of crime on today's scale. California is richer and more criminal than Britain . . .

No: the trigger of today's outburst of crime and violence was deeper. It lies in the era and attitudes of post-War funk which gave birth to the 'Permissive Society' which, in turn generated today's violent society.

The permissives scorned traditional standards. Bad art was as good as good art. Grammar and spelling were no longer important. To be clean was no better than to be filthy. Good manners were no better than bad. Family life was derided as an outdated bourgeois concept. Criminals deserved as much sympathy as their victims. Many homes and classrooms became disorderly – if there was neither right nor wrong there could be no basis for punishment or reward. Violence and soft pornography became accepted in the media. Thus was sown the wind; and we are now reaping the whirlwind . . .

I believe that by the 1990s we shall see the effects of a revulsion against the valueless values of the Permissive Society. The public are demanding stiffer sentences for criminals – and in the end they will get them. They will demand that television producers think about the effects of what they broadcast upon impressionable people – and in the end it will happen. They will insist upon traditional style in schools . . . I know that at the front of that campaign for a return to values of decency and order will be the Conservative Party: for we understand as does no other Party that the defence of freedom involves a defence of the values which make freedom possible without its degeneration into licence.

Index